Mom,

Christmas becomes increasingly memorable
when we get to enjoy the holidays together.
This book reflects the great example you
have set on us appreciating mass, our
Father + Religion.
    merry Christmas 07'
        Dave + Nanc

# *The Mass*

# *The Mass*

## *Its Rituals, Roots and Relevance in Our Lives*

Joan Carter McHugh

Lake Forest, Illinois

Nihil Obstat
  Reverend Brian J. Fischer, S.T.L.
  Censor Deputatus
  June 7, 2005

Imprimatur
  Reverend George J. Rassas
  Vicar General
  Archdiocese of Chicago
  June 8, 2005

The Nihil Obstat and Imprimatur are official declarations that a book is free of doctinal and moral error. No implication is contained therein that those who have granted the Nihil Obstat and Imprimatur agree with the content, opinions, or statements expressed. Nor do they assume any leagal responsibility associated with the publication.

All Bible quotations are taken from the Revised Standard Version, Catholic Edition. San Francisco, CA: Ignatius Press, 1966.

Published by:
Witness Ministries
825 S. Waukegan Road, PMB 200
Lake Forest, IL 60045
Tel: 847-735-0556 or 866-948-6377
FAX: 847-735-0911

ISBN: 1-892835-07-X

To my grandchildren:

Tommy McHugh III
Ryan McHugh
Aidan McHugh
Eva McHugh

Eleanor Ranke
Erin Ranke

and to Tommy and Sinead's child
expected in the fall, and to those grandchildren
who may come along later.

# Table of Contents

# The Concluding Rites

Christian worship is surely a cosmic liturgy, which embraces both heaven and earth. . . . The Lord has gone before us. He has already done what we have to do. He has opened a way that we ourselves could not have pioneered, because our powers do not extend to building a bridge to God. He Himself became that bridge. And now the challenge is to allow ourselves to be taken up into His being for all people, to let ourselves be embraced by His opened arms that draw us to Himself. He, the Holy One, hallows us with the holiness that none of us could ever give ourselves. We are incorporated into the great historical process by which the world moves toward the fulfillment of God being "all in all."

—Joseph Cardinal Ratzinger, Pope Benedict XVI
*The Spirit of the Liturgy*

The Adoration of the Trinity/Albrecht Duerer

# Preface

Our Savior reaches out and touches us today through the Mass, the sacramental ritual He instituted which allows us to enter into His passion and death, and to experience the mystery of the Resurrection in our own lives. This is the gift and teaching of the Catholic faith: that Jesus Christ is present to us during Mass in His Body, Blood, Soul and Divinity, and His love for us in the Eucharist impels Jesus to shower us with graces and blessings that fill us with His divine life which brings healing to our bodies as well as our souls.

Being Catholic and believing in the physical presence of the risen Christ in the Eucharist go hand-in-hand. Francis Cardinal George of Chicago explains this faith:

> The Eucharist brings the hope of resurrection into our lives, into our very bodies. No matter what sorrow or pain we may be struggling with, no matter how difficult we may be finding life or how overwhelmed with problems we may be, the Eucharistic presence of the risen Christ can touch us profoundly and intimately. We are not alone; Christ's victorious love enfolds us. Christ's triumph over sin and death becomes our own. This belief and this experience are at the heart of what it means to be Catholic. (*The Catholic New World*, March 27–April 9, 2005)

Cardinal George expresses the bottom line of this book: how our God walks with us, talks with us, lives with us, cries with us, and even dies with us, so that we can experience our salvation now, in every moment of every day. It is about the transformation of our lives, a process initiated by God when He sent His Son to earth to save us from sin and death and to lead us to a life of joy and abundance. It is a process of "slow fermentation," writes the late Fr. Josef Jungmann, S.J., one of the great liturgical historians of our time, in which Jesus Himself "works as leaven . . . a process which takes hold of individuals to reshape them according to His image." He is "fashioning a new humanity" Father Jungmann says, "to transform society into a holy people of God." He then offers a compelling reason to fulfill our Sunday Mass obligation: "The forces which drag us down towards the earth in our flight through this life are very strong, and we would surely crash if we were not raised up again and again by the powerful uplifting of our Lord and Master" (*The Meaning of Sunday*, 30, 31).

Within seconds of completing the final draft of this book, I got a call from my oncologist saying that my CT scan results looked pretty good. *Thank you, Jesus,* I whispered to God. Deep down, I felt a connection between my ten-year struggle with two deadly diseases, scleroderma and lymphoma, and the saving presence of the Risen Christ in the Eucharist. I am sure that each person reading this can relate to the daily battles we encounter against forces that seek to overwhelm us: crises of all kinds, job losses, failures, emotional and physical suffering, accidents, sickness, death and sorrows galore. How do we deal with these issues, if not through faith in a God who sent His own Son to rescue us and lead us to victory over the trials and setbacks of our human condition? It is an immense mystery to fathom, how God entered human life to sweep us off our feet into another world. The only way we can wrap our minds around this mystery is through faith, a precious gift, offered to every person on earth, but accepted today by so few. Foreseeing the apostasy and tremendous loss of faith in the Church caused Jesus to lament to His disciples, "Will the Son of Man find faith on earth when He returns?" (Lk 18:8).

It wasn't until junior year of high school that I began to realize the enormity of the gift of faith. I was at an away basketball game at one of our Sacred Heart sister schools, when a knee injury forced me to sit out the quarter. On my way to the water cooler I stopped in the chapel to make a visit. Sitting in the last pew, I carried on a silent conversation with the Lord in the tabernacle. Suddenly I was weeping, telling Him all my problems and asking Him to help me. After a few minutes I felt better and walked out of the chapel on a cloud, thinking: *I have just carried on a conversation with the Son of God and He is a personal friend of mine!*

Faith will never let us down. It is the one tool in our survival kit that will literally save our lives—spiritual and physical. When we discover that Jesus is real, that He is alive, and yearns for us to love Him—and to let Him love us—*our real life begins.* He infuses our life with meaning and joy. It is our faith that identifies us as sons and daughters of God; it helps us "find ourselves," which is to say, to become our best selves. Sadly, so many today live without faith and without knowing their true identity as God's beautiful, gifted, holy children. Without faith, we desperately try to satisfy our inner hunger for love and belonging by ourselves, in ways that often lead to addictive and/or sinful behavior that robs us of our freedom and joy. Stress and illness in our society is at an all-time high. Why? We think we can do and have it all—on our own steam. We burden ourselves with fear and anxiety because we mistakenly think we are in charge of our lives, and everyone else's.

Mass attendance among Catholics has dropped to an all-time low in many countries. For example, in 2004 it was estimated that only twenty-five percent of the registered members of Catholic households in my own Archdiocese of Chicago attended weekend services in their home parish. How has it happened that so many are bored, and worse, "don't get anything out of it," like the thirteen-year-old who complained to her mother: "Why do I have to go to church? It's boring. I don't pay attention. The priest says the same thing every week. I already know it all" (*America,* March 7, 2005).

What this teenager and many others so often fail to realize is that the Sacred Liturgy is our meeting ground with God, our eternal Father, through Christ. This is why the *Catechism of the Catholic Church (CCC)* calls it the source and summit of the Christian life, "the font from which all her power flows" (1074). In His death and resurrection, Jesus has shown us a place of encounter with God. That place is at the foot of our crucified and risen Lord at Mass, where we meet Christ in person, in a sacramental ritual that enables us to eat His Body and drink His Blood. In this way, we participate in the most intimate moments of Christ's life: in His dying, His rising from the dead and His ascension into heaven. He takes us by the hand, as it were, and lifts us out of the mire of darkness and sin, so that we can experience resurrection and freedom in our lives. The Lord saves us by inviting us to undergo the same kind of transformation He experienced.

The gift and mystery of the Eucharist is that Jesus thirsts for our love and feeds us with Himself so that we can go out and feed the world with His love. In this year which our late, beloved Pope John Paul II designated as the Year of the Eucharist (October 2004 to October 2005), I pray that *The Mass* will enable readers to find new meaning and hope for their lives through the Sacred Liturgy, and that they will share that hope with a world starving for the love of Christ.

Joan Carter McHugh  
April 3, 2005  
Feast of Divine Mercy

The Eucharist/Monsignor Anthony La Femina

The Son of God became man in order to restore all creation, in one supreme act of praise, to the One who made it from nothing. He, the Eternal Hight Priest who by the blood of His Cross entered the eternal sanctuary, thus gives back to the Creator and Father all creation redeemed. He does so through the priestly ministry of the Church, to the glory of the Most Holy Trinity. Truly this is the *mysterium fidei,* which is accomplished in the Eucharist: the world which came forth from the hands of God the Creator now returns to Him redeemed by Christ.

—Pope John Paul II
*On the Eucharist in its Relationship to the Church*

# Acknowledgements

What started as a very simple book three years ago grew, like *Topsy*, into a larger work demanding extensive research. Somewhere along the way we decided to make the book more "people friendly" by adding artistic images and photos. I say "we" because a team of people helped form and guide *The Mass* into the book you are about to read.

Special thanks go to my husband, Tom, whose enthusiasm for the vision of *The Mass* sustained me through all the dry times. He gave me the freedom to work long hours and patiently endured many late dinners waiting for me to come home from the library. I'd also like to thank Anne Tschanz, who is the right arm of our ministry. She read and reread the early chapters as well as umpteen revisions, adding insightful comments and suggestions on every page. When I was just getting started, my youngest son, Richard, offered to edit some chapters. He ruthlessly red-penciled my earliest efforts; he crossed out all the esoteric language and challenged me to write from my gut and trust my heart. Richard helped me find my "voice."

I am deeply grateful to two very special priests who stood watch over the entire text, protecting it from error and guiding its theological content. They are my friends and mentors, Fr. Patrick Greenough, OFM Conv., newly elected provincial of the St. Bonaventure Province of the Conventual Franciscans, and Fr. Larry Hennessey, Ph.D., professor of systematic theology at the University of St. Mary of the Lake Seminary, Mundelein, Illinois, and editor of *Chicago Studies*. If a book has a backbone, they are it! I also want to thank my new pastor, Fr. Larry Dunn, as well as deacon Jim Carroll who, along with Frs. Greenough and Hennessey, patiently posed for photographs and endured as many as three retakes on some shots.

I am also grateful to so many friends whose unbridled enthusiasm for this project fueled my commitment and bolstered my discipline. After Cheri Klock read a sample chapter, she put a fire under me to hurry up and finish it because she wants to give it to everyone in her Bible study—as well as everyone she knows and loves. Ethel Moran and Fr. Stephen McKinley, OFM Conv. also read sample chapters and offered valuable suggestions that I incorporated in the book. And finally, thanks go to Diane Healy who, at the eleventh hour, provided a much-needed photograph from our pilgrimage to the Holy Land.

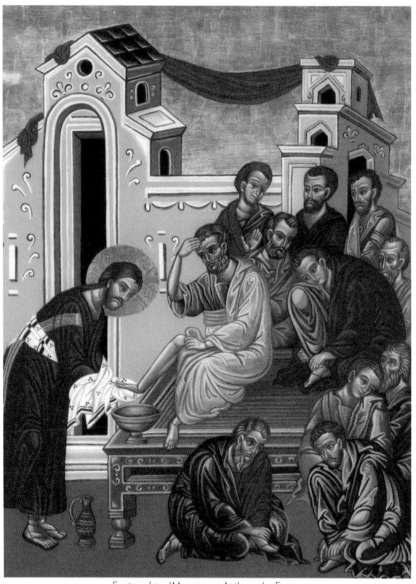

Footwashing/Monsignor Anthony La Femina

*A new commandment I give to you, that you love one another; even as I have loved you, that you also love one another. By this all men will know that you are my disciples, if you have love for one another.*

—Jn13: 34,35

Cathedral of the Madeleine, Salt Lake City, Utah/Richard Prehn

*Come, let us bow down in worship; let us kneel before the Lord who made us. For he is our God, and we are the people he shepherds, the flock he guides.*

—Psalm 95:6, 7

# Introductory Rites

*Entrance Song, Greeting, Penitential Rite,
Gloria and Opening Prayer*

## *Entrance Song*

When Catholics meet one another in the parking lot before Sunday Mass and exchange pleasantries, such as "Good Morning, how are you, I haven't seen you in a long time," we are simply individual people exercising our Christian responsibility to love our neighbor. But as soon as we cross the threshold of our church door, we have entered sacred space and are on holy ground. *Ekklesia,* a word in Greek meaning church, referred to an official gathering of people who came together to participate in a civic act, exercising their responsibility not as private individuals, but as citizens of a larger whole. In the same way, when Catholics gather for worship, they shed their private identity and form a community of baptized members of the Church to celebrate Jesus Christ in the Eucharist, the Sacrament of their salvation. Christ, as head of His Body, the Church, is represented by the celebrating priest.

But we often arrive preoccupied with the cares of the world—tired, absorbed in our own worries or problems, quite unaware of the gift of the celebration about to take place and of the people sitting beside us who have gathered for worship. The *Introductory Rites* are designed to welcome us, to wake us up to the wonder of the spiritual world we are now entering, and to the presence of our brothers and sisters who share our faith.

When we invite friends for dinner, we don't automatically sit down at the table. We first offer them a drink and perhaps an hors d'oeuvre, engage them in conversation and "break the ice," giving them time to relax and to get to know one another. We enter into a dialogue and exchange the latest news and happenings of our lives. It is similar when we go to Mass. Everything we do in this first part of the Mass—the *Entrance Song, Greeting, Penitential Rite, Gloria* and *Opening Prayer*—ushers us into a dialogue with God. We are preparing our hearts and minds to greet our Divine Guest in person—the Risen Lord Jesus Christ—in the Scriptures and in the Sacrament.

## EXPLANATION

When I was eleven or twelve, my friend Janet invited me to a service at a Methodist church. In those pre-Vatican II days, Catholics were not allowed to enter Protestant churches let alone participate in their services. Risking my mother's wrath if she found out, and overcoming my own anxiety (would I be struck dumb on the spot?), I went out of curiousity and because I had nothing better to do. We sat in a circle in the church basement and opened our song books. What happened next seared itself into my memory. Everyone sang a song called "Do Lord" with a spirit of excitement, love, joy and faith which invited total participation. The experience spoke volumes to my adolescent heart, showing me that singing to God is prayer.

> Are you looking for praises to sing? His praise is in the assembly of the saints. The singer himself is the praise contained in the song. Do you want to speak the praise of God? Be yourselves. Be what you speak. If you live good lives, you are his praise.
>
> —St. Augustine

Music was high on the agenda of the bishops during the Second Vatican Council (1962-1965). For centuries before the Council, the faithful took a back seat, so to speak, saying, and singing, very little. Churchgoers did more listening than singing, especially to a prescribed form of Gregorian Chant which was the same in every community around the world. This form of sacred music has always held a pride of place in the Church, and is enjoying a strong comeback today. The bishops reversed this trend, saying, "One cannot find anything more religious and more joyful in sacred celebrations than a whole congregation expressing its faith and devotion in song" (*Instruction on Music in the Liturgy,* 16). They called for a more active participation by the people and cited prayer and song as one of the four major ways in which Christ is present in the Church's liturgical celebrations. (The others were: "in the person of His minister . . . in the Eucharistic species . . . and in the word" (*Constitution on the Sacred Liturgy,* 113).

Every song we sing in church is designed to lead us into the heart of the mystery we are celebrating: God's intimate unconditional love for His Bride, the Church. Hymns stir our spirits, open us to God's presence and unify us as a worshipping community. Singing also introduces us to the mystery of the season or feast, sets the mood of the celebration and unites us emotionally in prayer. Ideally, singing should stir up deep feelings of gratitude for having been invited to the Lord's Supper.

The celebrant and ministers of the altar process to the sanctuary singing an *Entrance Song.* Like David dancing before the Ark of the Covenant, we greet our God and with joyful song "enter his

David Dancing before the Ark/James Tissot

*And David danced before the Lord with all his might; so David and all the house of Israel brought up the ark of the Lord with shouting and with the sound of the horn.*

—2 Sam 6:14-16

gates with thanksgiving, and his courts with praise" (Ps 100:4). While David expressed his heartfelt love for God's presence by dancing, the Church invites us to join in the procession by singing. It is a form of worship which one author describes as a gateway to our transformation in Christ, saying, "If we never dance before the ark, our alleluias are doomed to be very dull" (Fr. Peter E. Fink, S.J., *Praying the Sacraments,* 146). What he is saying, I believe, is that if we want our lives to change, we must pray the Mass with our hearts.

Christians have been processing since the earliest days of Christianity to publicly proclaim their allegiance to Christ. Four processions take place in the liturgy: at the entrance, the Gospel (from the altar to the ambo), the preparation of gifts and communion. "The procession is not just a means to arrive at the sanctuary," says Fr. Peter Stravinskas, founding editor of *The Catholic Answer*, "it has deep theological significance reminding all of the fact that the entire People of God is a pilgrim people *in via* (*CCC,* 769), on the road from here to eternity. In that sacred journey Christ is not only our final goal (symbolized by the altar), but He also accompanies us on the way—in the person of the priest" (*The Bible and the Mass,* 14). Our journey, which the procession symbolizes, takes us from being individual members of the body of Christ to being the body of Christ gathered around Christ, the Head of His Body, the Church.

The entrance procession includes those who perform a special liturgical role in the Mass such as concelebrants, deacons, lectors, cantors, altar servers or acolytes. The altar servers carry the cross, candles and thurifer (censer); the lector or deacon the Book of the Gospels. As the procession makes its way to the sanctuary, the congregation greets Our Lord in song. If there is no singing (such as at daily Mass) the spoken *Entrance Antiphon* replaces the *Entrance Song*. Formerly called the *Introit* of the Mass, this is the first part of the Mass spoken or sung aloud. It sets the tone and theme of the entire celebration.

Fr. Lawrence Hennessey venerates the altar.

When the priest, concelebrants, deacon and liturgical ministers enter the sanctuary, the presider approaches the altar which he reverences with certain devotional gestures. He makes a profound bow (or he genuflects as a sign of adoration to the Blessed Sacrament), he kisses the altar (he will also venerate the altar with a kiss at the end of Mass), and if he chooses, he incenses it. He offers these displays of deep respect to greet Christ our High Priest who is present in our midst symbolically as the "table of the Lord"

(1 Cor 10:21), known in the early Church as the *mensa altaris*, the name of the supper table on which our Lord instituted the Eucharist. The altar represents the Person of Christ who offered His Body and Blood to the Father for our salvation and through Whom we now offer this perfect act of oblation to God. Next to the Blessed Sacrament, the altar is the most sacred object in the church.

### Veneration of the Altar

Altar comes from the Latin *altare* (from *altus*, "high," and *ara* for table or place of sacrifice). In Roman times, *ara* was the small household altar; *altare* was the great monumental altar upon which public sacrifices were offered.

Today the altar represents two aspects of the same mystery: the altar of the sacrifice and the table of the Lord (*CCC*, 1383). As a symbol of Christ, it is the focal point of His sacramental presence. It is the place where Christ steps into our time and space, and, in the midst of the assembly of the faithful, offers His Father a perfect sacrifice of praise and thanksgiving.

Ancient rock in the Church of the Primacy of Peter in Capernaum, known as the *Mensa Christi*. Tradition cites this rock as the place where Jesus shared breakfast with the seven disciples on the shore of the Sea of Galilee after His resurrection.

The altar is usually made of stone to denote Christ, who is the foundation stone of His Church. In the Old Testament, it was prophecied that the Messiah would be the cornerstone of the spiritual temple, a temple which would be built of His people ("living stones") to take the place of the old Jewish temple with its imperfect sacrifices.

Just as the cornerstone unites two walls of a building, so does Christ unite all people into His Body, the Church. Christ Himself is called our altar, in whom and through whom the offerings of the faithful are consecrated to God. The altar is a symbol of both Christ who is the cornerstone, and of Christ present in His members.

Altars are essentially stone tables, or if made of wood, a small square stone known as an "altar stone" containing relics of the saints is imbedded into the altar itself. The main altar of the Cathedral of the Madeleine in Salt Lake City contains relics of St. Gratus, Bishop of Aosta in Piedmont, Northern Italy, who died in 457, and St. Fenusta, an early Roman martyr buried in the Roman catacombs. The relics signify the call to sainthood of all who approach Christ's table, and are a metaphorical link across space and time between every Eucharist.

Main altar at the Cathedral of the Madeleine, Salt Lake City, Utah, made of Carrara onyx.

The altar should be freestanding to allow the ministers to easily walk around it and so that Mass can be celebrated facing the people, a directive of Vatican II. It should be placed as a focal point where the whole congregation naturally centers its attention, and should be elevated slightly, a few steps above the floor of the Church. An altar-cross is always placed on or near the altar to establish the connection between the Mass and Calvary. The image of Christ crucified reminds us of His Passion, of which the Mass is a representation. It is also interesting to know that the altar slab or stone is often engraved with crosses, one on each corner and one in the middle. These five crosses represent the five wounds of Christ on the Cross.

The priest has the option of incensing the altar, a rite which adds solemnity and respect to the Sacred Liturgy. Rarely used today, we see the ritual most often during funeral services or Benediction of the Blessed Sacrament. Used in Old Testament worship and even by pagans, incense is made from woods or resins which have been heated and which give off a fragrant aroma. The magi used "frankincense" (a purer form of incense) to worship the newborn Christ. Since the reign of Constantine, Christians have used incense to symbolize the prayer of the human heart rising up to

God: "Let my prayer be counted as incense before thee" (Ps 141:2). If the celebrant censes the altar, he also censes the Book of the Gospels, the altar-cross, the ministers and the assembly.

It was Our Lord Himself who implicitly recognized the sacredness of the altar when He hurled His famous invective at the Pharisees, "You blind men! For which is greater, the gift, or the altar that makes the gift sacred?" (Mt 23:19). Christians have always recognized the sacredness of the altar and to this day retain the custom of touching to the altar things they want to put under God's protection, a practice which originated in the Old Testament: "Seven days you shall make atonement for the altar, and consecrate it, and the altar shall be most holy; whatever touches the altar shall become holy" (Ex 29:37).

One who honored this tradition was St. Thomas Aquinas (1225-1274), Doctor of the Church and one of her greatest theologians, whose faith the Lord rewarded by appearing to him. In response to a challenge put to him by the professors at the Sorbonne about the Real Presence of Christ in the Eucharist, he took the matter to prayer and penned a response, which he laid at the foot of the crucifix on the altar, offering it to God, as it were, for His approval. While the saint was deep in prayer, the other friars watched as the figure of Christ came down from the cross before their

Vision of St. Thomas Aquinas/Sassetta

eyes. Christ stood on the response, saying, "Thomas, thou has written well concerning the Sacrament of My Body" (G.K. Chesterton, *The Autobiography of St. Thomas Aquinas,* 137).

If the Eucharist is the "soul" of the Sacred Liturgy, singing is its heart. And yet people are reluctant to express their love for God in song. Despite the Council's changes and the liturgists' efforts to implement a "full, conscious and active" participation by the faithful, many people don't sing a word. I know I'm guilty of it, usually out of laziness or tiredness. Imagine how a child would feel at his or her birthday party if no one joined in singing "Happy Birthday" when the cake was presented. What a downer! It is the same at Mass. It would be hard to guess from our body language that the Mass is the most awesome celebration on this planet—an exchange of gifts between ourselves and the living God. We present our lives to God symbolically in the bread and wine which, at the Consecration, is united with Christ's perfect Gift to the Father—His sacrificial Body and Blood. In return,

> *Before all else, the church is the people. Long before there should be any mention of buildings, ministers, priests, bishops, popes, organizations, institutions, or moral codes, there should be mention of a community of hearts and souls, previously separated by many things, coming together. Jesus formed a community around himself, animated it, and then left it his word, his spirit, and the Eucharist. That community is the church and it is a particular kind of community, an apostolic one.*
>
> —Fr. Ronald Rolheiser
> *The Holy Longing*

God thanks us for our love by giving us a gift—Himself in Holy Communion. It is an exchange of love so sacred and intimate that there is nothing on earth to which it can compare.

The problem is deeper than just our unwillingness to sing. One of the Church's foremost theologians, our newly elected pope, Benedict XVI, former Prefect of the Congregation for the Doctrine of the Faith, has written extensively on liturgical music. He agrees that there is a problem in this area of our worship which he sees as part of the general crisis of the Church since Vatican II—a crisis which might stem from the underlying question of what the liturgy is. He refers to the rise of "utility music" over art music. Its roots, he suggests, stem from a cultural crisis in the West which has all but disowned Christian culture (in M. Francis Mannion, *Masterworks of God*, 177).

The derailment of liturgical music is an outrage, and very sad, considering our rich biblical heritage of sacred song. It's been more than a decade since Thomas Day's book, *Why Catholics Can't Sing*, came out, yet its message—that bad taste has triumphed over classic Catholic culture—still runs true. Unfortunately, mundane music seems to be the norm in many Catholic parishes today.

If our singing truly reflects our faith, we should witness to the world—in song—that we have come to celebrate Jesus Christ. As I write this, I recall my husband telling me about his years at a Jesuit prep school, when the student body began their day in the assembly hall on the second floor. One of the priests would order the students to open the windows—in the middle of winter—and sing at the top of their lungs. My husband remembers, with some emotion, the force of two hundred young men singing "Holy God We Praise Thy Name" and the impact that their voices must have had on unsuspecting pedestrians on the street below.

Would that our singing in church could witness to the Lord with such power and glory! "When man comes into contact with God," says Pope Benedict XVI, "areas of his existence are awakened that spontaneously turn into song." We need liturgical song, he says, because "man's own being is insufficient for what he has to express, and so he invites the whole of creation to become a song with him" (*The Spirit of the Liturgy,* 136). This beautiful image captures the essence of the *Entrance Song.*

## HISTORY

Everything we do in the Mass is built on the bedrock of Sacred Tradition. We know from Scripture that Jesus and His apostles sang hymns at the Last Supper: "And when they had sung a hymn, they went out to the Mount of Olives" (Mt 26:30, Mk 14:26). These were the songs of the *Hallel* (Psalms 113-118, thanksgiving songs sung after Passover) which the Jews traditionally sang at the end of the paschal meal. St. Paul encourages the Ephesians to "be filled with the Spirit, addressing one another in psalms and hymns and spiritual songs, singing and making melody to the Lord with all your heart" (Eph 5:18, 19).

We also find evidence of singing in the early Church from a famous letter that the Roman governor Pliny wrote to the Emperor Trajan about the year 112, telling of the Christian practice "to meet, on an appointed day, before sunrise, to sing together among themselves a hymn to Christ, as to a god" (in Daniel J. Sheerin, *The Eucharist,* 32).

As early as the fourth century, the presider processed to the altar and greeted the people. The entrance procession originated in the early days of the Roman Church when the pope walked in solemn cortege from the Lateran Palace to the designated church where Mass would be celebrated. The eloquent and fearless Bishop and Doctor of the Church, St. John Chrysostom (347-407), gives us a glimpse into the musical tradition of the early Church:

> As soon as the singing of the psalms begins, all the voices are united and are gathered into a harmonious canticle. Young and old, rich and poor, men and women, slaves and free men, we all sing the same melody. The musician plays the various chords of his zither but it is one melody that is heard: it is so astonishing that the power of the psalm and the inspired canticle produce the same result! . . . The prophet speaks, we all respond, together we form one choir. There are no longer slaves, free men, rich, poor, master, nor servant. The inequality which exists in the world has been pushed aside, forming a single choir with equal voices, earth imitating heaven. Such is the nobility of the Church! (In Lucien Deiss, *Spirit and Song of the New Liturgy*, 126)

The practice of antiphonal singing (two choirs answering each other) was introduced in the West by St. Ambrose (340–397). During a night of terror when his church was besieged by Arian troops, Ambrose barricaded himself in the church with his parishioners to prevent a takeover. To bolster the spirit of his people and calm their fears, he divided them into two choirs and directed them to sing hymns and psalms all night.

During the fifth and sixth centuries, sometimes called the Golden Age of Liturgy, singers from the *Schola Cantorum* (large choirs which usually performed in basilicas, cathedrals and other major churches) in Rome were grouped together at the end of the nave where they sang a psalm of entry, the *Introit*, antiphonally. Whole psalms were often sung to accompany the long and solemn procession which brought the pontiff to the altar. In those days, after he kissed the concelebrating bishops or deacons, the pope prostrated himself in front of the altar. Eventually, the singing was reduced to an antiphon

St. Ambrose baptizing Augustine/Carl Van Loo

alternated with a psalm verse, similar to what we have today in the *Responsorial Psalm.*

One who speaks with great personal conviction about the gift of liturgical singing is St. Augustine (354–430), who said, "He who sings prays twice." Doctor of the Church and one of the most beloved saints of all time, Augustine lived a wild and undisciplined life until the age of thirty, even fathering a child out of wedlock. He taught rhetoric at Carthage and Milan and became a Manichaean for several years, following a philosophy which taught of the great struggle between good and evil, but which featured a lax moral code. A summation of his thinking at the time comes from his *Confessions*: "God, give me chastity and continence, but not just now." Augustine finally broke with the Manichaeans and was converted by the prayers of St. Monica, his mother, and with the help of St. Ambrose of Milan, who baptized him.

Prior to his conversion, he would sit for hours, apparently unmoved, listening to the sermons of St. Ambrose in Milan. Years later, St. Augustine wrote in his *Confessions* that when the people rose to chant the psalms, his heart melted. Here are his own words:

> I wept at the beauty of Your hymns and canticles, and was powerfully moved at the sweet sound of Your Church's singing. Those sounds flowed into my ears, and the truth streamed into my heart: so that my feeling of devotion overflowed, and the tears ran from my eyes, and I was happy in them (Bk 9, 6).

What a beautiful testimony to the power of song to open our hearts to God!

## REFLECTION

I experienced that power at a Christmas concert given by the Irish Tenors. It was the December following 9/11, when the pain of the terrorist attack on the World Trade Center was still very fresh. The auditorium was packed and the mood was somber. Each song was like a prayer which reached into the deep recesses of our troubled hearts and called forth hope. And healing.

After two curtain calls, the three Tenors sang a final *God Bless America*. When they started singing, everyone was seated. A hushed silence enveloped the auditorium. People rose to their feet, at first one by one, then row by row, then section by section, until the entire place was standing. It was a tribute in song to God, acknowledging our need for His protection. Tears flowed freely. Although I didn't know anyone personally, my heart was breaking from the sheer amount of pain and suffering Americans had endured. The audience and the Tenors were one in spirit and sang with an emotional intensity reminiscent of the early Christians, who were so filled with the Spirit when they prayed that "the place in which they were gathered was shaken" (Acts 4:31).

If we could only sing like that in church! What happened at the concert is a good example of the sacred atmosphere singing is intended to create at Mass. As the celebrant and liturgical ministers make their way to the altar, we stand to greet our God in song. We proclaim our gratitude for being able to express our faith freely and openly in a country which was founded on Judeo-Christian values, and for the privilege of participating in the Lord's Supper. Lifting our souls to heaven, the faithful express themselves with one voice, one heart and one mind—the goal of every Eucharistic Liturgy.

# *Greeting*

He stood alone and tall in the high, wet grass at the end of the runway at the 8th Air Force base in England during World War II. He showed up everyday to bless our American pilots as they became airborne, and to welcome them home with the Sign of the Cross upon their return. A Catholic priest affectionately remembered as "the unknown priest of Buncher Eight," Fr. Ed Norkett is a spiritual legend in the Air Force. Most of our soldiers never met him or knew him personally, yet for the pilots who flew aerial combat missions deep into German territory he became a talisman who lifted his hand in prayer to send them off and guide them safely home. He was the harbor from which their planes departed and the beacon to which they returned. Although Father Ed always remained at his post, his spiritual presence flew with them on every mission.

Catholic Chaplain Fr. Edward Norkett, now in his nineties, is still active in the priesthood.

Such is the power of God's hand on our life, extended to bless and greet us in our coming and going. When we enter into the sacred space of our Catholic church to attend Mass, we bless ourselves with holy water, a gesture reminding us of our Baptism which places an indelible seal on our soul. When the bishop traces the Sign of the Cross on the forehead of an infant with holy oil, the gesture seals the child's relationship to Christ. Reborn as a *Christian,* we are saved by the Cross and the Sacrament of Baptism. We are redeemed, says St. John, by the blood of Jesus Christ and the water of baptism (1 Jn 5:6).

As the Mass begins, the priest stands with arms raised to welcome us, a gesture he renders in the name of Christ. We are headed on a spiritual mission, not into enemy territory but to a sacred Supper, where God invites us to participate in the Sacrament that won our salvation: the dying and rising of Christ.

How many times have I wondered what it must have been like to be at the foot of the Cross on Golgotha in 33 AD and witness our suffering Savior offer His Father every last drop of blood—and breath—for our redemption. When we eat His Body and drink His Blood at Mass, we are privileged to kneel before the altar of the Cross and unite ourselves to this unbloody representation of Christ's sacrifice. We stand in awe with Mary and John and all the saints in heaven and on earth and proclaim the mystery of our faith: *Dying you destroyed our death, rising you restored our life. Lord Jesus, come in glory.* The great mystery is that we become what we eat and drink—a new person in Christ—risen, free and transformed by His love.

At the beginning of the Sacred Liturgy, we sign ourselves with the cross, indicating who we are and what we're about. Like Father Ed reaching out to his pilots, the celebrant raises his arms in a gesture of greeting to formally welcome the faithful home in the name of the Lord.

## EXPLANATION

### Sign of the Cross

After the priest venerates the altar with a kiss, he proceeds to his presider's chair where he makes the Sign of the Cross, saying, *In the name of the Father, and of the Son and of the Holy Spirit,* to which the people respond, *Amen.* This begins the Sacred Liturgy.

It is fitting that this most sacred act of sacrifice—the Mass—should begin with a reminder of the Cross on which it was offered. The priest offers Mass in the name of the Trinity: Father, Son and Holy Spirit. The Sign of the Cross marks us as a community of faith, distinguishing us from members of a secular club or an organization. What we are really saying—and praying—is, *In the name of our loving heavenly Father who created us, in the name of Jesus, sent to redeem and heal us, and in the name of the Holy Spirit Who is continually sanctifying us.* This sacred gesture is used throughout the Mass: in the beginning, over the gifts during the *Eucharistic Prayer* and at the liturgy's conclusion.

The most important and frequently used sacramental of our Church, the Sign of the Cross is both a sign of our redemption and a sign of the Trinity: in one God there are three divine Persons, equal in all things and having only one Divine nature. When we sign ourselves, we recall our baptism which brought us into God's family, the Blessed Trinity. We can thank St. Patrick for helping us grasp the difficult concept of

Three Persons in one God. While he was explaining Christianity to the pagan Irish, he plucked a little plant that grew at his feet. Holding the shamrock before them, he pointed to the three leaves that made one plant, each leaf equal, distinct, separate, and yet only one plant. In this way, St. Patrick taught the Irish the meaning of the Trinity!

The cross is one of the oldest symbols in the world, dating back to pagan cultures. In the Christian era, the symbol of the cross is rooted in the meaning of Jesus, reminding disciples of every generation that God saves through the Cross. Since the day that Christ died and rose from the dead, Christians have equated the Cross with reconciliation between God and neighbor, with renewing life in this world and finding life in the next, and freedom from slavery to sin and selfishness. It is unclear when the prayer formula accompanying the signing originated, but we do know that the word for baptism was "crossing" or "sealing." The words of blessing accompanying baptism are taken from Jesus' command: "Go therefore and make disciples of all nations, baptizing them in the name of the Father, and of the Son, and of the holy Spirit, teaching them to observe all that I have commanded you" (Mt 28:18). To sign oneself with the Cross is to confess our Christian faith and hope in Christ, the Crucified one, "a stumbling block to Jews and folly to Gentiles, but to those who are called, both Jews and Greeks, Christ the power of God and the wisdom of God" (1 Cor 1:23). The Cross brings the power of Christ's blessing and protection to persons and objects, sanctifying them in His name.

Jesus asked His disciples to take up their crosses, saying: "If any man would come after me, let him deny himself and take up his cross daily and follow me" (Lk 9:23). We do that by "crucifying" our actions, our work, our problems, our joys, our very lives upon the Cross of Christ, offering them to Him for our sanctification. Discipleship begins with a reverent and intentional Sign of the Cross.

Author Bert Ghezzi has gifted Christians with an inspirational book, *The Sign of the Cross*, in which he offers anecdotes and insights about the transformative power of this holy gesture. Here is a sample story about a famous Soviet dissident and author:

> Alexander Solzhenitsyn leaned on his shovel and watched the gray clouds drag sullenly across the sky. A merciless wind tore at him through his prison garb. He felt as though

it penetrated to his soul. Every one of his bones and muscles ached. Hunger gnawed at his stomach. Years of hard labor in the Siberian work camp had ruined his health and stripped him of hope.

Solzhenitsyn could endure no longer. He dropped his shovel, left the work gang, and sat on a bench nearby. Soon a guard would command him to return to work. When he would ignore the order, the guard would beat him to death with his own shovel. He had seen it happen to others many times. A quick bloody death today, thought Solzhenitsyn, would be better than a slow death in a bleak, empty future.

He stared at the ground, waiting for the inevitable. Soon he heard footsteps and braced himself in anticipation of the guard's harsh words. But when he raised his eyes, instead of a guard he saw a gaunt, elderly prisoner standing before him. The old man said nothing but knelt in front of Solzhenitsyn. With a stick he scratched the sign of the cross in the dirt and then hurried back to work.

Solzhenitsyn looked at the cross, and as he reflected on it, a ray of light penetrated his dark thoughts. In that moment his perspective changed radically. He realized that he did not have to face the evil of the gulag and the Soviets on his own diminished strength. With the power of the cross, he could withstand the evil of not one but a thousand Soviet empires. (3, 4)

## Holy Water

When we make the Sign of the Cross, we bless ourselves with water which has been blessed by a priest, bishop or deacon. Holy water is used in the blessing of nearly everything which the Church wishes to sanctify. Its use was common in almost every ancient faith to denote interior purification. Among the Greeks and Romans, the sprinkling of water was an important feature in religious ceremonies. Cities were purified by its use during solemn processions. Fields were prepared for planting by being blessed with water.

Armies setting out for war were put under the protection of the gods by being sprinkled in a similar manner. Among the Egyptians, the use of holy water was even more common, the priests being required to bathe in it twice every day and twice every night.

Among the Jews, a ceremony of purification was required before entering the Temple to assist at the sacrifices, and this undoubtedly suggested the Catholic practice of placing holy water at the church door. This ancient custom constitutes a ritual cleansing (a reminder of our baptism) in preparation for Mass. When we leave church we once again bless ourselves with holy water, an action which reminds us to fulfill the great commission Jesus gave us: "Go, therefore, and make disciples of all nations, baptizing them in the name of the Father, and of the Son and of the holy Spirit, teaching them to observe all that I have commanded you" (Mt 28:19).

St. Teresa of Avila/Fray Juan Miseria

Carmelite nun and first woman Doctor of the Church, St. Teresa of Avila (1515–1582), valued holy water so much that she and her nuns carried it in gourds tied to their habits when they journeyed throughout Spain in oxcarts. Blessing herself with holy water was a source of great consolation, which she says gave her an "inward joy" and also made demons flee: "From long experience I have learned that there is nothing like holy water to put devils to flight and prevent them from coming back again. They also flee from the Cross, but return; so holy water must have great virtue" (in E. Allison Peers, *The Autobiography of St. Teresa of Avila*, 289).

I had just finished reading St. Teresa's autobiography before a pilgrimage to Fatima one year. The saint's devotion to holy water rubbed off on me, so that after the trip and before returning home, I bought the largest plastic jug I could find to fill with holy water.

Enroute to Chicago I changed planes at Dulles International Airport. When I checked in, I put the jug on the counter which aroused the curiosity of the ticket agent. I tried to tell her the entire story of Fatima while she was typing things into the computer. There was a long line behind me and I could tell they didn't appreciate my having a conversation with the United Airlines agent. She was extremely interested in Fatima and the holy water and ran in search of a receptacle for this precious water. I carefully poured some water into a little film container, then poured some over my fingers and sprinkled her with it while asking God to bless and protect her. I told her that this is a powerful sacramental of the Church, and to expect the Lord to bless her deeply when she blesses herself or others with it. I didn't even have to turn around to feel the hostile stares of a whole line of impatient, outraged passengers behind me!

### Greeting

The celebrant's greeting concludes the entrance procession. We have entered God's dwelling and the priest welcomes the faithful in the name of the Master of the house. By facing the congregation and greeting them, the celebrant brings to a focus what already has become apparent—that we are standing in the presence of the Lord to worship together. Extending his arms in a gesture of welcome, "the priest declares to the assembled community that the Lord is present" (*General Instruction,* 28), saying, "The Lord be with you."

This is a moment for us to pay attention and be present

Mary's Visit to Elizabeth/Carl Bloch

to the Lord. When someone drops by to visit, we welcome them and exchange polite greetings. A greeting is a show of hospitality which we usually engage in with gusto. It is inconceivable to think that when friends step through our front door we would somehow be distracted and not respond to their conversation. Yet we often miss the Lord's greeting at Mass because it is brief and we are not yet settled—and centered—in His presence. "The Lord be with you" is a salutation from the Lord Himself. It is only courteous that we reply, "And also with you."

The priest, facing the people, extends his arms and greets all present with one of three sayings taken directly from Sacred Scripture: "The grace of our Lord Jesus Christ and the love of God and the fellowship of the Holy Spirit be with you all," to which the people respond, "And also with you." The roots of this ritual are scriptural in that it is almost identical to the closing words of St. Paul's Second Letter to the Corinthians (13:13).

The celebrant has a second option of saying, "The grace and peace of God our Father and the Lord Jesus Christ be with you," to which the people respond "Blessed be God, the Father of our Lord Jesus Christ," or "And also

Fr. Laurence Dunn greets his parishioners.

with you." This is also scriptural, a form of salutation St. Paul used to begin most of his letters: "Grace to you and peace from God our Father and the Lord Jesus Christ" (Rom 1:7).

The celebrant's third choice is to say simply, "The Lord be with you," and the people answer, "And also with you." This was a common form of greeting in the Old Testament: "And behold, Boaz came from Bethlehem; and he said to the reapers, 'The Lord be with you!' And they answered, 'The Lord bless you'" (Ruth 2:4).

I am reminded of St. Peter's remark to Christ on the Mount of Transfiguration: "Lord it is good that we are here" (Mt 17:4). *It is good that we are here*, a community of saints united in Spirit who assemble to celebrate Jesus Christ. Jesus told His disciples that wherever two or more are gathered in His name, He will be with them (cf. Mt 18:20). His promise applies to us, too!

The bishops of the Second Vatican Council reinforced Christ's words, saying: "Christ is always present in his Church, especially in liturgical celebrations." Listing a number of ways in which Christ is present in His Church, they conclude: "Lastly, he is present when the Church prays or sings" (*Constitution on the Sacred Liturgy*, 7).

The *Greeting* should be formal and biblical because the "greeting and the people's response express the mystery of the gathered Church" (*General Instruction*, 28). What is that mystery? It is that we are invited to share in this preeminent prayer of the Catholic Church, to participate in Christ's own prayer addressed to the Father in the Holy Spirit (*CCC*, 1073). The late American liturgist Dr. Ralph Kiefer is one of many who object to presiders greeting the assembly with, for instance, an informal "Good morning, everybody" instead of "The Lord be with you." He sees a secular greeting as an inappropriate violation of the "ritual bond" already established by the song and procession. To change the *Greeting* into a flat statement sends a message that the biblical salutation (*The Lord be with you*) is somehow a barrier to communication or that it will bore the congregation (*To Give Thanks and Praise*, 109).

The *Greeting* and our response forms a real dialogue between the celebrant and the people, one which is a "precious reminder that the liturgical community is not just any kind of assembly," says English author, Fr. J.D. Crichton. "It is a dialogue with God through the presence of the Spirit" (*Christian Celebration: The Mass*, 70).

Famed French liturgist Fr. Lucien Deiss, C.S.Sp., composer, teacher, scripture scholar, and special advisor to Vatican Council II on the liturgy, sees the *Greeting* as "the descent of the Eternal into time, the descent of the tenderness of Jesus into human distress." He cautions that the exchange be an actual dialogue, so that the priest speaks to the people in an authentically human and expressive manner, eliciting a unanimous, joyful—and intentional—response from the congregation (*Spirit and Song of the New Liturgy*, 66).

After the *Greeting*, the priest, a deacon or a lay minister may say a few brief words to introduce the Mass of the day. He may mention a particular feast or refer to a special character or intention of the Mass, but it is not a time to expound on the life of a saint or explain the upcoming readings. The idea is to be very brief and stay within the sacred boundaries of the liturgical ritual to further unite the community and prepare them for communion with their Creator.

# HISTORY

A great deal of evidence in the writings of the Church Fathers shows that the early Christians looked upon the Sign of the Cross as a means of sanctifying all their actions by calling to mind the sacrifice of Christ on the Cross. Tertullian (160-230), a quick-witted lawyer and Father of the Church from Carthage in Africa, observes: "At each entry and departure from the house, when dressing, when bathing, when about to eat, when lighting lamps, when going to bed, on rising, on all occasions, they trace the sign of the Cross on their foreheads."

Reliquary containing pieces of the True Cross in the Basilica of the Holy Cross of Jerusalem in Rome.

Among the Jews in the Old Testament, a ceremony of purification was required before entering the Temple to assist at the sacrifices. Holy water stoups and fonts existed in the earliest days of the Church. Some examples made of marble, glass and terra cotta were unearthed in the catacombs while other urns and containers for holy water were discovered in ancient Roman churches and cemeteries.

According to the diary of Egeria, a fourth century Spanish nun, Holy Week services in Jerusalem included a rite for veneration of the Cross. This devotion spread to Rome to the Basilica of the Holy Cross in Jerusalem, where a piece of the True Cross was taken and placed in a reliquary which can be seen today. The relic of the True Cross as well as a nail used to crucify Jesus and two thorns from the Crown of Thorns was obtained by St. Helena, the mother of Emperor Constantine, who brought these treasures to Rome where she enshrined them in a chapel.

By the third century, the Sign of the Cross was customary in some forms of Christian liturgy. In the ninth century, the Church stipulated that the celebrant make the Sign of the Cross over the offerings at Mass with his thumb and two fingers extended.

For two millennia, Christians have passed on this sacred gesture of their heritage by which we profess our belief in Christ, in the hope of our salvation which flows from the Cross. We remind ourselves, and the world, that we are Christians and that our life is in God. How ironic that such an instrument of death—the Cross of Christ—is such a sign of life and hope! It has converted people in every age beginning with Longinus, the pagan centurian whose failing eyesight was restored during the Crucifixion when a drop of Our Lord's blood ran down his lance and touched his eyes. Tradition says that he gave up soldiering, converted to the faith, then became a monk and eventually a martyr. His statue stands in a place of honor in St. Peter's Basilica today, not far from the main altar.

In the very early days of the Church, when liturgical practices were developing, every community gathered around its bishop to celebrate Mass. As far as we know, there was no *Entrance Song,* and Mass began with the *Liturgy of the Word.* Scholars disagree as to whether it was customary to begin the service in the early Church with a liturgical *Greeting,* yet there is some evidence of a type of *Greeting* from the writings of the Church Fathers.

St. Augustine relates an amazing story in *The City of God* about a miraculous cure of a brother and sister which took place before Mass on Easter Sunday in 426. Evidence of a liturgical *Greeting* is included in the description.

> On all sides, the church was filled with cries of joy and thanksgiving. People ran to the place where I was sitting, already ready to come forward. Each one hurried after the other, the last one telling me as new what the first had already told me. Quite joyous, I gave thanks to God in myself when the young man himself arrived, well surrounded; he threw himself at my knees and arose to receive my kiss.
>
> We came forward toward the people. The church was full; it resounded with cries of joy: Thanks be to God! Praise

be to God! No one stays quiet; from the right, from the left, rose up cries!

I greeted the people. The acclamation started again with redoubled intensity. Finally silence was established and the passage from the Holy Scriptures was read which dealt with the feast. (in Lucien Deiss, *The Mass*, 16)

There is also evidence of a *Greeting* in the early Church in the writings of St. John Chrysostom (347-407), who is ranked as one of its greatest pastors: "The church is a house belonging to all. Once you have entered in before us, we too enter. . . . And when I say, 'Peace to all,' you answer, 'And with your spirit.'" He also complains of the noise that fills the church when "the president prays for peace, like a man entering his paternal home."

## REFLECTION

I never realized how much a simple greeting could mean until the memory of my dad's affectionate greetings to me throughout my life surfaced after his death. Like a king presiding over his kingdom, my father sat in his armchair in the living room while he sipped his scotch and soda and contemplated life. Each evening when I turned the key in the apartment door, my dad would be sitting there reading the newspaper. "Joanie!" he cried, his high-pitched voice revealing a depth of emotion. Startled by his enthusiasm, I'd giggle. We lived in entirely different worlds, yet I knew that my dad cared deeply for me. Years later, after marriage and four children, I'd ring the doorbell, let myself in with my key and there he would be in that same chair, rising to his feet while saying my name with such love. Ecstatic to see me and the children, he'd open his arms wide to scoop us up in his love.

Now that my dad isn't here anymore, I think about those greetings—his warm welcome and the joy that my presence brought him. "Joanie, I'm behind you a thousand percent," he'd always say to me. My dad gave me a small taste of the unconditional love which Our Lord wishes to give us when He greets us at the beginning of Mass.

# *Penitential Rite*

The first time I planted a vegetable garden I got out a shovel and started digging, thinking that I could just drop in the seeds randomly along the way. I had no clue as to the amount of preparatory work involved, such as tilling the soil, to properly prepare the earth to receive the seeds. At this point in the Mass, we are tilling the soil of our minds and hearts, preparing to receive Christ in His Word and in the Eucharist. What does this "tilling" mean, practically speaking?

The late Fr. Henri Nouwen, one of the most beloved spiritual writers of the twentieth century, offers a clarifying insight which came to him one night while he was watching a program on Dutch television. The speaker, he said, poured water on hard, dried-out soil, saying "Look, the soil cannot receive the water and no seed can grow." Then, after crumbling the soil with his hands and pouring water on it again, he said, "It is only the broken soil that can receive the water and make the seed grow and bear fruit."

"After seeing this," Nouwen said, "I understood what it meant to begin the Eucharist with a contrite heart, a heart broken open, to receive the water of God's grace" (*With Burning Hearts, A Meditation on the Eucharistic Life,* 32, 33).

During the *Penitential Rite* in the Sacred Liturgy, we have an opportunity to "break open" the hard soil of our hearts by admitting our powerlessness over sin and our need for a Savior. Like AA, which asks its members to work the Twelve Steps as a means of becoming accountable for their behavior by trying to change themselves instead of others, Jesus asks His disciples to "let go and let God," to seek a conversion of heart by surrendering our lives to Him. The Eucharist empowers our transformation, making us "one spirit" with Christ (cf. 1 Cor 6:17). Christ becomes really present in the Eucharist so that we may become His Body.

A story which powerfully illustrates the power of a personal encounter with Christ is found in the parable about the wealthy tax collector, Levi, who was sitting at his customs post when Jesus asked him to follow Him (cf. Lk 5:27-39). Levi immediately left everything behind, got up and followed Jesus. He had a change of heart, a conversion experience. Although he had a great deal of money and possessions, he had the humility to see his littleness in the light of God's greatness. Levi then invited all his rich tax collector friends, as well as the Scribes and Pharisees, to his home for a lavish banquet in honor of Jesus. These people complained to the disciples because Jesus dined with tax collectors and sinners. Jesus set them straight, saying:

The Feast in the House of Levi/Paolo Veronese

"those who are well have no need of a physician, but those who are sick. I have not come to call the righteous, but sinners to repentance" (Lk 5:31, 32).

In the same way that Jesus called Levi, He calls us today, to seek Him at Mass, a sacred banquet to which we have all been invited and where we can feast on the spiritual nourishment Christ gives us in His forgiving, healing love. It is by God's grace that we want a deeper conversion—even our attendance at Mass is a response to His desire to heal and transform us. The Scribes and Pharisees were too busy and important for Jesus. They had eyes that couldn't see and ears that couldn't hear because they didn't really want to know— the truth, that is. How blessed are we if we seek the truth and "drop everything" to follow the Lord!

## EXPLANATION

As our encounter with Christ in His Word and Sacrament draws near, the Church calls us to a moment of truth to see God as He really is—all-loving, all-merciful and all-forgiving—and to see ourselves and our sins "through a formula of general confession" (*General Instruction*, 29). As a people of God we have sinned, and we come to Mass to celebrate the Eucharist for the forgiveness of our sins.

The *Penitential Rite* is a means by which the community can acknowledge their need for a Savior, Jesus Christ, because of our collective and personal sinfulness. The Church provides this rite to make the communal sinfulness of all who have gathered manifest. We must not confuse this with sacramental confession (the Sacrament of Reconciliation), which is a sacrament in itself.

## What is Sin?

To admit our sinfulness presupposes an understanding of sin, a word and a concept which is spoken of very little today. In some circles people even make fun of it. A brief discussion here might help us to appreciate the meaning of this part of the Sacred Liturgy so that we can enter into it more deeply.

The word "sin" is not part of the vocabulary of atheists because they do not believe in God. We can grasp what sin is in relation to God's revelation of Himself and His plan for our lives. Only then can we see how we've abused our God-given freedom and gifts.

Do we understand our own sinfulness? St. Peter at times didn't. When he refused to allow the Lord to wash his feet, Jesus admonished him for not understanding his own need to be washed clean by the Lord's love: "If I do not wash you, you have no part in me," Jesus said to him (Jn 13:8).

One who did admit his sin was St. Paul, who struggled with an inner disorder which prevented him from properly loving God and others: "I do not understand my own actions. For I do not do what I want, but I do the very thing I hate. Now if I do what I do not want, I agree that the law is good. So then it is no longer I that do it but sin that dwells within me" (Rom 7:15–17). Most of us can relate to St. Paul's struggle.

What inside of us causes us to detour from the straight and narrow and take the low road which leads us away from what is good and truthful and loving? Like the San Andreas fault in California, a fracture in the earth's crust more than eight hundred miles long and many miles deep, we have an inner spiritual fracture running through our lives which we are always on the verge of falling into through our bad choices which separate us from God—and others. The Church describes this as the effect of Original Sin. What we have inherited from Adam and Eve is a propensity to abuse truth and goodness and love, choosing evil instead. Their first bad choice was to listen to the serpent who tricked them into believing they would be like gods. Underneath their choice was pride, the root of all sin, which says, "Not Your will, but my will be done."

We have the same tendency—to point the finger, to evade responsibility for what we have done and to cry "mistake." Adam blamed Eve and Eve blamed the serpent. Today the inclination is to place self on the throne and cover up our wrongdoing so that we don't have to admit blame and guilt. The *Catechism* defines sin as an offense against God which ruptures communion with Him and damages communion with the Church (*CCC*, 1440). Sin is not merely a developmental flaw or a psychological weakness or a mistake we make.

> *The great Hindu Mohandas Gandhi tells of a time when he deeply offended his father. His response was to make a clean confession to his father and, by so doing, the affection between them grew beyond measure. Gandhi adds that he made a promise never to commit that particular sin again. Repentance is the starting point in rebuilding any broken relationship.*
>
> —Bishop Robert F. Morneau
> *Paths to Prayer*

Jesus refused to perpetuate evil. He died and rose from the dead to free us from the effects of our bad choices, our sinful ways. He asks us to imitate Him by giving up the choices that separate us from God so that He can free us to be the people He intended us to be. We do that by asking God's forgiveness for the ways we have abused our freedom and hurt others or been hurt by them—and hurt ourselves. When we take responsibility for our sin and seek God's mercy, He pours His healing forgiveness into our fractured souls.

## Penitential Rite

We are about to encounter the Risen Christ in the Sacred Liturgy. Can we muster up the humility of Peter and allow Jesus to wash us clean with His love? The Church gives us this brief but important opportunity to open our hearts to the merciful, forgiving love of our Savior.

During the opening prayer of the *Penitential Rite*, the celebrant admonishes the community to recall its sins by saying one of three short prayers. For example, "Coming together as God's family, with confidence let us ask the Father's forgiveness, for he is full of gentleness and compassion" (*Sacramentary,* 360). A long silent pause is in order here to give the assembly a moment of reflection. The Missal, which contains the guidelines for every part of the Sacred Liturgy (known as the *General Instruction of the Roman Missal*), calls these moments of silence "sacred" and mentions the places where they are built into the Mass: during the *Penitential Rite, Opening Prayer,* in the *Liturgy of the Word* after a reading or the homily, and after *Communion.*

Following the pause, the celebrant chooses one of three forms of penitential prayers: the *Confiteor* or a set of penitential verses, and, almost always, a *Kyrie* litany. A prayer for forgiveness follows each form of the *Penitential Rite.*

The first formal penitential prayer is the *Confiteor* (from the Latin, "I confess"), a communal prayer which the celebrant has the option of saying at any Mass (Sundays, feast days, weekdays), although it seems to be more appropriate at certain times of the year such as Lent. In this prayer, we "*confess to Almighty God, and to you, my brothers and sisters, that I have sinned through my own fault in my thoughts and in my words, in what I have done, and in what I have failed to do*" (*Sacramentary,* 360).

Sin not only hurts our relationship with God, but weakens our bond with others. "It's like a tennis match," says the great Catholic convert, Fr. Ronald Knox. "Just as you apologize to your partner when you've made a perfectly rotten stroke at tennis, so when you have sinned you want to apologize to your fellow-

"I am mercy itself,"
Jesus to St. Faustina Kowalska.

Christians; you have let them all down" (*The Mass in Slow Motion*, 9).

In the remainder of the *Confiteor*, we ask the Blessed Mother and the whole heavenly court of angels and saints, as well as our brothers and sisters in Christ, to intercede for us before the throne of God. Then the priest invokes God's pardon, saying, "*May almighty God have mercy on us, forgive us our sins, and bring us to everlasting life*," to which the people assent by saying, "*Amen.*"

If the *Confiteor* is not recited, the celebrant may choose another form of penitential prayer—a two-fold exchange between the priest and assembly by which we acknowledge our sinfulness and ask for the Lord's mercy.

*Lord, we have sinned against you: Lord have mercy.*
   *Lord, have mercy.* (response)
*Lord, show us your mercy and love.*
   *And grant us your salvation.* (response)

A third alternative lists eight possible invocations structured around a three-fold litany of praise to the Lord. Here is a sample:

*Lord Jesus, you came to reconcile us to one another and to the Father: Lord have mercy.*
   *Lord have mercy.* (response)

*Lord Jesus, you heal the wounds of sin and division: Christ have mercy.*
   *Christ have mercy.* (response)

*Lord Jesus, you intercede for us with your Father: Lord have mercy.*
   *Lord have mercy.* (response)

After each invocation the people respond, *Lord, have mercy. Christ have mercy. Lord have mercy.* Then the priest says the absolution: *May almighty God have mercy on us, forgive us our sins, and bring us to everlasting life.* The people answer: *Amen.*

Integral to all three options of the *Penitential Rite* is the *Kyrie*, a Greek word which means Lord. Like the early Christians, we are proclaiming Jesus as the Lord of our life: "that at the name of Jesus every knee should bow, in heaven and on earth and under the earth, and every tongue confess that Jesus Christ is Lord, to the glory of God the Father" (Phil 2:10, 11). The acclamations, "Lord have mercy, Christ have mercy," which praise the Lord and implore His mercy, are some of the oldest rites in the Church's tradition. They are a combined act of contrition and hope, an acknowledgement of our sorrow and at the same time of our confidence in the goodness of Him whom we have offended. We know that Jesus loves us and has made us His own family and has the power to heal us and make us whole—and holy. And so with all our strength we call out to Him, *Kyrie eleison. Christe eleison. Lord, have mercy. Christ have mercy.*

### Sprinkling Rite

As an alternative to the *Penitential Rite*, there is an ancient custom known as the *Asperges,* a blessing and sprinkling rite which may be used at all Saturday evening and Sunday Masses. The word comes from the first word of the antiphon sung at the beginning of Psalm 51:9: "Cleanse me of sin with hyssop, that I may be purified." Popular since the Middle Ages, in the recent past the ritual was customary only at "High Mass." Now, if used at all, this moving and meaningful rite is used during the Easter season because it recalls our baptism whereby we die to sin and rise to new life with Christ.

After the priest greets the people, he blesses the holy water, asking the people to pray with him: "Dear friends, this water will be used to remind us of our baptism. Ask God to bless it, and to keep us faithful to the Spirit he has given us." A moment of silent prayer follows, after which the celebrant blesses the holy water, and, if he wishes, blesses salt (a sign of preservation and purity) which he mixes with the water. Then he sprinkles himself, the ministers of the altar, the clergy and the congregation as he walks through the church. Music accompanies the sprinkling and the rite ends with a beautiful prayer for the forgiveness of sins: "May almighty God cleanse us of our sins, and through the Eucharist we celebrate make us worthy to sit at his table in his heavenly kingdom. Amen."

## HISTORY

According to the *Didache,* the earliest known liturgical document (other than Scripture), confession of sin was already the practice of the first Christians at the beginning of second century. The *Didache* stated that on Sunday, the Lord's Day, people were to come together to break bread and to give thanks "after first confessing their sins" so that the sacrifice will be pure. The first words Jesus spoke when He began His public ministry were: "The time is fulfilled and the kingdom of God is at hand; repent, and believe in the gospel" (Mk 1:15).

The early Christians were keenly aware of their need to repent and open themselves to God's grace. A good example in Scripture is the humble tax collector who showed a childlike spirit of dependence, saying, "God, be merciful to me a sinner" (Lk 18:13). In contrast, the self-righteous Pharisee, who excused his own behavior and blamed others, went home stuck in sin because of his unrepentant heart. St. Paul, writing about thirty years after the Last Supper, warns the new Christians to examine themselves, "and so eat of the bread and drink of the cup" (1 Cor 11:28). And St. John, always getting to the

The Pharisee and the Tax Collector/James Tissot

heart of the matter, said, "If we confess our sins, he is faithful and just, and will forgive our sins and cleanse us from all unrighteousness. If we say, we have not sinned we make him a liar, and his word is not in us" (1 Jn 1:9, 10).

This is strong language. Yet in the ancient Roman Church, there was no *Penitential Rite* in the liturgy despite the fact that Christ asked us to reconcile with others before offering sacrifice (Mt 5:23–25). The *Confiteor* was added to the Mass in the later Middle Ages and first appeared as a private prayer said by the priest and ministers at the foot of the altar. In the early Eucharistic liturgies, the sacristy was in the back of the church. The priest said any introductory prayers (which were private) either in the sacristy or while he was processing to the altar. Later, when the sacristy was moved to the front of Church, these prayers passed over from private prayers to the public liturgy of the Church. Over the centuries, discussions ensued over the placement of the *Penitential Rite* in the Mass. It was placed at the beginning of the celebration after the *Entrance Song* and *Greeting,* where it remains to this day.

*Kyrios* (Lord) was the title given by the Romans to their emperors whom they deified. The Christians also used the term to acclaim their divine Master. The *Kyrie* is really a song, an ancient hymn which originated in the Greek-speaking East, perhaps in Jerusalem where the Spanish nun Egeria heard it sung about the year 390. Egeria went

to Jerusalem for Holy Week and noted in her diary that at the end of Vespers, one of the deacons read a list of petitions and "as he spoke each of the names, a crowd of boys stood there and answered him each time, *Kyrie eleison,* as we say, Lord have mercy; their cry is without end" (in Josef Jungman, *The Mass of the Roman Rite,* 334). A cry for help from the heart, the *Kyrie* was first sung in Antioch and Jerusalem as the people's response to petitions in a litany said by the deacon. St. John Chrysostom, who came from Antioch, prayed the *Kyrie* often.

The litany with the petition *Kyrie eleison* was introduced into the Roman Mass by Pope Gelasius (492-496). We know from a Church Synod held in Gaul (France) in 529 that the "blessed custom" of the

Pope John Paul II meets with Mehmet Ali Agca, who attempted to assasinate the pope on May 13, 1981 in St. Peter's Square.

*Kyrie eleison* had spread from east to west as far as Italy and Rome. Because of its frequent use, the *Kyrie* became universally known and loved. In the early Church, there were an indefinite number of cries for mercy which went on until the celebrant gave a sign for them to cease. When St. Gregory the Great was pope (590-604), he introduced the *Christe eleison* to the liturgy. He also dropped the long litany of petitions and fixed the acclamations at nine, invoking the Father, Son and Holy Spirit each three times. Before the introduction of the vernacular into the Mass after Vatican II, the penitential litany was said in Greek as a reminder of the Church's universality and ancient heritage. (Until the third century and possibly beyond, the whole Mass was in Greek). In our own time, Pope Paul VI simplified the *Kyrie* by reducing the invocations and response recited each time by the people to three.

## REFLECTION

On our thirty-sixth wedding anniversary, Tommy and I exchanged cards. Although I can't remember my exact words, I recall saying that my gratitude for him was deep, that his goodness to me and the children was a gift straight from the heart of God. Then he delivered the *coup de grace*. After professing his love, he asked me to forgive his shortcomings. I cried. Somehow when we seek pardon, the purity of our heart shows through. It takes real humility to ask for forgiveness, to become vulnerable to the soul of another.

This is what the *Penitential Rite* asks of us: to become little and vulnerable before God. Like children who look to their parents for their needs, God wants us to trust in His love and mercy.

"Mercy is not only the greatest attribute of God, but it is His very nature," says author and evangelist Fr. Robert DeGrandis, who shares some personal insights about God's mercy in his bestselling, *Healing Through the Mass.* "All my life I've been saying the *Kyrie Eleison* at Mass," he writes, until "finally it dawned on me, many years after I was ordained into the priesthood, 'Lord, have mercy'! I never heard it so deeply before." Father Bob brings the concept of mercy to life with a powerful image: "We are like sponges floating on an ocean of mercy, crying 'Mercy.' All we need is the capacity to receive, like the sponge. When a sponge has a capacity to receive, water rushes in and the sponge is filled. As we forgive, and receive His forgiveness, then we can soak up the mercy. Mercy means love and forgiveness in action." Father Bob places God's mercy in the context of the Eucharistic Liturgy:

> The Lord then holds you up tenderly to His Father, covered in His precious Blood and says, "Mercy." The accuser, the devil, interrupts angrily and asks, "But what about this, and this, and this?" The Father ignores the accuser, looks down at you and sees someone clean and free and whole, washed in the blood of His Son. His heart overflows with joy as He says, "Come, beloved of my Son." There is no time with God. Because He lives in the eternal now, He sees us in glory already, and is so happy with our presence. (43)

Jesus is about to come to us in the Eucharist. He wants us to share our pain and failures with Him so that He can remove the blocks which rob us of our freedom and joy. He wants to seal up our fractured souls.

Could it be that the reason children are so loveable is because they *receive* so easily? They are open and honest with their feelings and don't yet know how to put up barriers to block our attempts at loving them. Love isn't only about giving, it's about receiving. Perhaps that is why Jesus told His followers that we must become like little children if we are to enter the kingdom—open, honest, simple, vulnerable and trusting.

The two disciples on the road to Emmaus modeled these qualities when they shared their heartache and depression with Jesus, the "Stranger" who accompanied them for awhile. When Jesus broke bread with them at their home, He healed their sorrow. He led them to understand that the Messiah had to suffer brokenness before He could enter His glory. And so do His disciples.

Healing happens when we give God our hardened, unforgiving hearts and receive His heart of flesh which He opened on the Cross—where He released His forgiving Spirit as promised through His prophet Ezekiel: "A new heart I will give you, and a new spirit I will put within you; and I will take out of your flesh the heart of stone and give you a heart of flesh" (Ez 36:26). Are we open to receive Him?

# *The Gloria*

When my precious three-year-old Katie surprised me with a bouquet of freshly picked wildflowers one day, she was really giving me her heart. The purity of her gift touched me to the core. She tapped into an unending reservoir of love and I responded by nearly smothering her to death with hugs and kisses! In the same way, when we pray the *Gloria* at Mass, we are really giving God our hearts—by offering Him a bouquet of thanks and praise for His goodness and love.

Praise is a form of letting go which lifts us out of ourselves, helping us to focus on the majesty and grandeur of God. In this sense, it is unselfish, and when we pray in a spirit of childlike surrender we fulfill our noblest calling—to honor our Creator and Redeemer. Mass is the most perfect form of worship because we praise and thank God not for His gifts, but for Himself.

The whole earth is full of God's glory—a glory Jesus promised that we share through the indwelling presence of the Holy Spirit—Who comes laden with spiritual gifts so that we might experience healing and new life in all the little and big things of our daily lives. The greatest truth neglected in our Christian experience is the Indwelling Presence—the God of glory living within us—writes Paul de Jaegher, S.J., author of *One with Jesus*, reputed to be one of the late Mother Teresa's favorite books. This saintly woman, now called Blessed Teresa of Calcutta, was so close to Our Lord that at the end of each day she asked this question: "Lord, what did we do today

Pope John Paul II greets Mother Teresa.

together and what did I do alone" (in Sr. Francis Clare, *Glory to Glory*, 152). We so easily forget that God's majesty is hidden deep within our own hearts, where the Father, Son and Holy Spirit make their abode. Our God-in-residence wants to be present in every detail of our lives, empowering our thoughts, our words and our actions and healing our wounds and imperfections. In the second century, St. Irenaeus (125-203) made a statement which, remarkably, has stood the test of time: "The glory of God is man fully alive; the glory of man is the vision of God." If we want to become "fully alive," we have to be full of Life Himself—full of Jesus. When we pray the *Gloria* with every fiber of our being, we open ourselves to the Spirit of Love by which we "are being changed into his likeness from one degree of glory to another; for this comes from the Lord who is Spirit" (2 Cor 3:18). To reflect God's glory is to be filled with God's life. That is why Jesus came, to give us Life—in abundance (Jn 10:10).

## EXPLANATION

During the *Kyrie,* the mood is somber as we recall our sins and implore God's love and mercy. Now, says Fr. Ronald Knox, we need a bit of "cheering up." This happens when we sing the *Gloria in excelsis,* in which we express our joy, praise and adoration of "God the Father and the Lamb." Next to the *Eucharistic Prayer,* the *Gloria* ranks second as a great prayer of thanksgiving and praise which is the heart of our worship.

The atmosphere now changes to one of celebration, a difficult transition according to English pastor, Fr. Francis Randolph, who notes that it is not easy to convey this change of mood. At a chapel in Zimbabwe, he witnessed the *Gloria* as a burst of praise to God as the people jumped to their feet and broke into joyful song while pounding drums and rattles! (*Know Him in the Breaking of the Bread,* 58).

While expressing ourselves in this way is admittedly not our tradition, this prayer nevertheless deserves our full-hearted devotion in praise of God's infinite goodness and love. We do not pray the *Gloria* during Advent or Lent. During Advent we await our salvation, the coming of the Messiah on Christmas. One way this anticipation is emphasized in the Eucharistic Liturgy is to omit the *Gloria.* We realize the fulfillment of the promise when we sing out the *Gloria* on Christmas day and throughout the Christmas octave (eight days following Christmas). We do not sing or recite the *Gloria* in Lent because it is a penitential season, a time of purification and renewal when we ask God's mercy for our sins and failures. On Holy

Shepherd's Field, Bethlehem

*Then the glory of the Lord shall be revealed, and all mankind shall see it together; for the mouth of the Lord has spoken (Is 40:5).*

Thursday, the *Gloria* makes a sudden reappearance, but then it is not heard again until the Easter Vigil.

The *Gloria*, which is usually sung, is one of the Church's oldest and most cherished Christmas carols: *Gloria in Excelcis Deo*. On the night of our Savior's birth, a triumphant chorus of praise resounded from heaven, sung by "a multitude of the heavenly host praising God and saying, 'Glory to God in the highest and on earth peace among men with whom he is pleased!'" (Lk 2:13, 14). Peace is the Father's gift of grace which comes to us through Christ. In the *Gloria* we join our voices to those of the angels who assemble around the altar to chant God's praise as they once sang at the manger of the newborn Savior. Every Mass is, in a sense, a celebration of Christmas, for Jesus comes down on the altar under the humble appearance of bread as once He came as a child. Today He comes to us for the same reasons He came to Bethlehem—to restore to His Father the glory which our sin deprived Him of, and to give His people the peace which the world can not give. Such was Christ's redeeming mission, such is the Church's mission, and such is the mission of each of her members.

The first part of the *Gloria* focuses on God our heavenly Father. We sing: "Lord God, heavenly King, almighty God and Father, we worship you, we give you thanks, we praise you for your glory" (*Sacramentary*, 365). The next part is a tribute to the Son, the Lamb of God Who has taken away the sins of the world and is seated at the right hand of the Father. We ask Him for mercy and to receive our prayer for salvation. In a spirit of joyous welcome to the Savior, soon to be present among us in the Eucharist, we sing to Him as the Holy One, the Lord and the Most High. We conclude with words addressed to the Holy Spirit, who is praised in union with the Father and the Son.

The Greek church calls the *Gloria* "The Greater Doxology" (*doxa*, praise; *logos*, word) which means a verse or a hymn of praise to God, to distinguish it from another *Gloria*, the "Lesser Doxology" known as the "Glory Be:" *Glory be to the Father, to the Son and to the Holy Spirit.* The *Gloria* is a canticle of praise and thanksgiving for our salvation which we, the children of God, sing to the Blessed Trinity. Our worship acknowledges us as God's children who give our Father the most perfect form of adoration and thanksgiving possible—by offering Him the gift of His own Son in the Sacred Liturgy.

> The peace of Christ—which is Christmas—was sealed upon the Cross by the Sacrifice which is commemorated and continued in every Mass. In the Eucharist the angels' solemn declaration is made actual: it is the Sacrifice which gives to God the greatest 'glory' that He can receive from people: it is the Sacrament through which God grants to us the most bounteous graces. The *Gloria* throws into high relief the true purpose of the Eucharist, which is both a gift from God to us and an offering which we make to God.
> (Chevrot, *Our Mass Explained,* 44)

## History

The people of the Old Testament participated in their temple worship with great joy and enthusiasm. During all their important gatherings such as festivals, consecrations or dedications, the assembly expressed their enthusiasm with cries of "Amen!" "Alleluia!" or in refrains such as "Eternal is His love!" (Ps 136:1) in music and chant. Songs of cultic praise are dispersed throughout the psalter, the most famous of them being the "Little Hallel" (Ps 113–118), the "Great Hallel" (Ps 136) and the "Final Hallel" (Ps 146–150). Biblical scholars note that the singing of psalms usually accompanied the "sacrifice of praise" in the temple, which was a peaceful sacrifice followed by a joyful and sacred meal in the buildings adjoining the temple.

There are indications in the New Testament that Christians also integrated praise into their worship. The traditional glory of Yahweh becomes the glory of Christ: "Every day they devoted themselves to meeting together in the temple area and to breaking bread in their homes. They ate their meals with exultation and sincerity of heart, praising God and enjoying favor with all people" (Acts 2:46, 47). Their praise was distinctly Christian, since it was a response to Christ's gift of redemption.

*Meanwhile, as the 'Glory to God in the highest' was being intoned, the Lord Jesus, the Sovereign High Priest, sent forth toward heaven, to the glory of God the Father, a divine breath like a living flame. And at the words 'and on earth peace to men of good will' he breathed forth this same breath, like gleaming snow, over all those who were present.*

—St. Gertrude the Great

Scholars estimate that at the end of the first century there were roughly seven thousand Christians. Their decision for Christ naturally alienated them from certain social—and familial—structures. They kept a low profile, so to speak, save for some who fearlessly and openly proclaimed the Gospel. Two men who gave public witness to Christ were apprehended by the magistrate and ordered to be stripped and beaten with rods. Then they were thrown into the innermost cell of the prison where their feet were shackled to a stake. At midnight, still suffering from their bloody wounds, they began to praise God with prayer and song so that all the prisoners heard them. Their names were Paul and Silas—two disciples irrepressible in their witness for Christ.

What happened next is remarkable. "And suddenly there was a great earthquake, so that the foundations of the prison were shaken; and immediately all the doors were opened, and every one's fetters were unfastened" (Acts 16:26). When the jailer saw the doors of the prison wide open, he was going to kill himself, fearing that the prisoners had escaped. Paul and Silas remained with the jailer who converted on the spot, then accompanied him to his house where they baptized the whole family.

The frustrated magistrates finally gave up and asked Paul to leave the city. With his kind of faith, it is no wonder that God worked miracles.

Paul was driven by faith which was fueled by thanksgiving and praise. He models how our prayer must be preceded by thanksgiving:

> Have no anxiety about anything, but in everything, by prayer and supplication, with thanksgiving, let your requests be made known to God. And the peace of God which passes all understanding will keep your hearts and your minds in Christ Jesus. (Phil 4:6)

In the early Church, where most of the liturgical prayers were improvised, even by the faithful, many invocations and doxologies were patterned after those found in St. Paul's Epistles. In all probability, the *Gloria* was gradually composed of different acclamations joined together. It is one of the Church's oldest—and most beautiful—hymns, which is first found in the *Apostolic Constitutions* (c. 350–380), as a hymn in the morning office. Almost certainly of Syrian origin, the document is a fourth-century collection of independent, though closely related treatises on Christian discipline, worship, and doctrine, designed to serve as a manual of guidance for both clergy and laity. Among the Greek-speaking Christians, it was recommended by St. Athanasius (297–373) to the consecrated virgins for their morning devotions. Authorities have speculated as to whether this might be the hymn alluded to by the pagan governor Pliny in his famous letter to the Emperor Trajan, informing him that the Christians usually assembled early in the morning "to sing a hymn to Christ as to their God." Known in the Eastern Church as the *Great Doxology,* Pope St. Telesphorus (125-136) introduced it into the Mass for Christmas day. Like the *Kyrie*, it originated in the East where St. Hilary of Poitiers (d. 368) translated it and brought it to the West.

St. Augustine maintains that the human heart experiences its true identity and worth in praising God: "Man is one of your creatures, Lord, and his instinct is to praise you. . . . The thought of you stirs him so deeply that he cannot be content unless he praises you, because you made us for yourself and our hearts find no peace until they rest in you" (In R.S. Pine-Coffin, *Confessions*).

In sixth century Rome, the *Gloria* was introduced into the first Mass of Christmas which was celebrated before daybreak. Pope Symmacus (498-514) extended its use by allowing it to be chanted on Sundays and the feasts of martyrs. For a long time, it was the exclusive privilege of bishops to sing the *Gloria* on Sundays and saints' days, while the rest of the clergy were only allowed to sing it on Easter Sunday. By the twelfth century, the restrictions were withdrawn and replaced by the present custom of singing the *Gloria* on all Sundays except those in Advent and Lent. It is also sung on special days known as "solemnities" and "feasts."

## REFLECTION

In a booklet called "Advent Reflections," written by parishioners of Holy Cross Parish in Deerfield, Illinois, longtime member of the parish Gloria Squaglia shares a personal story to illustrate what "praise" means to her. She and her husband, Ralph, celebrated their fiftieth wedding anniversary by spending a week with their family. "The highlight of it all," she writes, "was the evening we gathered by candlelight. The children and grandchildren presented us with a beautiful book in which each one had written a letter to us sharing what part we have played in their lives. One by one they read their letters. It was a special time. We cherish the moment and the book—I guess we could call it our book of 'praise.'"

Gloria then suggests that just as we never get tired of praise or of hearing the words, "I love you," neither does God! While thank you is very important, she says, "praise might be a more perfect form of telling God we love Him." Theologians agree with her. I believe that the love and unity shared by the Squaglia family is what Jesus wants each of us to experience in our extended family of the Church, the Body of Christ.

Preparing to say goodbye to His disciples before His suffering and death, Jesus gives us an intimate glimpse into His own heart in a prayer He utters to His Father. Raising His eyes to heaven, Jesus prays that His disciples—those present and all those who would follow Him in the future—would become one, just as He and His Father are one: "The glory which thou hast given me I have given to them, that they may be one even as we are one, I in them and thou in me, that they may become perfectly one, so that the world may know that thou hast sent me and hast loved them even as thou hast loved me" (Jn 17:22–24).

God wants us to share in His glory, not only when we die, but

The Transfiguration/James Tissot

*Jesus said to her, 'Did I not tell you that if you believe you will see the glory of God?'* —Jn 11:40

now as we go about our daily lives. In the Old Testament, the *Shekinah* cloud of glory through which God manifested His presence was so strong that one literally could see it as a "cloud" by day and a "fire" by night. Today, we have a palpable experience of God's glory—which is to say His presence manifest in our lives—through the gift of His Holy Spirit whom we receive through the Sacraments: Baptism, Confirmation and Eucharist. The Spirit helps us live out our discipleship as members of the body of Christ by empowering us with His gifts so that we can be the hands and heart of Our Lord in the world. United as one Body in Christ, we are the Father's gift to Jesus and share in His glory.

How do we share in His glory? Sr. Francis Clare, a School Sister of Notre Dame, is a prolific writer with a charismatic healing ministry who tells down-to-earth stories about God's glory made manifest in our everyday lives. Of the many accounts of healing in her magnificent book, *Glory to Glory,* some that touched me the most were about prisoners. Her ministry is powerful because she does not act alone, but relies totally on the Lord.

Before setting out for the prison one day, she and another sister prayed for hours, praising God in a spirit of thanksgiving for what He wanted to do at the prison. She felt God saying to her, "Your only problem will be to believe what I am ready to do or to get in My way by claiming any of the glory." At the prison, each person they prayed for was set free—either physically, emotionally or spiritually.

When she prayed with Dave, a man filled with hate and eaten

alive with stomach ulcers, prayer was his only hope. His medical records showed recent transfusions of seventeen pints of blood. He drank a whole bottle of Maalox everyday just to eat bland food. Doctors told him there was nothing further they could do.

Sr. Francis Clare and her companion prayed for Dave, saying, "God, You are bigger than any hate and bigger than any ulcer. Heal Dave now. Thank you for doing it." When they returned to the prison the following week, Dave was standing at the gate glowing. He thanked them, saying that God had heard their prayers. All his hate was gone, as well as the ulcers. As proof, on Sunday morning he had sausage and bacon for breakfast and pizza for lunch. "The prison walls have disappeared," he said. "I know they are there physically, but they are not there for me for I'm free inside. But what is even greater" he said, "I have begun praising God and I can't stop!" (*Glory to Glory* 151).

Now *that* is the glory of God made manifest in our lives!

*Our deepest fear is not that we are inadequate. Our deepest fear is that we are powerful beyond measure. It is our light, not our darkness that most frightens us. We ask ourselves: Who am I to be brilliant, gorgeous, talented and fabulous?*

*Actually . . . who are you not to be? You are a child of God. Your playing small doesn't serve the world. There is nothing enlightened about shrinking so that other people won't feel insecure around you.*

*We were born to make manifest the glory of God that is within us. It's not just in some of us, it's in everyone, and as we let our own light shine, we consciously give other people permission to do the same. As we are liberated from our own fear, our presence automatically liberates others.*

—Quoted by Nelson Mandela
at his inauguration as President of South Africa
(in Marianne Williamson, *A Return to Love*)

# The Opening Prayer

"**P**rayer is a hunger," writes Fr. Edward Farrell, a well-known writer and spiritual director from the Archdiocese of Detroit. In the opening chapter of his classic book on prayer by the same title, he illustrates what he means with a story about St. Ignatius, who, on one of his journeys with his followers, hired a porter to carry their bags. Periodically, the group stopped and prayed together. The porter stood by watching, wondering what they were doing. As the days went by, he began to want to do what they were doing. When Ignatius discovered the porter's desire, he realized that this humble man was, through his desire to pray, praying the finest prayer of them all (*Prayer is a Hunger,* 8).

Father Farrell's example leads us into the heart of the mystery that is prayer. Of the many things that can be said about prayer, at the top of the list is the fact that it is a gift. As soon as we acknowledge our desire to pray, or that "we do not know how to pray as we ought" (Rom 8:26), we are ready to receive the gift of prayer (*CCC,* 2559). "If you knew the gift of God" (Jn 4:10), Jesus said to the Samaritan woman who came to the well seeking water, she would understand that Jesus wants to give her "living water" (Jn 4:10). The *Catechism* sums up the meaning of their encounter:

Jesus and the Samaritan Woman/Carl Bloch

> The wonder of prayer is revealed beside the well where we come seeking water: there, Christ comes to meet every human being. It is he who first seeks us and asks us for a drink. Jesus thirsts; his asking arises from the depths of God's desire for us. Whether we realize it or not, prayer is the encounter of God's thirst with ours. God thirsts that we may thirst for him. (2560)

We can look upon this part of the Mass, the *Opening Prayer*, as a gift from the Church. It is a call to prayer from the heart of God who speaks through the celebrating priest, inviting us to encounter Christ at the well of the Eucharist where we will receive "living water" (Jn 4:10). In this Gospel story, Jesus makes it quite clear where we can go to quench our thirst for love—to Him—who actually thirsts for us and comes to meet us now. We have an opportunity in the moments of silence after the celebrant says, "Let us pray," to return His love by becoming aware of His presence and sharing our needs and desire for Him.

Up to this point in the Mass, we have celebrated our faith in the *Entrance Song,* exchanged words of welcome with the Lord in the *Greeting,* admitted our sinfulness and implored God's mercy in *The Penitential Rite,* and sang (or recited) a hymn of praise and thanksgiving to God in the *Gloria.* In the *Opening Prayer (Collect),* we turn to God and, in a spirit of childlike dependence and humility, tell Him our needs. This concludes the opening part of the Mass in which we have been addressing the eternal Father, and forms a bridge to the next part, the *Liturgy of the Word,* wherein God will speak to us.

## EXPLANATION

With hands upraised according to the ancient *orante* figure seen on the walls of the Roman catacombs, the celebrant now summons the faithful to prayer, saying, "Let us pray." Fr. Ronald Knox compares *Collects* to what used to be called telegrams—today's e-mail. Like old school friends at a reunion dinner who e-mail their professor back home, the congregation now sends almighty God a joint message in honor of their gathering. Speaking in the name of the community, the priest includes all our wishes as well as those of the entire Mystical Body. United as one in faith and love, we express our dependence on God.

These prayers are appropriately called *Collects* because they contain the sum and substance of all favors asked by the priest, for himself and for the community. It is the first of the "presidential prayers" in the Mass. "Prayers addressed to God by the priest who, in the person of Christ, presides over the assembly, are said in the name of the entire holy people and of all present" (*Constitution on the Sacred Liturgy*, 33). Describing the *Opening Prayer* as the "prayer that gathers together" (it collects our petitions), the late professor of sacramental theology Msgr. Johannes Emminghaus likens it to a musical overture which summarizes the principal motif and atmosphere of the day. It sets the tone and focus of the liturgy and expresses the theme of the celebration, be it a Sunday, feast day, a fixed season, memorial of a saint or remembrance of the dead (*The Eucharist, Essence, Form, Celebration* 128). The *Sacramentary* contains hundreds of *Opening Prayers* for every type of liturgy, be it Sundays, weekdays, feast days, weddings, funerals and so forth.

A moment of silence follows the celebrant's call to prayer, similar in nature to the pause during the *Penitential Rite* which gave us a chance to reflect on our sinfulness and our need for God's mercy. Now the Church provides another pause to give the faithful an opportunity to place themselves in God's presence and gather together their personal petitions which they want to present to God. The celebrant "collects" their petitions into a prayer which he recites in the name of the congregation.

When English Bishop Vincent Nichols concelebrated an early morning Mass with the Holy Father in his private chapel in the Vatican, he describes this pause in the liturgy which "seemed to last almost five minutes." In his insightful book, *The Gift of the Mass*, he admits that, at first, he was distracted, wondering what had happened. But then, he says, "I gave myself to the silence. The longer it lasted the deeper it became and the more I was taken up into the prayer it contained." The pope, he realized, was listening to the Holy Spirit, "asking and permitting the Holy Spirit to fill his mind, his consciousness, his heart." At the end of that celebra-

Pope John Paul II prays in his private chapel.

tion of Mass, Bishop Nichols came away thinking he had never been anywhere in which a sense of the suffering of the world was so keenly felt. "It seemed to me," he said, "in that small chapel there was a concentration of awareness of the pain, despair, and violence that is such a common part of humanity's experience" (22–24). Bishop Nichols goes on to say that, for the Holy Father, this was truly a "universal prayer"— as it must be for us. "We are united in one formal prayer, the *Collect,* which is, for that day, the common prayer of the Catholic Church throughout the world." (24)

What can we take from this story which will impact our own prayer? It encourages me to imitate the Holy Father by listening deeply for the voice of God within. When the celebrant says, "Let us pray," that is our cue to create a space in ourselves, an openness and a receptivity to the Holy Spirit. This can be a moment of profound communion which makes us one with God and with the whole Church—our family, friends and brothers and sisters around the world for whom we pray. God alone knows the depth of the world's need for Him. It is a gift to be able to consult with Him during this pause in the liturgy.

The *Opening Prayer* begins with an invocation to God our Father, praising Him for a certain quality or attribute. The celebrant may then recognize the mystery being celebrated on a given Sunday or feast. The prayer concludes with a petition to God for the special grace expected from this Eucharistic celebration while paying homage to the Trinity. The celebrant may speak or sing the *Opening Prayer* of the day, which summarizes the desires in the hearts of the assembly. He "collects" them and presents them to God the Father through Christ, in the Holy Spirit.

We pray in the name of Jesus, asking Him to accept our prayers and place them before His eternal Father. We take Jesus' words literally: "Where

Fr. Lawrence Hennessey reciting the *Opening Prayer.*

two or three are gathered in my name, there am I in the midst of them" (Mt 18:20) and trust His promise: "Whatever you ask the Father in my name he may give it to you" (Jn 15:16). We believe that when our prayer rises to the throne of God, it is welcomed by the Risen Christ, who "lives to make intercession" for us (Heb 7:25).

*Opening Prayers* have been called "perfect" prayers. They are spiritual gems which contain lofty doctrinal content notable for their economy of words. They read like poetry, expressing the prayerful desires of the congregation with harmony and cadence. They were written to be sung, thus their language flows like rhythmic prose. Although some of the pristine beauty of the ancient Roman *Collects* has been diminished by their translation into modern English, they are admired for their simplicity, beauty of style and directness. They carry a depth of meaning which lends itself to prayer and meditation.

The *Opening Prayer* for the Feast of the Body and Blood of Christ (Sunday after Trinity Sunday) provides a good example:

> Lord Jesus Christ,
> you gave us the Eucharist
> as the memorial of your suffering
> and death.
> May our worship of this sacrament
> of your body and blood
> help us to experience the salvation
> you won for us
> and the peace of the kingdom
> where you live with the Father and
> the Holy Spirit,
> one God, for ever and ever.

## HISTORY

When the persecution of Christians ended and Mass could be said in public, the faithful would gather in one church known as the *ecclesia collecta* (the assembly church), where they would say a prayer. From there the pope led the procession to another, larger church, the "station" church, where Mass was celebrated. For centuries, this opening prayer was called the *collect* (Latin *collecta*, gathered, assembled, collected together), offered for the faithful who *collected* for the celebration of Mass. Eventually, when the gathering and the procession were discontinued, the Church preserved the *Collect* at the opening of the liturgy, where it remains as the chief prayer of the day.

In the infant Church, all the prayers of the Eucharist were improvised by the officiating priest, including this prayer. Eventually, when it became necessary to give more structure to the liturgy, many of the *collects* were written down. This was done between the fifth and seventh centuries, and although the authors are unknown, the most beautiful of them were drawn from the *Sacramentary* of Pope St. Leo the Great (d. 461).

One spiritual writer compares the authors of these prayers to artists who created the magnificent mosaics displayed in Rome's ancient churches. Tiny stones of many colors were carefully put together, each stone just correct, and the result makes modern artists despair of ever copying them. These *collects* were

The "Orante" posture/Catacombs of St. Pricilla

*I stretch out my hands to you; I thirst for you like a parched land.*                    —Ps 143:6

fashioned by minds which sought to express the greatest amount of beauty in the fewest words.

At the end of the *Collect*, the people answer *Amen* by which they give their approval, their agreement. *Amen* is a Hebrew word which means "really and truly," "so be it," "I agree." St. Augustine spoke to his listeners about asking favors from God in the *Collect*, saying: "Do we ask him for all these things in vain? No! For you have wittingly subscribed to it by saying *Amen*. Your *Amen*, my brethren, is your signature, your approbation, your assent." St. Jerome (342–420), the great Doctor of the Church and Biblical scholar who spent thirty years revising the Latin text of the Bible into the Vulgate, records that the faithful of Rome said *Amen* so loudly and in so great numbers that it sounded like "a clap of thunder."

## REFLECTION

The *Opening Prayer* provides us with a perfect opportunity to center ourselves and, in faith, to ask God for our personal needs. Not that He doesn't already know them, because He does! But I believe He wants us to come to Him *through His Son*, assuring us that "if you ask anything of the Father, he will give it you in my name. Hitherto you have asked nothing in my name; ask, and you will receive, that your joy will be full" (Jn 16:23, 24). "This is the very heart of intercession," says Mother Nadine Brown, founder of a community of men and women dedicated to intercessory prayer. "It's prayer at its best because we have access to the throne room of God through Jesus anytime" (*Interceding with Jesus,* 34, 35).

> Indeed if we consider the unblushing promises of reward and the staggering nature of the rewards promised in the Gospels, it would seem that Our Lord finds our desires, not too strong, but too weak. We are half-hearted creatures, fooling about with drink and sex and ambition when infinite joy is offered us, like an ignorant child who wants to go on making mud pies in a slum because he cannot imagine what is meant by the offer of a holiday at sea. We are far too easily pleased.
>
> —C.S. Lewis, *Weight of Glory*

To illustrate the importance of having such access to God, she tells the story of Queen Esther in the Old Testament, who went to the king, without an appointment—which meant certain death. The king who hated the Jews, had approved a plan to destroy the entire Jewish race in one day. Esther, who was Jewish (though the king didn't know it), and whom the king loved more than all his other wives, arrayed herself in royal attire and entered the king's throne room, faint with the fear of her own demise. The king not only didn't refuse her, but handed Esther a golden scepter and asked her what she wanted. She pleaded with him to spare her life and the lives of her people, a request which he readily granted. Esther is credited with saving the Jewish race from extinction.

Just as Esther's intimate relationship with the king gave her the courage to approach the king with her needs, so does our relationship with God empower us to come face-to-face before Him to present our requests. In John's Gospel, Jesus describes the intimacy of our relationship, saying that we are as close to Him as a vine is to its branches: "If you abide in me, and my words abide in you, ask

Esther before Ahasuerus/Gregorio Pagani

whatever you will and it shall be done for you" (Jn 15:7). Unlike Esther, we need never be afraid to be in the King's presence.

Our moment has arrived. The Church provides us this opportunity in the *Opening Prayer* to have a word with the King of Kings and Lord of Lords—who not only welcomes us with open arms, but who anticipates—and answers—the prayers of our heart. God is reaching out to us with a golden scepter, Himself in the Eucharist, asking us what we want. Nothing is too good for us because we are children of a King. We lack for nothing.

# The Liturgy of the Word

*First Reading, Responsorial Psalm, Second Reading, Alleluia, Gospel, Homily, Profession of Faith and Prayer of the Faithful*

## Introduction

In the *Introductory Rites*, we have been conversing with almighty God. We have sought God's forgiveness in the *Penitential Rite*, praised Him in the *Gloria,* and petitioned Him for our needs in the *Opening Prayer.* Up to this point, we have done most of the talking, so to speak. We now enter into the first part of the Mass, *The Liturgy of the Word,* wherein God will speak to us. The *Scripture Readings, Responsorial Psalm, Homily, Profession of Faith* and *Prayers of the Faithful,* comprise the *Liturgy of the Word.*

The Bible tops the best-seller lists every year. Why? Because it is the greatest love story ever told, written and directed by God under the inspiration of prophets, evangelists and apostles such as Moses, David, Amos, Isaiah, Matthew, Mark, Luke, John and Paul, people who allowed their lives to be transformed by listening to God's voice and saying *yes* to Him. It has been called God's love letter to His children, which He entrusted to the minds and imagination of these scribes—kings, fishermen, poets, teachers and prophets—very human but spiritually heroic authors who attracted the attention of the Hebrew people and the surrounding nations, the Gentiles, to believe in the power and promise of God's Word.

When we go to Mass on Sunday (or during the week) and hear the Scriptures proclaimed, it is as if we are sitting around the kitchen table reading a love letter from someone very dear to us. That "Someone" is the eternal Father who chooses Sacred Scripture as a means of revealing Himself to His children and making known to us the mystery of our salvation. God's Word is the bedrock of our faith. That belief, as expressed in the *Baltimore Catechism* of years ago, is that God made us to know, love and serve Him in this world so that we could be happy with him in the next.

How can we know God? We can know Him through His sacred Word, much as we can know a fiancee whose long distance love letters reveal something of the

God the Father/Pompeo Batoni

essence of the person we love. "Knowing" in the biblical sense is being in a love relationship with a person, in this case, God. He enters into a dialogue with us in Scripture, asking us to trust in His providential, forgiving, unrelenting and unconditional love.

God's incredible love for His people was tenderly expressed by the prophet Hosea, who compared the relationship between Yahweh and Israel to a marriage. Yahweh loves His people despite the fact that they have been unfaithful, and, like Hosea's wife, have prostituted themselves before other gods. Just as Hosea could not give up his wife even when she played the harlot, so Yahweh could not renounce Israel, who had been betrothed to him. God would chastise, but it would be the chastisement of the jealous lover, longing to bring back the beloved to the joy of their first love.

To read the Bible is to trace the hand of God through human history and see His divine plan emerge in the story of our creation, fall and redemption. Scripture presents the story of our salvation beginning with God at work in the life of Israel in the Old Testament. The Bible is not one book, but a whole collection! Forty-five books make up the Old Testament, which covers a sweep of history from the creation of the world to about 200 BC. ("Testament" is a translation of the Hebrew word meaning "covenant" or "agreement.") Its books include poetry and history, prophecy and law, which tell the story of God's loving but often troubled relationship with His people.

The New Testament consists of twenty-seven books. The evangelist wrote four accounts of His life—the *Gospels*. Matthew, Mark, and John knew Christ personally. The Book of Acts tells the story of the beginning of the Church and of its expansion to all corners of the earth. To give guidance and direction for the growth of the fledgling Church, Paul and other disciples wrote letters or epistles to the communities of believers. In

The Four Evangelists/Jacob Jordaens

the face of great suffering and evil, St. John, in the Book of Revelation, calls upon Christians to remain steadfast in their faith and trust in Jesus' promise that He will be with us always.

Our salvation story is about God forming a people for Himself because He loves us so much. The "Good News"often appears to us too good to be true. God wants us for Himself and will stop at nothing, including sending His Son to die for us, to show us the depth of His commitment and love. "It is God's love and His power by which we and all the human race can be redeemed," say popular authors and retreat directors Frs. Richard Rohr and Joseph Martos, "but as long as we still see this as something that God will do without our participation in His suffering, we do not yet have New Testament faith":

The final level of faith to which God calls us is a total and unreserved yes to His request to be present in and to the world through us. He desires to love others unconditionally in and through us. He wants the full redemption of humanity to occur in each of us so that the salvation of the world can be brought about through us. The Church's function is to be the eyes and ears, mouth and hands of God in the world, a body through which the power of divine love can transform the world. This call is a summons to live at the deepest level of faith. (*The Great Themes of Scripture*, 125)

The whole point, say the authors, is to become so attuned to God's voice that He will guide all our decisions and actions. We don't have to worry about making mistakes, they say, because God will correct us if we are always listening. If we stumble and fall, He will be there immediately to catch us. When we live life at this level of faith, we realize that God does not demand great things of us; He wants only to be great in us. If we allow it, God will even do great things through us. But we ourselves do not have to *make* them happen. We only have to surrender and trust at every step. We only have to stand on His promise and wait for it to be fulfilled in our lives, choosing in accordance with that promise (129).

We are called to realize the Good News in ourselves, that God is truly present to us in the here and now of our daily experiences and decisions. If we take His words to heart, they will convert and sanctify us, re-creating us into the person He has called us to be.

This is undoubtedly what led the bishops at Vatican II to emphasize Scripture's place of prominence in the Mass; they wanted "the whole world to hear the summons to salvation, so that through hearing it may believe, through belief it may hope, through hope it may come to love" (*Dei Verbum*, 1). During the *Liturgy of the Word*, we have a God-given opportunity to listen to the voice of God.

One of the primary aims of the Vatican Council was to restore "full, active and conscious participation" by all the people. To this end it instituted changes in all areas of the Sacred Liturgy, including the introduction of the vernacular instead of Latin.

Of the sixteen documents produced by the Council, one of the most important was the *Constitution on the Sacred Liturgy*, in which the bishops said, "the treasures of the Bible are to be opened up more lavishly so that a richer fare may be provided for the faithful at the table of God's word" (*Constitution on the Sacred Liturgy*, 51). Their efforts led to a sacramental and biblical renewal within the Church, the likes of which hadn't been seen since the Council of Trent in the sixteenth century.

The *Liturgy of the Word*, a phrase that originated at the Council, now enjoys a prominence that it never had before. The Lectionary, which was published in 1969, contains the complete texts of the biblical readings and chants for the *Liturgy of the Word*. The Lectionary was arranged so that the faithful would be exposed to a greater variety of readings.

Prior to the Council, the cycle of readings was the same year after year; in fact, the faithful were never exposed to many parts of the Bible. The *Liturgy of the Word* no longer ends with the *Gospel*, but continues with the *Homily* and ends with the *Prayers of the Faithful* (*General Intercessions*), allowing the people an opportunity to respond personally to God's Word. The language gap that existed for centuries has been closed, thus allowing the faithful to enter more actively into the dialogue of the Mass.

The Lectionary divides the Sunday Scripture readings into three-year cycles. One year, the Sunday readings will be almost all Matthew (Cycle A), another year all Mark (B), and the third year emphasizes the Gospel of Luke (C). The Gospel of John is reserved primarily for the Christmas and Easter seasons, with the exception of John 6, the great "Bread of Life" discourse, which occurs in the middle of the Markan cycle.

The Scripture readings for weekday Masses are divided into a two-year cycle of odd and even years. For example, in 2004 we were in Year II; in 2005 we are in Year I. Then in 2006, we will go back to Year II. This method doubles the number of Scripture readings that we hear at daily Mass during a two-year period.

There is one more interesting point. If a person reads the Liturgy of the Hours (the Office of Readings) and attends daily Mass for three years in a row, they will have read or heard almost the entire Bible. Even if they do not pray the Liturgy of the Hours, they probably will have encountered seventy to eighty percent of the Bible.

# *The First Reading*

The Old Testament readings are like a treasure chest filled with precious spiritual gems—expressions of God's self-revelation to the Jewish people in preparation for the coming of the Savior. The Bible records the real-life experiences of our ancestors who, despite their disobedience, were favored with God's unconditional love and deliverance from bondage. Even though the stories describe events which took place thousands of years ago in an Hebraic culture which is unfamiliar to us, it is the same God who speaks through the prophets of the Old Testament to men and women like ourselves—people who had a hunger for God just as we do. His message to them about faith and covenant, sin and salvation, is as relevant to us today as it was to the ancient Israelites. The promises He made to them are the same promises He makes to us. He comes into the midst of our hopes and dreams, needs and problems, fears and struggles, to offer us direction and insight, hope and healing, faith and salvation.

We speak of the Bible as God's *living* word. In the Old Testament, God utters a word (as in the story of creation) and the word is already an action that is accomplished. God spoke and the heavens were made. In Hebrew, the word *dabar* means to create as well as to speak. God spoke and there was light. Creation was not a one-time event. God is creating and re-creating us at every moment of our existence. We are called to realize the Good News in ourselves: that God is truly present to us in the here and now of daily experiences and decisions. If we take His words to heart, they will convert and sanctify us, re-creating us into the person that He called us to be.

## EXPLANATION

After the *Opening Prayer,* the lector goes to the ambo (also called the lectern) for the *First Reading.* Chosen for its relationship to the *Gospel,* the *First Reading,* which is taken from the Old Testament, is often a prophecy whose fulfillment is proclaimed in the *Gospel,* the third reading of the same Liturgy. There is a continuity between the Old and New Testaments. In St. Augustine's words: "In the Old

Allegory about the Old and New Law/Jerome Wierix

Testament the New is hidden, in the New Testament the Old appears." The *Catechism* describes a unity between the Old and New Testaments which proceeds from the unity of God's plan and His Revelation: "Christians therefore read the Old Testament in the light of Christ crucified and risen" (CCC, 129).

For example, there is a thematic parallel between the Old Testament and the Gospel as found in the Mass for the Feast of the Epiphany: the Old Testament passage (Is 60:1-6) announces the homage to be paid to God at Jerusalem by the peoples of the East; in his Gospel, Matthew recounts the coming of the Magi to pay tribute to the Messiah (Mt 2: 1-12). The revelation of the previous two thousand years is brought to completion in the person and life of Jesus, God's *living* Word, who reveals Himself to us and calls us into a personal dialogue.

Nowhere is this more beautifully illustrated than in the New Testament *Epistle to the Hebrews,* in which the author addresses the early Christian converts who are in danger of apostasy from their Christian faith. He asks his listeners to reflect on the eternal priesthood of Christ, a priesthood that fulfills the promise of the Old Testament. He calls them to persevere in faith and holds up to them the saints of the Old Testament who were powerful witnesses of their faith: Abel, Enoch, Noah, Abraham, Isaac, Jacob, Joseph and Moses. He adds the examples of Gideon, Sampson, Samuel, David and the prophets. Surrounded by "so great a cloud of witnesses" (Heb 12:1), the author of this Epistle urges his listeners to "run with perseverance the race that is set before us, looking to Jesus the pioneer and perfecter of our faith" (Heb 12:2). All of these people trusted in God's promises and all were rewarded by God for their faith.

Fr. Raniero Cantalamessa, professor of early Christian theology and preacher to the papal household, explains the connection between the Old and New Testaments this way:

> The New Testament does not diminish the status of the Old Testament, but promotes it, making it pass from "the letter" to "the Spirit," transfiguring it into a "ministry of glory" (cf. 2 Cor 3:7). By his death and resurrection, Christ opens the hitherto sealed Old Testament and reveals its true content: "Then," after Easter, "he opened their minds to understand the Scriptures" (Lk 24:45). (*The Mystery of God's Word*, 10)

The result, says Father Cantalamessa, is that today we hear Christ's voice even when we read the Old Testament, because the Law, the Prophets and the Psalms "speak of him" (cf. Lk 24:27; Jn 5:39). "The liturgy" he says, "expresses this conviction by having us listen at Mass to one page from the Old Testament and one from the New" (10).

## HISTORY

The early Christians clearly understood this relationship between the Old and New Testaments. For example, St. Ambrose:

> Drink from the springs of the Old and New Testaments, since in the one as in the other you drink Christ. . . . Drink Christ, by drinking his words: the Old Testament is his word and the New Testament is his word. The Sacred Scriptures are drunk and the Sacred Scriptures are eaten when the sap of the Eternal Word descends into the veins of the spirit and into the powers of the soul. . . . Drink this word, but drink it in its proper order: first drink it in the Old Testament, then drink it straightway as well in the New. (in Cantalemessa, *The Mystery of God's Word*, 10)

In the earliest days of the Church, a deacon used to call the congregation to attention before the *Reading,* saying: "Be silent and listen attentively." That the congregation needed to establish silence and order, we can tell from a remark of St. Ambrose: "How difficult it is to procure silence in the Church when the lessons are being read." The people had to stand, and it is no wonder that they grew tired and inattentive! Whole psalms were chanted between the readings. Eventually shortened, the psalms survive today in the form of the *Responsorial Psalm* and *Alleluia.*

The *Readings* have been used since the beginning of Christianity. They were taken from the ritual of the synagogue service (Jewish houses of worship) during which the worshipers read prayers from the Old Testament—extracts from the Law and the Prophets—and sang psalms, followed by a homily. Jesus taught in synagogues throughout Galilee; Paul preached in synagogues in Damascus and refers to synagogues in every city he visited in Asia Minor. When the early Christians began celebrating their own liturgies, they kept the same pattern as the synagogue service: prayers, readings, chants, homily, with the addition of a Eucharistic meal.

The ancient Church referred to the *Liturgy of the Word* as the *Lessons.* We learn from St. Hippolytus of Rome (d. 236) that on weekdays, when there was no communal celebration of the Eucharist, the priests and deacons went to a place appointed by a bishop to explain the Scriptures to the people and to pray with them. St. Augustine in his *Confessions* tells us that his mother, St. Monica, used to go to church twice a day, in the morning and the evening, to hear the word of God and to pray.

Theologians surmise that there were three Scripture readings in the infant Church. They were read "as long as time allows," according to St. Justin Martyr (d. 165), reputed to be a great defender of the faith. In addition to the books of the Old Testament, Christians read the letters (*Epistles*) sent to the different communities by early disciples of Christ, and the first written accounts of the life of our Savior (*Gospels*).

Today, two thousand years later, our *Readings* follow the same pattern. On Sundays and major feast days, there are always three readings. The *First Reading* is taken from the Old Testament (except during the Easter season when the first reading is taken from the Acts of the Apostles), the second from the writings of St. Paul and other disciples (*Acts, Epistles, Revelation*) and the third is always the *Gospel*. On weekdays, there are only two readings within a two-year cycle, the second of which is always the *Gospel*.

## REFLECTION

When we gather as a community of faith and listen to the Word of God, the Scriptures retell the story of our salvation. In the course of the Sacred Liturgy, the Word of God comes alive. It ceases to be a simple story of the past and becomes *our* story.

The author of Hebrews tells us: "For the word of God is living and active, sharper than any two-edged sword, piercing to the division of soul and spirit, of joints and marrow, and discerning the thoughts and intentions of the heart" (Heb 4:12). Unlike human words, God's word is powerful because it *effects* what it proclaims. His word penetrates to the innermost parts of a person, forcing one to come to grips with what really matters. You might say it forces truth to the surface.

St. John equates the Word of God with *life* (Jn 1:4), a truth Jesus affirms: "The words I spoke to you are spirit and life" (Jn 6:63). In the Prologue of his Gospel, St. John proclaims: "In the beginning was the Word, and the Word was with God, and the Word was God" (Jn 1:1). Speaking of Christ—as God—he says, "And the Word became flesh and dwelt among us" (Jn 1:14).

Vatican II theolgian Fr. Louis Bouyer expands this point, suggesting that God *invades* our human life with His divine life through His Word: "God speaks to us most personally through Christ Who reveals Himself in a Word which is the most personal form of communication possible—since it is itself a Person" (*Life and Liturgy*, 105).

Father Bouyer is saying that word of God is somehow God Himself. This means that if we let the Word of God inform our lives, it will live in us and we will bear powerful fruit.

St. Paul recognized the power of God's word to change lives: "I am not ashamed of the good news: it is the power of God saving all who have faith" (Rom 1:16). Another who equated God's word with power was the great prophet Isaiah:

For as the rain and the snow come down from heaven and

return not thither but water the earth making it bring forth and sprout, giving seed to the sower and bread to the eater, so shall my word be that goes forth from my mouth; it shall not return to me empty but it shall accomplish that which I purpose and prosper in the thing for which I sent it. (55:10-13)

When God speaks a Word to us in Sacred Scripture, it is like a promise that will not come back to Him empty, but one that will fulfill its intention. He wants us to respond to His voice like the young Samuel, who finally realized God was calling him and said, "Speak, for thy servant hears" (1 Sam 3:10). Just as the Lord transformed Israel's history through Samuel's prayer, so will He heal and transform our lives. If we are open to *receive* God's word, it will convert and sanctify us, forming us into a new person in the image and likeness of Jesus (cf. 2 Cor 17).

My own life over the past ten years bears testimony to the fact that God's Word is filled with promise and will accomplish what it says. One day I experienced the life-giving power of God's word when I was the lector at morning Mass. The Scripture reading opened me to the depth of a personal struggle I was facing, bringing consolation and a feeling of God's closeness. The Old Testament reading spoke to me so strongly that I came home and wrote about it in my journal.

In this reading, King Hezekiah (2 Kings 19) received a threatening letter from the King of Assyria, who destroyed cities and people at will. Hezekiah took the letter from the messenger, read it, then went up to the temple of the Lord, and spread-

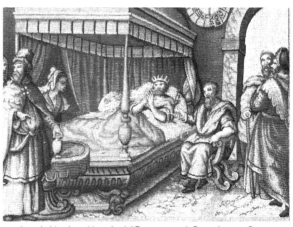

Isaiah Healing Hezekiah/Guasparri di Bartolomeo Papini

ing the letter out before him, prayed in the Lord's presence. He asked God to save him and his people from this evil man, so that all the kingdoms of the earth would know that the Lord is God. God heard his prayer and saved the city from destruction. Once again, Hezekiah turned to the Lord when he became mortally ill, and God heard his prayer and healed him—adding fifteen years to his life.

*Today that is my exact prayer, Jesus. 'Persistent malignant lymphoma' is what I've got in my stomach. Lord, now it begins, my fight for life, but life as You will it for me. First, scleroderma and now cancer. Jesus, help! It occurs to me that great saints suffered many infirmities. That's a consolation to me save for the fact that I'm not a great saint! But I do want to be.*

*Now in this sacred temple of Your Church, like King Hezekiah, I offer You this new evil which threatens to take my life. Please, Lord, hold my hand and walk with me to give me strength and direction. Now I have something to give You! I offer it to you Jesus. Please take this cancer/sickness and use whatever suffering and pain it brings to shower graces on my family, my children and husband. Please give them new life and new love of You through this—and new faith, especially in the Eucharist.*

The emotional impact which the Old Testament reading had on me told me that God was speaking to me personally. I felt connected to King Hezekiah, to the threat he received from the evil king and to his reliance on the Lord to save him and his people. The Scripture passage set my own experience in bold relief, highlighting my fear of cancer and my need for God. What it really did was to open me to the Lord, reassuring me of His closeness. As a lector I felt privileged to pass on the hope to others that the Lord and Savior of the world—almighty God—speaks directly to us through His holy Word.

# The Responsorial Psalm

The Church recognizes the importance of the *First Reading* by following it with a few moments of silent reflection, so that we can begin to discern the voice of the Holy Spirit. These silent pauses in the Sacred Liturgy allow the seed of God's word to take root in our minds and hearts, enabling us to worship God in a real spirit of praise and thanksgiving.

Following this brief pause, we sing the *Responsorial Psalm*. Since the earliest days of the Church, the *Liturgy of the Word* began with Scripture readings, followed by singing that ended in prayer. The whole point of the readings and the singing is to unite us in prayer. That is why we have come together. The *Responsorial Psalm* prepares our hearts for prayer.

The Psalter is the most ancient songbook of the Church. It is a collection of 150 poem-prayers, half of which were probably composed by King David, a "skillful harpist" (1 Sam 16:18), whom Samuel dubbed the "sweet psalmist of Israel" (2 Sam 23:1). Known to the Hebrews as "The Book of Praises," these psalms were set to music and sung by pious Jews in the Temple for their religious ceremonials. In the synagogues at the time of Jesus, the Jews followed the reading of Scripture with the singing of psalms, a practice the early Christians adopted for their liturgical worship. Jesus emphasizes the prophetic importance of the psalms

King David Playing the Harp/Domenichino

when He spoke to the two disciples on the road to Emmaus, saying that "everything written about me in the Law of Moses and in the prophets and psalms must be fulfilled" (Lk 24:44).

The psalms are one of the most familiar and beloved parts of the Old Testament. They inspire us to get in touch with our own deepest feelings and aspirations because they express a whole range of emotions which we, too, experience: love, joy, praise, gratitude, longing, pleading, anger, distress, guilt, sorrow and betrayal. Saints in every age have had a deep devotion to praying the psalms. St. John Chrysostom regarded the psalm refrains as precious pearls that he urged the faithful to meditate on and sing to themselves and their friends and relatives, because they would bring great peace and consolation to troubled souls. He often preached on the psalms and encouraged their memorization.

Fr. Josef Jungmann notes that in one of his sermons, St. John Chrysostom said, "Most of you know dirty songs, but who of you is able to say even one psalm?" (*The Early Liturgy*, 168). St. Augustine also preached about the psalms, calling them a "treasure-house of good teaching." There is a record in the office of St. Patrick's Feast day on March 17, saying that he used to worship God by genuflecting three hundred times a day, a devotion he practiced in conjunction with praying the entire Psalter, 150 psalms (in Josef Jungmann, *The Liturgy of the Word*, 59). St. Gertrude's community of nuns understood that praying the psalms was very beneficial for the souls of the faithful departed, so they recited the Psalter for these souls before Mass. In one of her many conversations with the Lord, St. Gertrude asked Him about this practice that often "caused more weariness than devotion." He encouraged her to pray the psalms because of His great desire to deliver souls, and assured her that He released many souls depending on the zeal and fervor of those who pray for them:

> Even as a prince, who had been obliged to imprison one of his nobles to whom he was much attached, and was compelled by his justice to refuse him pardon, would most thankfully avail himself of the intercessions and satisfactions of others to release his friend. (*The Life & Revelations of St. Gertrude*, 530, 531)

## EXPLANATION

We now celebrate in song Jesus Christ present in the Scriptures. "Prayed by Christ and fulfilled in him," says the *Catechism,* "the Psalms remain essential to the prayer of the Church" (2586). The *Responsorial Psalm* is a response from the heart for God's goodness to us, for His love and presence in His Word just proclaimed.

In the *First Reading*, God speaks to us; in the *Responsorial Psalm*, we respond to God. The community uses God's word as a response to God's word.  The psalm-response is closely related to the liturgical time of year or the particular feast that is being celebrated. The psalm draws out the meaning of the *First Reading*. It stimulates reflection on God's love and prolongs the reading, suggesting thoughts that should arise from what has just been read.

According to Fr. Lucien Deiss, the psalm response, which was buried and almost lost under the weight of thirteen centuries of history, has now been resurrected and restored to its place of honor in the liturgy. He speaks with the authority one who participated in the Council as a liturgical consultant. Vatican II reinstated the *Responsorial Psalm* to a position of special importance in the Mass. *The Instruction on Music in the Liturgy* underlines its significance:

Dawn Isaiah, leading the *Responsorial Psalm.*

"The song after the lessons, be it in the form of gradual or responsorial psalm, has a special importance among the songs of the Proper. By its very nature, it forms part of the Liturgy of the Word. It should be performed with all seated and listening to it—and what is more, participating in it as far as possible" (33).

There are different ways of incorporating the *Responsorial Psalm* in the liturgy. The first and most popular is for the cantor to sing the verses of the psalm from the ambo, while the congregation responds with an antiphon after each group of verses. Although rarely done, in some churches the cantor may sing the psalm straight through without a response. While this can be very beautiful, the disadvantage is that the people have no part in it. Yet another way is for the congregation to divide into two sections, so they can alternate singing the psalm verses. And finally a reader, or even the celebrant, may read the psalm, and the people answer by singing the antiphon. Historically, antiphons began as alternate chants in which two choirs responded to one another; today antiphon designates the verse that begins and ends the psalms.

## History

We can only imagine the pomp and circumstance that accompanied the singing of psalms in the Old Testament and in the Jewish synagogues of first century Palestine. The color and ceremony of Israelite worship must have been magnificent. Psalm 68 gives us a taste of its splendor: "Your procession comes into view, O God, your procession into the holy place, my God and king. The singers go first, the harpists follow; in their midst girls sound the timbrels" (Ps 68:25, 26).

In the Jewish synagogue liturgies at the time of Christ, the psalms were sung by trained voices with a great variety of musical accompaniment. Even Jesus sang psalms. "After singing a hymn, they went out to the Mount of Olives" (Mt 26:20). The first Christians no doubt drew their inspiration from the singing of those "psalms, hymns and spiritual songs" to which St. Paul alludes when he urges the Ephesians to be filled with the Spirit, "singing and playing to the Lord in your hearts" (Eph 5:19).

Until the middle of the fourth century, the *Responsorial Psalm* was the principal form of chant that followed the readings. Chanting the psalms between the readings may have originated to add variety and to break the monotony of the lengthy reading of the Scriptures. In the early Church, the Scriptures were read continuously, beginning at the point where they previously stopped. A soloist sang the psalm from beginning to end (unlike today when we sing only parts of a psalm and a response), and after each verse or group of verses the community joined in with a recurring refrain, often taken from the psalm itself that served to emphasize what had been read. Later, an antiphonal method of singing arose in monasteries in which the assembled community was divided into two choirs, and the psalm verses were chanted alternately by each choir. "Antiphon" comes from a Greek word meaning "answering voice." It originated in Antioch and was cultivated by St. Ambrose, who introduced antiphonal singing in Milan around 380. A special choir of singers known as the *schola cantorum* specialized in antiphonal singing.

Up to the time of St. Gregory the Great in the late sixth century, the psalms were chanted by deacons, whose qualifications for the diaconate included a good voice and a thorough knowledge of music. Some deacons were promoted to the episcopate on the basis of their vocal talent. St. Gregory discontinued this custom because deacons cared for their voices to the detriment of their other duties. Good voices were held in higher regard than moral character.

The psalm response was once known as the *Gradual,* or step-psalm, because, according to an early practice, it was sung from a lower step (Latin, *gradus*) of the ambo. The higher step was reserved for the *Gospel.* The ambo was a small raised platform in the church from which the Scriptures were read. Its roots go back to the Old Testament, where the reader positioned himself in an elevated place so everyone could see him:

> Ezra the priest brought the law before the assembly. Standing at one end of the open place that was before the Water Gate, he read out of the book from daybreak till midday. And all the people listened attentively to the book of the law. Ezra the scribe stood on a wooden platform that had been made for the occasion. (Neh 8: 2-4)

## REFLECTION

One day during Mass, the reading of a psalm spoke to me so clearly I came home and wrote about it in my journal. The psalm was taken from the second chapter of the Book of Jonah, a prophet whom God called to proclaim His word to the Ninevites, the traditional enemy of Israel. (Random psalms like this one which are not part of the Book of Psalms are found throughout the Old Testament). Jonah recoiled from this task and tried to escape by boarding a ship bound for Tarshish, going in the opposite direction. When God sent a huge storm to stop him, he was cast overboard and swallowed by a big fish, inside of which he remained for three days and nights. From the belly of the fish, Jonah said this prayer to God:

> Out of my distress I called to the Lord,
>     and he answered me;
> From the midst of the nether world I cried for help,
>     and you heard my voice.
> You will rescue my life from the pit, O Lord.
>
> For you cast me into the deep, into the heart of the sea,
>     and the flood enveloped me;
> All your breakers and your billows
>     passed over me.
> You will rescue my life from the pit, O Lord.
>
> Then I said, "I am banished from your sight!
> Yet would I again look upon your holy temple."
> You will rescue my life from the pit, O Lord.
>
> When my soul fainted within me,
> I remembered the Lord;
> My prayer reached you
>     in your holy temple.
> You will rescue my life from the pit, O Lord (Jon 2: 3-5, 8).

*For days now, I, like Jonah, have tried to escape You Lord, avoiding You at every turn. There is a part of me that no one sees, like the dark side of the moon. It is numb and seeks only comfort and security. I wonder if I am all talk and no substance. I fall so easily into fits of self doubt and laziness. These days I turn on the TV to watch the latest news in our war against terrorism. I have become almost obsessed with the news, feeling insecure and somewhat fearful of what will happen next.*

*Today I am on a flat plateau and need Your grace to lift me up. Like Jonah I want to hide instead of reach out to others. I think I'm tired, physically weary and beaten down somewhat by the surgeries and persistent health problems that haunt me. Maybe I feel a little sorry for myself. I offer my pain to You, but I'm no great martyr. I would just as soon be made well and whole on the spot, rather than limp around and worry that scleroderma and cancer are slowly overtaking me.*

*I guess I'm in a desert. It's flat, dry, boring and without meaning. I know enough to value this time as a gift, to thank You for the lesson which this experience is designed to teach me.*

*It was really Your mercy which allowed Jonah to spend three days in the belly of the fish. Down deep*

Jonah and the Whale/Annie Lykes Lucas

*Jonah was running from you because of his selfishness. He did not want to preach to the Ninevites. He did not want You to forgive them because of his own narrow vindictiveness of mind. He was angry and his anger almost killed him, but for Your mercy. He complained to You because of the unexpected success of his mission; he was bitter because instead of destroying his enemy, You led these people to repentance and spared their lives.*

*Jonah was about as human and self-centered as they come, yet You loved him and called him to be your instrument. You reached out to the people of Nineveh, evil as they were, because you loved them. This gives me hope, that no matter how human and sinful I am, You reach out to me with love and healing. Your wide open arms extend to embrace the whole world, especially your children caught in the grip of oppression and terrorism.*

*You have a mission for each of us. I beg for the grace to follow Your will, Lord, no matter where it leads.*

# *The Second Reading*

One of my favorite movies of all time is *Oh God!*, starring John Denver as a reluctant reporter-evangelist, a modern-day prophet, and George Burns, who plays, well, God. The gist of the movie is that God constantly appears and speaks to John Denver—just as He did to the prophets and evangelists—telling him that He loves and cares for His people and that with His help, the world will work out. George Burns plays a very congenial and benevolent God, who uses John Denver to spread His messages to the world. Risking his credibility, his job and his future, Denver relays God's messages with a childlike trust in His words. The film touched me deeply because, behind the parody, was the truth and reality that God is always trying to get our attention by speaking His Word to us—if we only have listening hearts.

## EXPLANATION

The *Second Reading* is taken either from one of the Epistles, from the Acts of the Apostles, or from the Book of Revelation. The Epistles were letters that St. Paul and other disciples sent to the first Christian communities to encourage and guide them in their new faith. Written by St. Luke, the Acts of the Apostles presents a broad survey of the Church's development from the resurrection of Jesus to St. Paul's first Roman imprisonment. Luke describes the emergence of Christianity from its origins in Judaism to its growing position as a religion of worldwide status and appeal.

The Book of Revelation, also known as the Apocalypse (Greek for "revelation"), is the last book of the Bible in which St. John writes letters to the seven churches in Asia Minor, to encourage and strengthen them in their time of suffering and persecution. It is also an account of his mystical visions written in symbolic language intended for all generations of Christians who, in the face of apparently insuperable evil, are called to believe that the ultimate salvation and victory will take place at the end of the present age, when Christ will defeat the kingdom of Satan and come in glory in the parousia (Second Coming of Christ).

The great Anglican convert Fr. Ronald Knox urges us to look at the Epistles of the New Testament as personal letters sent to us from St. Paul, St. Peter, or one of the other apostles. He likens the epistle (from the Latin, *epistola*, or letter) to a kind of letter written from a long distance, perhaps from a son in China or elsewhere, which consequently should be read out loud for the benefit of the whole family at breakfast.

A seminarian reads an Epistle of St. Paul at an outdoor Mass in Antioch, where followers of Christ were first called "Christians." Celebrant is Fr. Peter Damien Akpunonu. Fr. Robert Korbel, photographer.

The Church presents the Letters of the New Testament spread out in a semi-continuous cycle over three years. On Sundays and major feast days, the second reading is always taken from the New Testament. Unlike the connection between the Old Testament reading and the Gospel, the text for the second reading is not necessarily related to the other readings. But during certain seasons, passages are selected which correspond to the particular time of the liturgical year. During the Christmas season, for example, there are repeated readings from the First Letter of John. Written at the end of the first century in response to false ideas about Jesus, St. John defends the simple truth of the Gospel with compelling clarity and conviction.

While the *Responsorial Psalm* follows the *First Reading*, the *Second Reading* concludes with a sung acclamation (if it is not sung, it is omitted) in preparation for the *Gospel*.

## History

For centuries, the Roman liturgy used the term "epistle" to designate the reading that preceded the *Gospel,* even when this reading was not taken from a New Testament letter. Usually, there were only two readings during the Eucharistic Liturgy, the *Epistle* and *Gospel.* In the early Church, "a reading from the Apostle" meant a Pauline reading.

The Apostles and other disciples of Christ sent epistles or letters to their congregations and sometimes to such individuals as Timothy, Titus and even Philemon, the slave owner, in order to clarify what Our Lord said and meant, and what He wished His followers to practice. St. Paul traveled great distances throughout Asia Minor converting many to the faith. Because he was often unable to retrace his steps, he sent them letters written on papyrus rolls of parchment, instructing, guiding, encouraging and correcting his newly made converts.

Imagine the excitement at Corinth when a messenger arrived with a letter from St. Paul. The bishop would be advised, then word would spread from house to house that a letter had come from Paul that would be read at a meeting later that evening. Everyone gathered in anticipation of what Paul had to say. Perhaps the bishop would comment on Paul's words, then he would make copies

Saint Paul/Claude the Elder Vignon

to send to nearby towns, where Christians would gather to hear Paul in the same spirit. Thanks to the faith and fortitude of these first converts, these letters circulated far and wide to small groups scattered throughout the Roman Empire and even to Christians in hiding.

In the Epistle of the Mass, we hear an echo of the apostolic teaching that is a guidepost for us on our faith journey. When we gather for Mass on Sunday, we listen to the Epistles just like the early Christians did, who "devoted themselves to the apostles' teaching" (Acts 2:42). The Epistles give witness to the early Church living its

Christian faith, directed to followers of Jesus like us, who were de-
sirous of maturing in the practice of their faith and growing in virtue
and love. To the extent that we draw closer to Christ and His teaching through Scripture, we, too, will grow in faith and holiness.

When Paul wrote to Timothy from prison, he urged him to rely
on the power of the Scriptures, on proclamation of the word and on
sound doctrine:

> But as for you, continue in what you have learned and
> have firmly believed, knowing from whom you learned it
> and how from childhood you have been acquainted with
> the sacred writings which are able to instruct you for sal-
> vation through faith in Christ Jesus. (2 Tim 3:14-16)

In the face of opposition, hostility and even the defection of many
to whom the *Gospel* had been preached, Paul charges Timothy to be
strong in preaching the word: "Preach the word, be urgent in season
and out of season, convince, rebuke, and exhort, be unfailing in pa-
tience and in teaching" (2 Tim 4:2).

There is power in the word of God because it is a *living* Word—
a concrete manifestation of Christ's presence in the here and now.
Jesus asked His disciples to *believe* in His word because we would
know the truth which would make us free (cf: Jn 8:31). "Thy word is
a lamp to my feet, and a light to my path" (Ps 119:105), cried the
psalmist, rejoicing that God's word directs and guides human life.
When we *digest* God's Word, it transforms our lives.

## REFLECTION

I recently came across a story about someone whose life was
transformed because he heard the voice of God speaking to him in
Scripture. It gave me a new appreciation of God's Real Presence in
Sacred Scripture, a gift that I pass along to you.

In the preface of a small book entitled *The Our Father,* written by
my good friend, Fr. Bill McCarthy, who co-directs My Father's Retreat House with Sr. Bernadette Sheldon in Moodus, Connecticut,
Father Bill tells how, during a low point in his life, he reached out to
a priest-friend who told him a story that changed his life.

It seems that this priest was going through a dry period in his priesthood. He decided to isolate himself in a cave in Spain, seven thousand feet above sea level, to seek intimacy with God. He remained in this desolate place (which had a sacred reputation) for nine months, living on bread and water, and using oil for his lamp that an old man brought to him. Prayer, for him, was usually a one-sided affair, in which he did the talking then listened for God's answer.

In the early part of his retreat, he struggled through loneliness, fear, guilt and even disbelief, wondering if God was even there. Then he became keenly aware of his complete solitude and aloneness and grew very still. In this deep silence, he heard the words: *Brennan, I love you, and I called you here to be alone with Me. And even though you're passing through many fiery temptations, you shall not be burned. And though you are overwhelmed with many worries and fears, you shall not be drowned. For you are precious in My eyes and honored. I forbid you to be afraid.*

After this stream of thoughts, a page number from the Bible came into his mind. With great anticipation, he opened the Bible to that page, and in utter amazement read the words from Isaiah:

> Fear not, for I have redeemed you; I have called you by name, you are mine. When you pass through the waters I will be with you . . . when you walk through fire you shall not be burned, and the flame shall not consume you . . . Because you are precious in my eyes, and honored, and I love you . . . Fear not, for I am with you. (Is 43: 2-5)

Then and there, this priest realized two simple truths: first, that Jesus Christ was alive and well and living in his own heart; and second, that this Jesus was speaking to him from within his own thoughts. He could talk to Christ, then he would listen, and Christ would talk back to him. He developed a very intimate, personal relationship with God who lived in his heart.

One day in prayer, the Lord took him into an ecstasy and said to him through his own thoughts: *You are my beloved son upon whom my favor rests. I'm going to use you very simply, lovingly and powerfully among my people.*

Finally, after nine glorious months alone with Christ, the Lord sent him home with a very simple but powerful message: *Go and tell every single person that you meet that I love them with my whole heart and my whole soul. I love them regardless of their weaknesses and their sins. I love them and I want to be Lord of their hearts. And if they surrender their poor battered hearts to me, I promise that whatever they ask the Father in My Name, I will give to them. And the miracles that I've done before I shall begin to do in their own lives* (*Our Father*, 3, 4).

Father Bill left the encounter with his priest friend "changed forever." And so will we be transformed by the words God will speak to us in Sacred Scripture—if only we will open ourselves and allow Jesus to be the Lord of our hearts.

While we may not go to a cave in the mountains of Spain, we are, in a sense, like mountain climbers scaling the face of Everest. The peak is the Sacred Liturgy, which the *Catechism* describes as "the summit toward which the activity of the Church is directed; it is also the font from which all her power flows" (*CCC*, 1074). All our prayers and efforts culminate in this privileged place of encounter with God. The bishops at Vatican II took pains to remind us of the different ways Christ is present to His Church in liturgical celebrations: in the body of the faithful gathered in His name, in the celebrating priest, in the Sacrament of the Eucharist, and "in His word since it is He Himself who speaks when the holy scriptures are read in Church" (*Instruction on the Worship of the Eucharistic Mystery*, 9).

The Church is careful to point out that while Christ is present in a real manner in the ways just enumerated, His sacramental presence in the Eucharist is, according to our beloved Pope John Paul II, "a most special presence" (*On the Eucharist in its Relationship to the Church*, 21). In his encyclical, he cites the words of Paul VI, who writes that Christ's presence in the Eucharistic species "surpasses all the others," because the Eucharist contains Christ Himself" (Paul VI, *Mystery of Faith*, 17).

When we listen to the Word of God at Mass, Christ is speaking to us just as intimately as He spoke to Father Bill's priest friend in the cave. In the Sacred Liturgy, God feeds us by His Word in Scripture and His Body in the Eucharist. If we are open to *receive* His word, we are receiving the life of God Himself. Through this extraordinary gift, our lives will be renewed and transformed, both personally and as a community.

# *Alleluia*

Reading the history of the early Church can be a very sobering, even frightening, experience. Evil and disasters similar to those of the first and second centuries abound today; only the names of the dictators have changed. Early Roman emperors such as Nero, Domitian, Marcus Aurelius, Hadrian, Decius, Valerian and Diocletian ruthlessly persecuted the followers of Christ in an attempt to wipe out Christianity. These despots were the forerunners of modern dictators such as Stalin, Hitler, Pol Pot, Milosevic, Osama bin Laden and Saddam Hussein.

One of the cruelest dictators was Nero, who blamed the Great Fire of Rome in the year 64 on the Christians, to deflect blame from himself. The Roman historian Tacitus records that Nero "inflicted the most exquisite tortures" on the Christians, who were:

> Covered with the skins of beasts, they were torn by dogs and perished, or were nailed to crosses, or were doomed to the flames. These served to illuminate the night when daylight failed. Nero had thrown open his gardens for the spectacle, and was exhibiting a show in the circus, while he mingled with the people in the dress of a charioteer or drove about in a chariot. Hence, even for criminals who deserved extreme and exemplary punishment, there arose a feeling of compassion; for it was not, as it seemed, for the public good, but to glut one man's cruelty, they were being destroyed. (*The Annals of Tacitus*, 304)

Sometimes it is difficult to reconcile the sheer amount of suffering and evil in the world with the Good News Jesus proclaims in the Gospel. We stand to sing the *Alleluia* in preparation for His coming to us in His Word. We wonder, does God really care or know the extent of the persecution His Church is undergoing all over the world? The answer is a resounding, "yes."

St. Luke reports that when Jesus entered Jerusalem for the final time, what He saw caused Him to weep over the city, because He knew the devastation that would descend on the world as a result of people not accepting Him (cf. Lk 19:41 ff; Lk 21). Jesus cautioned His disciples to "watch at all times, praying that you may have strength to escape all these things that will take place, and to stand before the Son of man" (Lk 21:36).

During the reign of the emperor Domitian (81-96), the beloved disciple of the Lord, St. John, when he was very old and exiled on the island of Patmos (near Turkey), had a

Jesus Wept/James Tissot

*O Jerusalem, Jerusalem, killing the prophets and stoning those who are sent to you! How often would I have gathered your children together as a hen gathers her brood under her wings, and you would not! Behold, your house is forsaken and desolate (Mt 23:37).*

series of visions. He recorded the visions in the *Apocalypse,* now known as the Book of Revelation. He said his message was "the revelation of Jesus Christ" (Rev 1:1) which God gave him through an angel. He records the pictures he "saw" in his visions, coded in mystery and symbolism, whose meaning certain community leaders learned to decipher to share with the faithful. John's message would be unintelligible to prying Roman persecutors.

The whole point of these visions and St. John's message is to give hope and fortitude to the Church Suffering. He was speaking to the early Christians as well as to those in every age and at the end of the world, who would usher in the Second Coming of Jesus.

St. John had a vision of the beginning and end of history, of Christ who is the Alpha (beginning) and the Omega (end), of the Lover who created us out of love, who redeemed us with His very life, and who sanctifies us for His glory. While the struggle of Christ and His followers against Satan and his cohorts continues, the outcome should not be in doubt because Christ has won the victory and claimed us for Himself. We await our deliverance from evil and a great wedding banquet in heaven, where the Church Triumphant will be joined to Christ. We will sing the great victory song which St. John heard the entire church singing to celebrate the marriage of the Lamb, the union of the Messiah with the saints in heaven. "Hallelujah! Salvation and glory and power belong to our God. . . . Let us rejoice and exult and give him the glory" (Rev 19:1, 7). In John's vision, the redeemed rejoice over God's victory over evil and sing rapturous praises celebrating God's boundless love: "Then I saw the heavens opened, and behold, a white horse! He who sat upon it is called Faithful and True. . . . He is clad in a robe dipped in blood, and the name by which he is called is The Word of God (Rev 19:11, 13).

The Angel Showing Jerusalem to St. John/G. Dore

"Jesus is the rider on the white horse" says Fr. Alfred McBride, "who gallops ahead of us to lead us to absolute love and joy. He is the Word of God who knew best what would save us. That is why "the armies of heaven, arrayed in fine linen, white and pure, followed him on white horses" (Rev 19:14) (*The Second Coming of Jesus*, 152, 153).

In the Sacred Liturgy, Christ's followers have a foretaste of God's absolute love, revealed to us in Word and Sacrament. Jesus, "Faithful and True" (Rev 19:11), comes to us in the holy *Gospel,* teaching us the way of salvation. Like the people in Scripture who find the buried treasure or the pearl of great price, we, who have found Christ through faith, can rejoice that we have found life—life eternal—which begins here on earth. We, like the early Christians, are willing to make any sacrifice for this *life,* knowing that we will triumph over Satan because of our fidelity to Christ.

We prepare for God's coming by singing the *Alleluia,* an ancient and beloved acclamation of praise. With profound gratitude we rise to our feet to glorify God with a full heart—contemplating Him in His Word and preparing to receive Him in the Eucharist.

## EXPLANATION

Two Hebrew words, one for praise (*hallelu*), and the other for God (*Yah,* an abbreviation for the divine Name, rendered *Yahweh*), unite to form *Alleluia*, which means: "Praise to the One who is!" Today we say, "Praise the Lord." *Alleluia* is used five times in the New Testament Book of Revelation, where it is sung by a "great multitude" in heaven that resembles a magnificent chorus who joyfully celebrate the Lord.

*Alleluia* is an ecstatic cry of joy praising Our Lord who comes to proclaim the good news of salvation. Usually taken from the *Gospel*, the acclamatory verse is both a reflection on the Word of God and a preparation for the *Gospel*. It attunes our minds to hear Christ speak to us in His own words.

Musically, this rite is a very beautiful part of the Mass that is sung by the cantor or choir and repeated by the congregation. One of my favorites is the *Celtic Alleluia*: "Father we praise you as Lord, all of the earth gives you worship, for your majesty fills the heavens, fills the earth. *Alleluia, alleluia, Alleluia, alleluia."* If the *Alleluia* is not sung, it is omitted and replaced by a moment of silent reflection.

Since the fourth century, the honor of proclaiming the *Gospel* has been reserved to the deacon or priest. We stand as a sign of respect when we sing the *Alleluia,* not because of the chant, but to honor the *Gospel*, the good news of the resurrection of Jesus. We are about to celebrate the victory He has won for us which will transform our lives.

During the entrance procession, the deacon or lector raises the Book of the Gospels to eye-level as a sign of distinction and respect, then places it in the middle of the altar. This, in itself, is a sign of great honor, as the altar has always represented Christ, Himself. During the singing of the *Alleluia,* the deacon or celebrant solemnly processes with the Book of Gospels from the altar to proclaim it from the ambo.

On solemn occasions during the singing of the *Alleluia,* the Book of the Gospels may be venerated with incense; usually by two acolytes or altar servers who hold lighted candles and flank the reader.

A word about the ambo is in order because it, too, deserves great respect. The ambo is the place we celebrate the presence of Christ in His Word. There are two tables, said St. Augustine: the Table of the Word, and the Table of the Eucharist. Both represent Jesus Christ. At the altar, Jesus Christ is shown present under the appearances of bread and

Ambo in St. Patrick's Church, Binghamton, New York. Designed by the author's grandfather, ecclesiastical architect, Domenico Borgia.

wine. At the ambo, the same Lord is shown present in his Word. Church architects often show the importance of the relationship between the altar and the ambo by constructing them out of the same material.

Today, the *Alleluia* is sung in every season except Lent, when it is replaced by another acclamation of praise, such as "Praise to you, Lord Jesus Christ, King of endless glory!" Fr. Lucien Deiss disagrees with the substitution, arguing that the original meaning of *Alleluia* ("Praise the Lord present in his Word") is valid for all occasions, including those of penance and sorrow. He cites an example from St. Jerome, who tells us that the *Alleluia* at the funeral of Fabiola was so loud that it made the roof of the church tremble! (*Spirit and Song of the New Liturgy,* 141).

Pope John Paul II recently spoke about the *Alleluia* during a general audience. He offered his reflections on a canticle from the Book of Revelation, "The Wedding of the Lamb," that is recited every Sunday except in Lent during evening prayer of the Liturgy of the Hours. He noted that the word "alleluia" is used frequently throughout the canticle as a bridge linking heaven and earth.

The Church on earth sings her song of praise in harmony with the song of the just, who are already beholding the glory of God. A channel of communication is established between history and eternity, which originates with the liturgy. . . and culminates with the liturgy in heaven, which our brothers and sisters who have preceded us on the road of faith have already achieved. (*National Catholic Register,* September 26, 2004)

## HISTORY

*Alleluia* appears frequently in the Old Testament psalms of praise and thanksgiving, including the Hallel (Psalms 113-118) that Jesus recited at the Last Supper. (From *Hallel* comes *Hallelujah.*) In the Book of Tobit, when the inspired writer describes the glory of the heavenly Jerusalem, of which the splendor of the earthly city is but a faint image, he says: "The streets of Jerusalem will be paved with beryl and ruby and stones of Ophir; all her lanes will cry 'Hallelujah!' and will give praise, saying 'Blessed is God, who has exalted you for ever'" (Tob 13:17, 18). The Jews did not just proclaim the *Alleluia* with their lips; they did so with their whole being as a sign of gratitude to God for the awesome wonders He had worked among them. In the New Testament, the *Alleluia* is only found in the Book of Revelation. There it is part of a victory song, sung by the entire church, celebrating the "marriage of the Lamb," the union of the Messiah with the community of the elect (Rev 19:5–10).

The *Responsorial Psalm* and the *Alleluia* are the oldest songs in our Eucharistic liturgy. The *Alleluia* was both said and sung in the early Church and was used outside of church, as well. St. Jerome heard the farm laborers of Bethlehem sing it while they ploughed the fields. He also introduced the *Alleluia* into the Roman Church at the time of Pope St. Damasus (366-384), where it was sung only once a year, on Easter, to emphasize the triumph of Christ's resurrection. St. Jerome observed that in the Eastern churches, lamps were lighted at the *Gospel* as a sign of joy, a custom that eventually made its way into the Roman Church. Incense was also burned before the *Gospel* reading.

"The 'Alleluia' is like the song of the wayfarer," St. Augustine wrote in one of his sermons. "Therefore, as we walk this road that is so exhausting, let us strive for that homeland in which there will be rest, in which all the present concerns will have disappeared, and in which only the 'Alleluia' will remain."

Eventually the *Alleluia* found its way into all liturgies thanks to St. Gregory the Great, who extended its use to all the Sundays and feasts of the liturgical year, except in Lent. And then it was noticed by its very absence.

Soloists who performed the *Alleluia* in the early Church were accustomed to vocalize the last vowel with a prolonged and ornate extension called a *jubilus*. St. Augustine explains its spiritual meaning:

> At harvest time, either in the fields or the vineyards, the people first begin by expressing their joy in the words of a song. But when their joy becomes so great that it can no longer be expressed in words, they forget the text and start to "jubilate." When a "jubilus" is sung it seems as if the heart is working hard to express what cannot be expressed. Who deserves this jubilation more than God who is indescribable? If, then, you cannot explain what you mean and at the same time you must speak, what else can you do except to rejoice (jubilate)? The heart rejoices without words and its joy is not limited by words. (in Deiss, *Spirit and Song of the New Liturgy*, 142)

In this way, the early Christians rejoiced in their faith, enabling their deep feelings of joy and love to spill over in song.

## REFLECTION

When my husband, Tom, and I were in Rome for the installation of our cardinal, Francis George of Chicago, we spent a delightful evening with Fr. Paul Cioffi, S.J., who taught courses on the Eucharist to the seminarians at the North American College. We had a mutual interest in the Sacred Liturgy, which we talked about nonstop. Sadly, Father Paul recently died, but left us a legacy of his love of the Eucharist in *Gospel Spirituality and Catholic Worship*, a book he co-authored with Fr. William Sampson, S.J., in which they offer much food for thought about how the celebration of the Eucharist can be spiritually fulfilling for both priest and laity.

Like the Lord whom he loved so much, Father Paul uses stories to convict his readers. He wants to encourage us to believe in a God more concerned for our happiness than we are ourselves, no matter what may appear to happen on the surface, a concept the following story illustrates:

> Imagine young Charles, away at boarding school. Christmas is near, and on Friday, Charles will go home for two weeks. But on Monday, his mother calls with bad news: Great Aunt Sophie is ill, and she must go to Paris and stay with her. Charles will have to remain at school for the holiday.
>
> Charles is devastated. After that call, it seems to him that all his fellow students can talk about is going home for the holidays. His teachers tell one dumb joke after another. Classes are dull and boring. Charles is an alien in a world of jollity.
>
> Then on Wednesday, his mother calls again. Great Aunt Sophie has taken an unexpected turn for the better. Mother will be at school to pick him up on Friday after all.
>
> All Charles has are his mother's words, a promise. But he enjoys school immensely that day. His teachers are witty. Classes challenge him. He has fun with his schoolmates. Even the food tastes better. Nothing at school has really changed. It is Charles who has been transformed by words of promise he trusts. He does not wait for Friday to be happy—he is happy now. (31)

Father Paul's premise is that faith enables us to experience *now* what the future promises. "Those who believe the promises of Jesus," he says, "find their lives invaded by anticipatory joy" (31).

Someone who does believe in the promises of Jesus and who experienced this "anticipatory joy," is theology professor and popular Catholic author Scott Hahn. Before his conversion to Catholicism, he had a deep curiosity about the Mass. Despite the fact that his Protestant training led him to believe that "the Mass was the ultimate sacrilege a human could commit," Hahn often attended Mass. Sitting in the back pew next to his beloved Bible, he realized that the Scripture readings were all familiar—Isaiah, psalms, Paul— and seemed to fit so well in the context of the Sacred Liturgy. When the priest raised the white host at the consecration, Hahn says he felt all his doubts drain away as a prayer surged from his heart: "*My Lord and my God. That's really you!*" (*The Lamb's Supper*, 8).

I will let him share his experience of the Mass as it relates to the *Book of Revelation* in his own words:

> I would return to Mass the next day, and the next day, and the next. Each time I went back, I would "discover" more of the Scriptures fulfilled before my eyes. Yet no book was as visible to me, in that dark chapel, as the Book of Revelation, the Apocalypse, which describes the worship of the angels and saints in heaven. As in that book, so in that chapel, I saw robed priests, an altar, a congregation chanting "holy, holy, holy." I saw the smoke of incense; I heard the invocation of angels and saints; I myself sang the alleluias, for I was drawn ever more into this worship. I continued to sit in the back pew with my Bible, and I hardly knew which way to turn—toward the action in the Apocalypse or the action at the altar. More and more, they seemed to be the very same action. (9)

The Book of Revelation, Hahn realized, was not about the end of the world or some future promise, but it was about the gift of God's eternal life which He gives to us now in the Eucharist.

At Mass, we prepare not for the Second Coming of Christ in the heavenly Jerusalem, or for the arrival of our mother at boarding school, but for our encounter with the Living God in the Eucharist. When we stand to sing the *Alleluia,* we, like Scott Hahn, are overwhelmed with joy and gratitude that Christ is really present in Word and Sacrament. And like Charles at boarding school, we are happy because we know that Christ is coming in Communion to rescue us and bring us "home." We celebrate our imminent encounter in song, rejoicing in a God who will do anything—including be nailed to a Cross and die—to lead us to the new life He has prepared for us. That new life is the life of God Himself that He gives us in the Eucharist: "This is the cup of My blood, the blood of the new and everlasting covenant" (*Sacramentary*, 549). We sing *Alleluia* to thank and praise God for not making us wait for our reward, but for letting us taste our future glory now as we feast on the pure unconditional love of God in the Eucharist.

# *The Gospel*

Fr. Ronald Rolheiser, a popular theologian and author who writes for Chicago's *Catholic New World,* headlined a recent column, "How to Listen and Hear God Say 'I Love You.'" Intrigued, I read further.

Father encourages us to pray in such a way that our prayer opens us to hear God say, "I love you." "These words addressed to you by God," he says, "are the most important words you will ever hear because, before you hear them, nothing is ever completely right with you, but, after you hear them, something will be right in your life at a very deep level." His words spoke truth, and I read on. "Nothing will heal us more of restlessness, bitterness, and insecurity than to hear God say: 'I love you.'" Father Rolheiser sums up this thought by saying that prayer is not meant to change God, but us. "And nothing changes us as much for the good as to hear someone say that he or she loves us, especially if that someone is God" (*Catholic New World*, April 13-20, 2003).

Christ in the Synagogue/G. Dore

Where do we go to hear God say, "I love you?" A cave in Spain, like the one Father Bill's priest-friend had, is really out of the question; but all of us have access to Sacred Scripture, and in particular, to the *Gospels,* where Jesus not only tells us in words how much He loves us, but proves it in His actions. How blessed we are to have such a clear picture of the person, of the conversation and actions, of the life and passion of our

Lord and Savior as described by eye-witnesses under the inspiration of the Holy Spirit. Although Jesus lived two thousand years ago, we can meet Him again in the *Gospels* and accompany Him through the scenes of His life, listening to Him speak to us as we go.

When Jesus spoke, everyone listened with a sense of wonder and anticipation of what He would say. Scripture tells us that "All the people hung upon his words" (Lk 19:48), and "early in the morning all the people came to him in the temple to hear him" (Lk 21:38). Jesus was an exceptional speaker who drew crowds around him; his listeners "all spoke well of him and wondered at the gracious words which proceeded out of his mouth" (Lk 4:22). Jesus captivated His followers by telling stories to teach them about the kingdom. The people were able to relate His stories to their lives in such a way that they found new meaning and direction for their own stories. His love healed and converted His listeners.

Today, we have the same opportunity as those first Christians. In many African churches, when the priest reads the *Gospel*, the congregation responds with shouts of joy and exultation because they believe that God is speaking to them personally. We can learn from them! In the *Gospel,* Christ calls us to new life and hope—in Him. He wants to re-write our stories in the light of His love for us. Listen carefully for His "I love you." You will hear it when you pray the *Gospels* with your heart.

## EXPLANATION

The proclamation of the *Gospel* is the climax of the *Liturgy of the Word*. After a prayer asking God to cleanse his heart and his lips in order to announce Christ's words worthily, the celebrant sings or says the *Gospel*. The word "Gospel" (from the Anglo-Saxon *Godspell* or "God story") means literally "good news." When Christ was born, the angel appeared to the shepherds, saying: "Be not afraid; for behold, I bring you good news of a great joy which will come to all the people; for to you is born this day in the city of David a Savior, who is Christ the Lord" (Lk 2:10, 11). As Christians, we celebrate the coming of the Messiah, who was prophesied in the Old Testament, and was born to us in order to save us from our sins and lead us to eternal life with His Father in heaven.

After Jesus was baptized, He "came into Galilee preaching the gospel of God: 'The time is fulfilled and the kingdom of God is at hand; repent, and believe in the gospel'" (Mk 1:14, 15). The good news is that the kingdom of God, which Jesus came to establish, is made present in Jesus' forgiving sins, healing the sick, feeding the hungry and raising the dead. He is the anointed one who stood in the temple and read from the Book of Isaiah: "The Spirit of the Lord is upon me, because he has anointed me to preach good news to the poor. He has sent me to proclaim release to the captives and recovering of sight to the blind, to set at liberty those who are oppressed, to proclaim the acceptable year of the Lord" (Lk 4:17-19). Jesus asked His disciples to spread this message to every person on earth, saying: "Go into all the world and preach the gospel to the whole creation" (Mk 16:15).

Jesus Unrolls the Book in the Synagogue/James Tissot

*Today this Scripture has been fulfilled in your hearing* (Lk 4:21).

"The gospel of your salvation" (Eph 1:13) is about to be proclaimed by the Risen Lord through the priest or deacon. While lectors or ministers may proclaim the other readings, from earliest times the reading of the *Gospel* was reserved to a deacon or priest. Special marks of reverence are accorded the Book of the Gospels to distinguish it from the other readings. The honors paid to the *Gospel* book correspond to those given to the altar: kiss, bow, incense, and procession with candles and acolytes. From the time of the Apostles, the faithful have stood as a sign of respect to acknowledge that Christ is present and speaking to them. Actually, the tradition of standing dates back to the Old Testament: "And Ezra opened the book in the sight of all the people, for he was above all the people; and when he opened it, all the people stood" (Neh 8:5).

At the ambo, the deacon or priest opens the Book of the Gospels and says: "The Lord be with you. A reading from . . . " and makes the Sign of the Cross on the book and on his forehead mouth and breast. The faithful do likewise, signing our forehead to show that we understand and believe what the Gospel teaches, our lips to signify that we are ready to spread the good news, and our breast to show that we will hold Christ's teaching close to our heart and give witness to the *Gospel* in our everyday lives.

Deacon Jim Carroll reading the Gospel.

After the reading, the priest or deacon kisses the book and says inaudibly, "May the words of the gospel wipe away our sins." Does the word of God have the power to forgive sins? Jesus addressed this issue when He said: "Amen, amen, I say to you, whoever hears my word and believes in the one who sent me has eternal life and will not come to condemnation, but has passed from death to life" (Jn 5:24). The Word of God is Life itself. Using the image of the vine and the branches, Jesus invites His disciples who have accepted His life-giving word to abide in Him so that they will produce fruit: "If you abide in me, and my words abide in you, ask for whatever you wish, and it will be done for you" (Jn 15:7).

We will produce "fruit" to the extent that we allow God's word to live in us and form us into a more perfect image of His Son, Jesus Christ. In the Old Testament, when God called the prophets to proclaim His word, He asked them to physically eat the scroll of the law, to eat their Scriptures:

> "'Son of man, eat what is offered to you; eat this scroll,
> and go, speak to the house of Israel.' So I opened my mouth,

and he gave me the scroll to eat. And he said to me, 'Son of man, eat this scroll that I give you and fill your stomach with it.' Then I ate it; and it was in my mouth as sweet as honey." (Ezek 3:1-3)

Fr. Ronald Rolheiser explains the symbolism. The idea, he says, is that "they should digest the word and turn it into their own flesh so that people will be able to see the word of God in a living body rather than on dead parchment." He argues that in order to bring God to others, it is simply not enough to hand someone a Bible or some religious literature. Rather, it is a matter of "transubstantiatiing God, the way we do with the food we eat." Father Rolheiser clarifies the meaning:

> We have to digest something and turn it, physically, into the flesh of our own bodies so it becomes part of what we look like. If we would do this with the word of God, others would not have to read the Bible to see what God is like, they would need only to look at our faces and our lives to see God. (*The Holy Longing,* 102)

What a challenge! When we listen to the reading of the *Gospel* at Mass, perhaps the image of eating the scroll and Father Rolheiser's insights will help us *ingest* the words of Scripture so that they will live in us and inform all our actions. In this way we will be preaching the *Gospel* with our lives, and others will know us by our "fruit" (see Mt 15:16).

## History

At first, the *Gospel* was proclaimed orally through the preaching of the Apostles. In his historical account of the Church during its crucial first three hundred years, the ancient historian Eusebius writes that St. Mark composed his *Gospel* at the request of the Christians living in Rome, who asked to have a written record of the preaching and teaching of St. Peter, of whom Mark was a disciple. St. Peter is said to have given his approval to Mark's writings that were to be read consecutively in the churches. St. Clement of Rome (c. 96) gives witness to this claim, as does Bishop Papias of Hierapolis (Eusebius, *The History of the Church,* 101-104).

Egeria, who left us a record of the liturgies of the fourth century, tells us that incense was burned during the reading of the *Gospel* so that the aroma filled the whole church. The Church Fathers also leave us a rich assortment of testimony describing the reverence paid to the *Gospel* in ancient liturgies.

On fire for the Word of God, St. Ambrose encourages us: "The Word of God is the vital sustenance of the soul; it feeds it, pastures it, and guides it; nothing can keep the human soul alive except the Word of God." In 406, St. Jerome wrote that so many candles were lit in broad daylight during the *Gospel* reading in all the churches of the East that it seemed as if "the sun shines with all its brilliance; but their flame is not intended to dispel darkness, it is a sign of joy." In Rome, the lector processed to the ambo with acolytes bearing candles, incense, torches and bowls of fire.

St. Jerome, who spent years in Bethlehem translating the Bible from the original Greek and Hebrew into Latin (the Latin Vulgate), looked upon God's word as His sacred Real Presence: "I think that the Gospel is the body of Christ and that the Holy Scriptures are his doctrine. When the Lord speaks about eating his flesh and drinking his blood, certainly this can mean the mystery (of the Eucharist). However, his true body and blood are (also) the Word of the Scriptures and its doctrine." And although Origen (185-253) is not counted as one of the Church Fathers, he is considered one of the most eminent writers of early Christianity. As a young man he memorized many passages of the Bible, which he shared in his sermons. His deep respect for the Word of God is evident in his writings:

> You who are accustomed to take part in divine mysteries know, when you receive the body of the Lord, how you protect it with all caution and veneration, lest any small part fall from it, lest anything of the consecrated gift be lost. For you believe, and correctly, that you are answerable if anything falls from there by neglect. But if you are so careful to preserve his body, and rightly so, how do you think there is less guilt to have neglected God's Word than to have neglected his body? (in Raniero Cantalamessa, *The Mystery of God's Word*, 14)

In his usual straightforward style, St. Augustine urged his

*One very simple discipline for contemplative prayer is to read, every evening before going to sleep, the readings of the next day's Eucharist with special attention to the Gospel. It is often helpful to take one sentence or word that offers special comfort and repeat it a few times. . . . I have found this practice to be a powerful support in times of crisis. It is especially helpful during the night, when worries or anxieties may keep me awake and seduce me into idolatry. By remembering the Gospel story or any of the sayings of the Old or New Testament authors, I can create a safe mental home into which I can lead all my preoccupations and let them be transformed into quiet prayer.*

—Fr. Henri Nouwen
*The Only Thing Necessary*

listeners to "listen to the Gospel as if the Lord Himself stood before us." "The Gospel is the mouth of Christ," he wrote. "He is seated in heaven, but he does not cease to speak on earth."

At first, the *Gospels* were read continuously, irrespective of the day or time of the year. This was probably due to the Church's desire to have all of the Scriptures read within a certain time frame. Long passages were read until the bishop gave a signal for the reader to stop. At the next assembly, the reading would be resumed where it had previously stopped. Pope St. Damasus (c. 306 384) was the first to organize the liturgical year and to make a selection from the Sacred Books of passages that were more appropriate, either to the mystery celebrated, or to the spirit of the season. Thus arose our present-day *pericopes* or passages.

The *Gospel* is one of the greatest treasures of the Church, and the books in which the sacred words are contained have been the object of veneration for centuries. The book containing the very words of Christ was treated as if it was Christ, Himself. Before printing was invented, monks spent years writing out the holy words in exquisite calligraphy on precious parchment, ornamenting the pages with delicate illuminations, binding them in sumptuous leather covers, ornamented with gold or ivory or precious stones. Oaths, then and now, were often sworn on the Book of the Gospels, both in ecclesial and secular law. The one swearing laid a hand on the book while reciting the formula of the oath: "By the help of God and his holy gospel, which I touch with my hand." In eighth century Rome, all the clergy kissed the *Gospel* book after the proclamation. (Occasionally the entire assembly was allowed to kiss it.) Today, it is the only liturgical book which is kissed and incensed, and on which the Sign of the Cross is made.

## REFLECTION

To the extent that we are open and eager to receive God's Word, it will transform our lives—a message which Jesus imparted to His followers in the *Parable of the Sower.* In this story, God is the sower, the seed is His word, and the ground is every human being. Jesus emphasizes the various types of soil on which the seed falls, which is to say the dispositions with which people receive His Word.

Our Lord cites three examples of people who would react to His Word negatively, and one who would be enriched by His Word. The former are those who never accept the "word of the kingdom" (Mt 13:19); those who believe for awhile but fall away when the going gets rough; and those who believe, but in whom the Word is choked by worldly anxiety and riches. Last, but not least, are those who respond to the Word and produce fruit abundantly: "As for what was sown on good soil, this is he who hears the word and understands it; he indeed bears fruit, and yields, in one case a hundredfold, in another sixty, and in another thirty" (Mt 13:23).

After telling this story, Jesus "called out, 'He who has ears to hear let him hear'" (Lk 8:8), so eager was He that the people take His words to heart. Are we among those who take His words seriously or are we like the people who "listen without hearing"? (Mt 13:13). Are we really listening with our hearts as well as our ears? I believe that if we expect God to speak to us, we will surely hear Him.

In my own experience, God speaks to me even when I don't expect to hear Him! At daily Mass one day, the *Gospel* was about Jesus driving the moneychangers from the Temple. The celebrant preached a powerful homily on our need to be pure temples of the Holy Spirit. I stayed afterward to reflect on the reading because it stirred something inside of me. I felt moved to pray to the Holy Spirit to help me clean out my "inner house" so to speak, and replace all the negative emotions with God's love and joy. I asked the Lord to purify my thoughts and desires, so that He would find a worthy dwelling in me, and so that I could give Him true love.

No sooner did I say this prayer than an incident that happened the day before with my husband popped into my mind. He had forgotten a promise he made to me. It was nothing big, in fact it was rather small, but when I realized it, I was angry. The stress and pain I experienced was out of proportion to the actual happening.

A few days later, I related this incident to my spiritual director, Father Bob, who asked me, "Who didn't follow through?" meaning in my past, probably in my family of origin. He urged me to go back to a memory of someone not being present, of feeling disappointed.

I closed my eyes and saw myself as a baby, feeling lonely and panicked that no one was going to care for me. I couldn't count on getting my needs met, and I began to cry. A deep feeling like I didn't matter seemed to be at the bottom of this.

Father Bob prayed, asking Jesus if this was true. In the quiet of my heart, I saw Jesus in the Temple, filled with rage, driving the money-changers from His Father's house. Then Jesus showed me His rage at what had been done to me. He

Jesus Clears the Temple/Carl Bloch

came into my childhood home and ranted and raved at the hurts and abuse I had suffered. He was angry that I hadn't been cared about in the way He wanted. As a temple of God, I was not reverenced.

Then I questioned Jesus as to why He would be so angry with my mother and father who were doing their best to care for me, despite their own wounds. Father Bob suggested that maybe Jesus wasn't angry with them, but with what made them wounded. Then I could appreciate Jesus' anger and watched Him as He drove out the spirits of neglect and disappointment from our family tree. Father Bob prayed, asking Jesus to go back through my family of origin and my ancestors to drive out these spirits who were keeping me in such bondage.

The Lord led me to a wound that was still causing pain so many years after the fact. Father Bob called on Jesus who came into my inner temple and drove out the spirits of neglect and abuse. In my imagination, I saw and felt the love of Jesus who drove out the lie that I didn't matter, just as He drove out the moneychangers who were buying and selling in His Father's temple. The Scripture story and my story merged together, bringing the Lord who healed me.

This is what Christ means when He says: "The words that I have spoken to you are spirit and life"(Jn 6:64). He wants to bring life to those "dead" parts of us, resurrecting and freeing us from the sins and wounds of our past. Jesus promised, "If you continue in my word, you are truly my disciples, and the truth will make you free" (Jn 8:31, 32).

God's word is a *living word*, which means that His teaching is timeless—it is as relevant today as it was to the people of His time. When we have the same strong faith as the woman suffering from hemorrhages, who reached out to touch the cloak of Jesus trusting she would be healed, Jesus will also cure us, saying, "Daughter/Son, your faith has made you well; go in peace and be healed of your disease" (Mk 5:34). We can join Jesus and His disciples in a boat on a stormy lake, and watch with wonder as He calms the storm—and our fears. We can dine with Jesus at the home of Martha and Mary, and offer Him the hospitality of a listening, centered heart that so endeared Him to Mary. We can recall the scene in the Upper Room where Jesus asked His disciples to remember His death in a ritual of eating and drinking—a sacred rite we memorialize at every Mass— which enables us to intimately encounter Our Lord, in His dying, and His rising. As He hangs on the Cross, we can listen as He forgives the penitent thief and His executioners—and us—for all the times we've failed Him. He overcame death and sin, and won for us a life of blissful freedom and joy. This is a gift He gives freely to His followers who believe in Him and live by His words.

# The Homily

A s Catholics growing up in the fifties, we were not allowed to attend any Protestant services or even watch Billy Graham on TV. Although my dad was raised Catholic, he didn't practice his faith and therefore did not allow these restrictions to effect him. After dinner I'd be in my room doing homework when I'd hear the familiar background music of a Billy Graham Crusade on TV (later in life my dad was hard of hearing and he'd turn the volume way up on the TV). I would steal into the living room for a peek, and was always moved to see hundreds of people walking forward to give their lives to Christ.

What they experienced is known as *metanoia,* a conversion of the heart and mind to Christ—the goal of our spiritual journey. Their lives would never be the same, thanks to the Holy Spirit working through the words of a dynamic preacher, who prepared the soil of their hearts to receive the seed of God's word (see Lk 8:11). This should be the intent of every preacher—to open the ears of the faithful to hear God's truth and their eyes to see God's light, so that they might conform their lives to His. Good preaching nourishes our conversion, which is a lifelong process of becoming, by which we are recreated into a new person. For a sermon to bear such fruit requires two things: one, a preacher so in tune with God's Word that he can shine it like a laser beam into the inner struggles and conflicts of his parishioners, bringing them God's healing light, and two, a congregation alert to their need for God and open to His transforming grace.

On Pentecost, the Holy Spirit lit a fire in the hearts and minds of the apostles to bear witness to Christ in Jerusalem and Judea, in Samaria, and to the ends of the earth (Acts 1:8). Faithful disciples of every generation take the torch and, like Olympic runners, continue to pass on the word of salvation to all generations of believers. The Church, through the indwelling power of the Holy Spirit, has been witnessing to Christ for two millenia, preaching the Good News of salvation in Jesus. Interpreting God's Word is a responsibility the Church entrusts to bishops, priests and deacons.

## EXPLANATION

A good homilist is like a locksmith who comes to the house to open a door whose owners have misplaced the key. In a matter of moments, he will find the right master key, which will unlock the door and let the people into the warmth of their home. A faithful homilist carries a master key with him at all times—the Holy Spirit— who can maneuver His way into the rustiest locked hearts!

Homily connotes a meeting of minds and hearts—as in a conversation with a group of people. It is the privilege of the priest to engage in a "heart to heart" discourse with his flock, to break open the Scriptures in order to apply God's Word to our everyday lives. The homilist should take his inspiration from the biblical texts of the Mass to reveal the presence of Jesus speaking to His people today. The homily is not meant to be a familiar chat about anything at all; it is nothing less than the proclamation of the Word of God made relevant to the lives of the faithful.

There must be a homily on Sundays and holy days of obligation; it may be omitted only "for a serious reason." The homily "is recommended on other days, especially on the weekdays of Advent, Lent and the Easter season, as well as on other feasts and occasions when the people come to church in large numbers"(*General Instruction*, 42). There should be no proclamation of the Word without a homily and, according to Fr. Lucien Deiss, it should be "real," which is to say "authentic." This does not necessarily mean long, he says, but it must be "of practical benefit to the celebrating community" (*The Spirit and Song of the New Liturgy*, 167).

The Church distinguishes between the Eucharistic homily, which can only be preached by the ordained, and lay preaching which is authorized by the pastor or a bishop for programs of a catechetical nature. Lay men and women preachers are a great gift to the Church, giving a variety of talks for vocations, fund drives, Communion services and the like. While there may be valid reasons for lay people to preach the homily, the Church only allows bishops, priests or deacons to preach the Eucharistic homily. Fr. John Burke, O.P., who teaches homiletics at the Pontifical Faculty at the Dominican House of Studies in Washington, D.C., explains that the priest is "the leader of the worshipping community," and that "the homily is an act of

Christ precisely as high priest of the New Covenant which He established at the Last Supper; it is an act of Christ making us holy, carrying with it the special grace for worship." This grace, Father Burke says, "does not depend on the person, but on the power of Christ," to which he adds, "even bad homilies by the power of Christ give us grace to grow in holiness" ("The Gift of the Priestly Homilist," in *Homiletic & Pastoral Review*, 17).

Elsewhere in the same article, Father Burke quotes Fr. Joseph Fox, who explains the homily as a "liturgical act of Christ":

> The homilist acts sacramentally in the place of Jesus the priest by rendering through his words an act of worship, as prophet, proclaiming and explaining the word of God, as King, he addresses the Body of Christ authoritatively as head and pastor. (18)

The priest has a unique and privileged role: to stand in the place of Christ and to preach in His name. Vatican Council II cited preaching as "the first task of priests as co-workers of the bishops to preach the Gospel of God to all men." Their role, the bishops said, is "Not to teach their own wisdom but the Word of God and to issue a pressing invitation to all men to conversion and to holiness" (*Decree on the Ministry and Life of Priests*, II, 4).

## History

Homilies trace their roots to the Old Testament. About four hundred years before the birth of Christ, during the period of restoration following the Babylonian Exile, the priest-scribe Ezra preached a homily to the returning Jewish exiles who were celebrating the Feast of Tabernacles:

> And all the people gathered as one man into the square before the Water Gate; and they told Ezra the scribe to bring the book of the law of Moses which the Lord had given to Israel. And they read from the book, from the law of God, clearly; and they gave the sense, so that the people understood the reading. (Neh 8: 1, 8)

Ezra's explanation of God's word stirred the people so deeply that they ate and drank and celebrated with great joy, "for they understood the words that were declared to them" (Neh 8:12).

Just as Ezra applied the Scriptures to the lives of the people, so did Jesus when He read from the scroll of the prophet Isaiah in the synagogue of Nazareth. After reading the text of Isaiah 61, He rolled up the scroll, gave it to the sacristan, and sat down: "And the eyes of all in the synagogue were fixed on him. And he began to say to them, 'Today this scripture has been fulfilled in your hearing" (Lk 4:20, 21). His hearers "wondered at the gracious words which proceeded out of his mouth" (Lk 4:22).

Jesus was a masterful storyteller. He told parables which spoke to the problems and conflicts of people, promising the Holy Spirit to help solve them. He awakened their deepest hungers, offering Himself as Bread to fill them. His stories converted the lives of His followers because He spoke the truth with love. Unafraid of popular opinion, criticism or church polls, Jesus called a spade a spade, never flinching from taking a stand on matters of faith

Jesus Speaking in the Treasury/James Tissot

and morals. His disciples followed in His footsteps, choosing torture or imprisonment over silence. After Peter and John healed the crippled beggar at the Beautiful Gate of the Temple, they were ordered to stop speaking in the name of Jesus. Their reply? "We cannot but speak of what we have seen and heard" (Acts 4:20). Peter's forceful preaching attracted large crowds; one day he spoke with such power and boldness that three thousand people came forward to be baptized (cf. Acts 2: 41).

In Antioch, when Paul and his companions entered the synagogue on the Sabbath, the Jewish officials urged them to speak to

Paul preaching at Athens/Raphael

*But how are men to call upon him in whom they have not believed? And how are they to believe in him of whom they have never heard? And how are they to hear without a preacher? And how can men preach unless they are sent? As it is written, 'How beautiful are the feet of those who preach the good news!'* (Rom 10:14-16).

the people after the Scripture readings: "Brethren, if you have any word of exhortation for the people, say it" (Acts 13:15). At Troas, on the first day of the week the Christian community gathered for a Eucharistic liturgy, when "Paul talked with them, intending to depart on the morrow; and he prolonged his speech until midnight" (Acts 20:7). Preaching was the heart and strength of Paul's ministry. If Sampson's power was his hair, Paul's power was his preaching! In Macedonia, where Paul and his disciples went because of a vision, a group of women gathered outside the city gate to hear him preach. One of the women, Lydia, who was a dealer in purple cloth, listened to him "and the Lord opened her heart to give heed to what was said by Paul" (Acts 16:14). She and her whole household were converted.

In the earliest days of the Church, anyone in the congregation could speak in the assembly, even a Christian visiting from another city. By the second century, that changed, so that preaching became the responsibility of the bishop who invariably addressed the faithful in a sermon based on the passage of the Gospel. Bishops would even write out their sermons to be delivered by priests or deacons in the outlying churches, when the bishop himself was unable to attend. For a period of time, a sermon followed each reading. Sermons became popular with St. Augustine, who preached twice weekly and who, apparently, didn't like poorly fashioned homilies. Trained in classical speaking, St. Augustine encouraged his catechists to learn from the persuasive rhetoric of his day.

At the request of a deacon in Carthage, St. Augustine wrote some instructions on what to do when he saw people yawning or showing signs they'd rather be somewhere else. He advised the deacon to get their attention with an anecdote or a moving story, and even to let them sit down (it was the custom to stand). And lastly, he advised: "If you wish to cure their boredom, be sparing with the medicine. Hurry, promise that you will soon finish, and finish very quickly" (in Chevrot, *Our Mass Explained,* 73).

St. Justin Martyr describes a homily that followed the Scripture readings in the earliest description of the Mass: "When the reader pauses the president (bishop) addresses the people, exhorting them to imitate the beautiful things they have heard." Origen, another eminent defender of the Christian faith and a forceful homilist, distinguished between a sermon and a homily, saying that a sermon followed the style of classical rhetoric which relied on biblical texts to prove a doctrinal point, whereas the homily was more of a pastoral explanation and application of the scriptural Word to the lives of the faithful (N. Abeyasingha, *The Universal Catechism, A Homily Sourcebook,* 14). Elsewhere, Origen describes the nature of a homily: "It is not a time to comment, but to edify the Church of God and to move inert and nonchalant hearers by the example of the saints and mystical explanations."

In fourth century Jerusalem, several priests preached one after the other followed by the bishop who spoke last. During the pontificate of Pope St. Leo the Great in 453, lay preaching was forbidden because of rampant heresy. Among the great homilists who were Church Fathers were Origen, Gregory Nazianzus and John Chrysostom in the East, and Ambrose, Augustine and Leo the Great in the West.

For a time during the Middle Ages, the homily lost its pride of place—and meaning—in the liturgy. Priests removed their maniples (a linen cloth carried on the left arm used as a napkin to wipe the face or hands of the celebrant and ministers), as if to suggest that what they were about to say was extraneous to the liturgy. They often read a homily from one of the Church Fathers or expounded on some point of doctrine unrelated to the Scripture readings of the day. The pulpit became a platform for theological debate, denunciations of heresies, and devotional, moralistic tales from the lives of saints.

By the nineteenth century, the homily in the ancient patristic sense began to revive; but it wasn't until Vatican II that preaching took its rightful place in the Mass following the Scripture readings, and its content was to flow "from the sacred text" (*Constitution on the Sacred Liturgy*, 52). In one of the shortest, but most important documents to come out of Vatican II, the bishops explained how God's revelation comes to us through the living Word of God—to teach, nourish and transform us. To this end they directed "all the preaching of the Church must be nourished and ruled by Sacred Scripture" (*Dei Verbum*, 21).

## REFLECTION

Have you ever gone to Mass and listened only half-heartedly to the homily, when suddenly, the priest says something which strikes at the heart of a problem with which you've been dealing? I often experience these little "wake up" calls, which I take as a word from the Lord who is speaking to me through the priest's homily. This is in accord with Vatican II, which stated that behind every homilist is God Himself, who preaches His Word to us.

Every homilist has the awesome responsibility of proclaiming God's word so that it will nourish our faith and call us to a deeper conversion. Tired of seeing his parishioners reach for the bulletin or look at their watches during his homilies, and hearing a perfunctory, "Nice sermon, Father," after Sunday Mass, Fr. Dominic Grassi, pastor of St. Josephat Church in Chicago, decided to do something about it. He shares candidly in *Still Called by Name, Why I Love Being a Priest* his growth in learning how to inspire his listeners and make an impact on the congregation. He went from theology lectures to word-for-word memorization to speaking from the center aisle to headaches—before, he says, the Spirit led him to the "theology of story." He discovered that a preacher needs to be familiar with not only the word of God, but also his own story of faith and the stories of the people with whom he shares his thoughts. Once he learned to make these connections, Fr. Dominic's homilies eventually became "a kind of spiritual dance with my story touching the stories of the people to whom I preached. And together we explored and shared the mystery of *the story*, found primarily in Scripture, but also found in human history." Now, if his parishioners come out of church on Sunday and simply say to him, "Nice sermon, Father," Fr. Dominic knows he failed. But, he says "if they start enthusiastically sharing their stories and insights with me, then I'll know that we're dancing. And there is no better feeling" (82-84).

It seems Father Dominic found the secret of good preaching: to enable the congregation to find *themselves* in his stories. When we connect our story with God's story, we find new meaning, or hope, or insights, or resolve to change our lives. We have the same problems and needs as our Christian ancestors who found hope and healing in the words of Jesus. When we reach out in faith to touch—and be touched by Jesus—He will heal us the same way He did the people in the Gospels: the leper (Mk 1:41), the paralyzed man (Mk 2:11), the woman with a hemorrhage (Mk 5:29), the daughter of Jairus (Mk 5:39), or the deaf-mute (Mk 7:35). These, and thousands

The Daughter of Jairus/Louis S. Glanzman

more, experienced miracles of physical, emotional and spiritual transformation, a gift promised to us if only we have the faith to trust in the Word of God.

A parishioner of Holy Trinity Church in Washington, D.C., experienced such a miracle—the healing of her marriage—after listening to a powerful homily on forgiveness given by her pastor, Fr. William Byron, S.J., on the Feast of the Holy Family. Father Bill is the former president of Catholic University and the University of Scranton, a prolific author and dynamic preacher. The parishioner and her husband were separated and headed for divorce. He wanted reconciliation, but she was on the fence. Then she listened to Father Bill's compelling description of "family," modeled, of course, on the Holy Family.

Fr. William J. Byron, S.J.

Father Bill introduced his homily with some age-old wisdom which the celebrating priest used to share with couples before they exchanged their wedding vows: "Let the security of your wedded life rest on the great principle of self sacrifice. Sacrifice is usually difficult and irksome: only love can make it easy and perfect love can make it a joy." "Love," said Father Bill, "is another word for sacrifice."

Although this quote no longer introduces Wedding Liturgies (what a pity!), Father Bill gave what must have been a stirring homily on sacrifice and forgiveness as "the bedrock of happy and holy families." He urged his parishioners to adopt the words from the days *Second Reading* as a sort of family creed or charter:

> Put on then, as God's chosen ones, holy and beloved, compassion, kindness, lowliness, meekness, and patience, forbearing one another and, if one has a complaint against another, forgiving each other; as the Lord has forgiven you, so you also must forgive. (Col 3:12-14)

After speaking about the pain of alienation in our families and society, Father Bill suggested that the way to heal our family wounds and tighten family structures is to learn to forgive—and forget. He urged that we imitate the Lord, which he said means "giving and restoring, reinstating and forgetting, when reinstatement and restoration are not deserved."

Three years later, Father Bill received a letter from a woman he didn't know who told him how his homily on the Feast of the Holy Family had changed her life. She explained that she and her husband were married at Holy Trinity in 1972. "Like most long unions," she wrote, "we encountered a rocky period in our marriage, leading to a separation in June of 2000. In December of 2000, on New Year's Eve, he approached me about a reconciliation."

Reacting to the proposal with "pain and anger," she admitted that she was "very undecided." On the following Sunday she attended Mass, "where you gave a sermon on forgiveness. You gave me much to think about." Shortly thereafter, she said she began meeting with her husband to begin "talking and exploring our mistakes." "Forgiveness is not an easy, instant accomplishment, and I owe you a great appreciation for opening my eyes to that."

Her letter continued:

> in the summer of 2002, we traveled to Ireland to celebrate my fiftieth birthday. Unbeknownst to me, he had arranged with the parish priest for us to renew our vows at the Catholic Church in Kinsdale, County Cork. It became the highlight of our trip and an opportunity for us to renew our devotion to each other with Christ's blessing.

Two months later, her husband died in an auto accident. "Although our reconciliation was short, I am indebted to you for teaching me the importance of forgiveness and love in my life" (Homily, *The Feast of the Holy Family*).

Father Bill shared this moving testimony when he visited us one beautiful summer day. He emphasized the importance of the Scripture readings, adding that he often repeats the words of Scripture throughout his homilies. I asked him why. "Because there is great power in the Word of God," he said. St. Paul, one of the greatest preachers of all time, would heartily agree: "So faith comes from what is heard, and what is heard comes by the preaching of Christ" (Rom 10:17).

# Profession of Faith

I've noticed that in my hometown of Chicago, when the crowd sings the National Anthem at a Blackhawks hockey game, the intensity of emotion is so strong, it is spectacle in itself. Even before the singing ends, the crowd expresses their spirit of support with sustained applause and shouts of jubilation. I will never forget the moment I realized just how unique this is to Chicago. When my youngest son, Richard, played hockey, we were in the Winnipeg ice arena waiting for the players to come out on the ice. We stood to sing the Canadian National Anthem. The people sang "Oh Canada" in a normal tone of voice; the quiet decorum was in such stark contrast to what goes on in Chicago; it didn't feel like we were at a hockey game!

What the National Anthem is to our country, the *Profession of Faith* is to Catholicism—a stirring tribute of praise. Although we don't shout and applaud during the Sacred Liturgy, we express the spirit of the Church that Christ founded when we profess our faith by reciting the *Nicene Creed*. It summarizes what we believe and is a form of worship in which we proclaim our allegiance to our God—Father, Son and Holy Spirit.

The great John Henry Cardinal Newman (1801-1890), one of the most illustrious of English converts to the Church, held university students in Dublin spellbound with his inspiring talks about the Catholic faith. When he spoke of the *Creed,* he compared it to a psalm, a prayer that lifts our hearts and minds to God. For two thousand years, the Church has protected and defended her identity as "one, holy, catholic, and apostolic" by living and dying by the words of the *Nicene Creed.*

## EXPLANATION

*Creed* is from the Latin *credo*, which means, "I believe." *Credere* comes from *cor* and *dare,* meaning to give one's heart. Faith and love are like two sides of the same coin; they are connected. Before he says the *Creed* on Sundays and holy days at my parish, our assisting priest extends his arms in a gesture of invitation: "Having heard the word of the Lord, let us renew the faith of our baptism when we were marked for life by the Holy Spirit's compassionate love and called to live forever in the family of Jesus Christ." Moved by the Word of God and aware of our identity as God's children, the community, united in one heart and mind, gives public witness to the faith of our Baptism, our Sacrament of Belonging.

There are several varieties of *Creeds*. The oldest and shortest used in the Latin Rite, known as the Apostles' Creed, is the one we still use today at baptisms. Named because "it is rightly considered to be a faithful summary of the apostles' faith" (*CCC*, 194), this was the only *Creed* used during the first three hundred years by the Latin Church. It was this *Creed* which St. Ambrose, St. Augustine and other Church Fathers urged the faithful to say daily, morning and evening, to protect themselves against heresies and attacks of the devil. A second and much longer creed is the Athanasian Creed, composed in the late fourth century to combat heresies that denied the Trinity. A third form of faith profession is the *Nicene Creed* that we say today at Mass.

The *Nicene Creed* was composed in the fourth century in the course of the first two ecumenical councils, Nicea in 325 and Constantinople in 381; at Nicea to counter the heresy of Arianism that denied the divinity of Christ; at Constantinople to protect the divinity of the Holy Spirit. Together they form the Catholic/Christian understanding of the basic doctrines of the Church, a belief that "remains common to all the great Churches of both East and West to this day" (*CCC*, 195).

The *Creed* follows the *Gospel* in which Christ has proclaimed the "words of eternal life" (Jn 6:68). The community responds wholeheartedly to the story of our salvation proclaimed in the Scriptures and explained in the *Homily*, saying, *We believe*. When Jesus said to His disciples, "Who do you say that I am?" (Mt 16:15), He wanted to know if they really believed Him to be the Messiah. The Church gives the congregation an opportunity to respond to the same question. Like the apostles, we are called to testify to the truth, to proclaim our faith in Christ and His teaching, and to give an account "of the hope of the gospel" (Col 1:23).

We stand as a sign of respect when we say the *Creed,* which is divided into three parts: "The first part speaks of the first divine Person and the wonderful work of creation; the next speaks of the second divine Person and the mystery of his redemption of men; the final part speaks of the third divine Person, the origin and source of our sanctification" (*CCC*, 190).

We begin the *Creed* by professing our belief in the Father: *We believe in one God, the Father, the Almighty, maker of heaven and earth, of all that is seen and unseen.*

The word, "one," was no doubt inserted to forever put to rest ancient beliefs in false gods, and to firmly establish monotheism as a primary tenet of the Christian faith. As Christians, we believe that God is one, just as Jews and Muslims do. But God is not only our Creator, He is our almighty, all-loving and all-merciful Father, who welcomes us as His sons and daughters into the bosom of the Trinity, His own Divine Family. Jesus knew God as His *Abba*, Father, who loves us in the same way He loves Jesus. When a voice from heaven said: "You are my beloved Son; with you I am well pleased" (Mk 1:11), God the Father acknowledged His Son in public for the first time

The Voice From Heaven/James Tissot

*"Now is my soul troubled. And what shall I say? 'Father, save me from this hour'? No, for this purpose I have come to this hour. Father, glorify thy name." Then a voice came from heaven, "I have glorified it, and I will glorify it again." The crowd standing by heard it and said that it had thundered. Others said, "an angel has spoken to him" (Jn 12:27–30).*

and confirmed His mission of salvation. When Jesus taught His disciples to pray, He taught them to say, "Our Father." When Jesus appeared to Mary Magdalene on Easter Sunday, He told her to go to His disciples and tell them that He will be ascending "to my Father and your Father, to my God and your God" (Jn 20:17).

The next part of the *Creed* focuses on Jesus—on His origin, birth, death and resurrection. This is fitting because Christianity is based on the mystery of the Incarnation, the Son of God-made-man. Or, to look at this a different way, if the Incarnation were proved untrue, Christianity would be no more.

We should also note that the *Creed* confirms the oneness of the Father and the Son; they are not two Gods, but one; they are the Son of God, namely Jesus, who is *one in being with the Father.* We say: *We believe in one Lord, Jesus Christ, the only Son of God, eternally begotten of the Father, God from God, Light from Light, true God from true God, begotten, not made, one in Being with the Father.* In the words of the *Catechism*, "The Christian faith confesses that God is one in nature, substance, and essence" (*CCC*, 200).

The third part of the *Creed* focuses on the divinity of the Holy Spirit: *We believe in the Holy Spirit, the Lord, the giver of life, who proceeds from the Father and the Son. With the Father and the Son he is worshiped and glorified. He has spoken through the Prophets.*

Who exactly is the Holy Spirit? The Church teaches us that He is the Third Person of the Blessed Trinity, but how do we *know* Him? If we look to the saints, they relate to Him as a Person. St. Teresa of Avila described prayer as a dialogue, a conversation between the soul and the Holy Spirit. When I first became seriously ill, I felt a desire to know the Holy Spirit. In the ten years I've been struggling with scleroderma and cancer, I've begun to recognize the promptings and urgings of the Holy Spirit deep within my own heart. The Holy Spirit is Jesus living inside of us. When we are baptized we are "born of water and the spirit" (Jn 3:5), branded with an indelible mark that identifies us as a child of God. We enter the kingdom of God and actually share in God's own Spirit-life.

## History

The *Nicene Creed* initially developed out of the baptismal liturgy in fourth century Palestine, perhaps in Caesarea. The neophyte preparing to receive the Sacrament of Baptism had to memorize certain faith statements and repeat them to the bishop prior to his baptismal celebration. In response to the triple questioning of the priest about the three persons of the Trinity, the catechumen confessed his personal belief, saying, "I do believe" as he was being immersed in the baptismal waters. The questions posed to the catechumens, such as, "Do you believe in God the Father Almighty, Creator of heaven and earth?" became known as "rules of Faith" or "Symbols," short and sharply defined statements of belief, which at once proclaimed the orthodox faith, and at the same time discouraged its distortion from error and heresy. These summaries of belief (one each for the Father, the Son and the Holy Spirit), gave shape to the

Baptismal font for immersion. Sixth century, Basilica of St. John, Ephesus, Turkey.

Creed. The Creed was spoken in the singular ("I believe") because it acknowledged an individual's faith.

The Creed gives expression to the essential beliefs of Catholicism, which in the first three hundred years was severely challenged by heresies, especially that of Arianism, which began with Arius (260-336), a popular priest in the church of Alexandria who taught that Christ was not divine and therefore could not be one in essence with the Father. Leading the opposition was a brilliant young deacon from Alexandria, St. Athanasius (297-373).

Determined to settle the dispute, the recently converted Christian Emperor Constantine ordered the first General Council of bishops to be held in the city of Nicaea in Bithynia in 325. Three hundred and eighteen delegates attended. We can imagine the long hours, days, and possibly weeks the bishops spent on the precise wording of the Creed. Every word was debated and forged from heated discussions. With the eyes of the world focused on them, Arius and St. Athanasius each fought for their beliefs, the latter suggesting the word "consubstantial," designating that the Son was of the same substance as the Father.

The word "consubstantial" (Greek, *homoousios*) was adopted and became an important bulwark of the faith. The Creed beautifully and clearly asserts the divinity of Christ:

*We believe in one Lord, Jesus Christ,*
*The only Son of God,*

*Eternally begotten of the Father,*
*God from God, Light from Light,*
*true God from true God,*
*begotten, not made, one in Being with the Father.*
*Through him all things were made.*

The Council closed with a state banquet given by Emperor Constantine. Arius and his followers were banished, but they managed to keep the heresy alive for many years. St. Athanasius became the bishop of Alexandria and spent his life vigorously defending the Church from this heresy, an effort which earned him the title "Father of Orthodoxy."

At the Council of Constantinople in 381, words were added to the *Nicene Creed* that declared the divinity of the Holy Spirit. This was done in order to nullify the efforts of Archbishop Macedonius and his followers who taught that the Holy Spirit was not God, but only a creation like the angels but on a much higher scale. Thus today we say: *We believe in the Holy Spirit, the Lord, the giver of life, who proceeds from the Father and the Son. With the Father and the Son he is worshiped and glorified. He has spoken through the Prophets.* Since the wording of the *Creed* stems from the two Councils, it is technically referred to as the *"Niceno-Constantinopolitan Creed."*

Despite the work of the Councils and the development of the *Creed,* Arianism continued to spread its false teaching far and wide. Catholics, however, were undeterred. St. Ambrose wrote a letter to his sister, St. Marcellina, in which he tells her that one Sunday, he had just finished explaining the *Creed* to people about to be baptized, when soldiers invaded his church. He told her that he remained at his place and began to say Mass.

The *Creed* was first introduced into the Eucharistic liturgy in Antioch in the fifth century; this practice eventually spread to Spain, Ireland, England, Gaul and Germany. The prayer first appeared at Mass in Spain as a protest against the Arians when the Third Council of Toledo, in 589, ordered it to be sung immediately before the *Our Father.* In this early period, the *Creed* was chanted in Latin to what some describe as the most majestic and moving music in all of Church liturgy. Following the reappearance of Arianism in France (then known as Gaul), Charlemagne (742-815), King of the Franks, arranged for the *Creed* to be inserted into the Mass of his church at Aix-la-Chapelle. When the German Emperor Henry II was crowned in Rome by Pope Benedict VIII in 1014, Henry was somewhat shocked by the fact that the *Creed* was not sung after the *Gospel* during his coronation, as was the practice in Germany. The pope explained that it was unnecessary because Rome had never suffered the plague of heresy. Eventually Pope Benedict VIII acceded to the Emperor's desire and inserted the *Creed* into the Roman Mass.

The *Creed* marked the end of the Mass of the Catechumens when those who were not baptized Christians had to leave the church. A deacon dismissed them, saying, "Let the catechumens withdraw." The unbaptized were not permitted to share in the Eucharist for they did not yet share in the priesthood of Jesus Christ. This ceremony disappeared in the eighth century when the practice of baptizing infants became practically universal. It has been reinstated today as part of the Church's practice, known as the *Rite of Christian Initiation of Adults*, of bringing adults into the Catholic Church.

## REFLECTION

Our Lord laid the foundation of His Church by preaching "the kingdom of God," which lives today in the words of the *Gospel,* in the creeds of the Catholic faith and in the hearts and minds of His disciples around the globe who practice what Jesus taught.

When we say the *Creed* week after week in church, it can almost become mechanical. Often, we recite the words automatically, without thinking what they really mean. If we took a moment to reflect on what the *Creed* meant to our Christian ancestors who went to their death rather than renounce their faith in the "one, holy, catholic, and apostolic church," it might help us open our hearts a little wider to say our own deep "Yes" to the Lord and the Church He founded. What a privilege it is for us to to recite the *Creed;* to do so in freedom, at least in the United States, is a gift that I, for one, take for granted.

We have already seen that Christianity thrived in the early Church despite brutal persecution. In the first three centuries, hundreds of thousands of Christians went to their deaths because they refused to worship pagan gods. Attendance at Christian worship was a crime punishable by death, yet Christians gathered weekly for the Eucharist. Incredibly, the Christian faith grew, causing Tertullian to make his poignant remark, "The blood of the martyrs is the seed of the Church."

St. Maximilian Kolbe offers his life in place of another prisoner.

As horrible as that persecution was, author George Weigel in his epic biography of Pope John Paul II, notes that the pope "has regularly reminded the world that the twentieth century is the greatest century of martyrdom—faithful witness unto death—in Christian history." Of the thousands who have shed their blood for the *Gospel,* the pope, explains Weigel, pays special tribute to a Polish Franciscan priest:

> No martyr of the twentieth century has been, for John Paul, a more luminous icon of the call to holiness through radical, self-giving love than Maximilian Kolbe. Kolbe was the "saint of the abyss"—the man who looked straight into the modern heart of darkness and remained faithful to Christ by sacrificing his life for another in the Auschwitz starvation bunker while helping his cellmates die with dignity and hope. (*Witness to Hope,* 447)

Torture and persecution of Christians is still rampant today. One of its most insidious forms is a pervasive and pernicious philosophy of secular humanism that seeks to undermine our religious beliefs. Rooted in a rejection of God and of absolute truths, powerful forces today are actively campaigning to eliminate Christianity from our culture. We are called upon to wage an equally powerful campaign for religious freedom and social justice.

When we recite the *Creed,* we stand with our brothers and sisters in Christ, Christians from around the world who have articulated their Catholic faith for two millennia. Fr. Basil Pennington, a leading writer on spiritual topics who has traveled the world to proclaim the Gospel message, recalls a "cosmic moment" from his student days in Rome, when seventy thousand seminarians stood in the immense cavern of St. Peter's Basilica. He remembers:

> We are all colors—red, yellow, black, white, tan, brown. We are from many more nations than one can readily name. We babble in many languages. Then—and it always seemed suddenly—the Vicar of Christ is in our midst, and the whole vast throng, as if with one voice, sings out mightily, so that the gilded vaults high above us seem to roll with echoes: *Credo in unum Deum......Credo in unum Dominum Jesum Christum....Credo in Spiritum Sanctum Dominum....* The Church Universal, gathered around its one Supreme Pastor, proclaims its one faith. Every creed ever said, even in the smallest of congregations in the most remote of mission chapels, in jungle huts or in Siberian prison camps, on battleships or on the summit of Tabor, is one with this creed being proclaimed at the heart of Christendom—and with the creed we proclaim today in our parish church....It is the expression of the mind and heart of the one body of Christ: We believe! (*The Eucharist, Yesterday and Today,* 24)

Sr. Teresa Benedicta of the Cross (Edith Stein).

The moment we say, *We believe in one God, the Father Almighty, maker of heaven and earth, of all that is seen and unseen,* Father Pennington says, "we enter into a great current that will flow until the end of time" (24). How truly blessed we are to be able to stand up in church and step into that current, joining millions of Christ's disciples, past and present, who gratefully live, and willingly die, by the words of the *Nicene Creed.*

One who did step into that current was the Jewish Carmelite Sister Benedicta of the Cross, known to the world as Edith Stein. Not even her deep love for her mother could keep her from embracing the Church Christ founded, which she did wholeheartedly and for which she ultimately gave her life. In what George Weigel cites as one of the great sermons of his pontificate, Pope John Paul II eulogized this "daughter of Israel in our century" at her beatification Mass in Cologne on May 1, 1987:

> On leaving their convent [in Echt], Edith took her sister by the hand and said, "Come, we will go for our people." On the strength of Christ's willingness to sacrifice himself for others, she saw in her seeming impotence a way to render a final service to her people. A few years previously she had compared herself with Queen Esther in exile at the Persian court. In one of her letters we read: "I am confident that the Lord has taken my life for all . . . I always have to think of Queen Esther who was taken from her people for the express purpose of standing before the king for her people. I am the very poor, weak, and small Esther, but the King who selected me is infinitely great and merciful. (*Witness to Hope,* 541)

When the nuns were clearing Edith's room at the convent, they found a small picture. On the back, Edith had written down her desire to offer her life for her fellow Jews. Her prayer was answered.

We pray for people who suffer any kind of persecution for Christ, and ask God to give them—and us—the endurance and strength to persevere in our faith. Like the father of the epileptic in the *Gospel* to whom Jesus said, "All things are possible to him who believes"(Mk 9:23), we cry out to the Lord in the twenty-first century, "I believe; help my unbelief!" (Mk 9:24).

# *Prayer of the Faithful*

Have you ever attended a Mass where someone offers a heartrending prayer for a sick relative or friend during the *Prayer of the Faithful*? It can be a very moving experience. One day, amidst the spontaneous prayers for the sick and needy in our parish, an unfamiliar voice uttered a cry for healing which surely pierced the heart of God. Faltering speech belied the inner boldness of a faith-filled grandmother who pleaded with God to help her three-year-old granddaughter through open-heart surgery. The momentary silence was deafening as each person stole into a quiet corner of his or her heart to implore God's mercy for this woman's granddaughter. Everyone in church felt her pain and anguish. I imagined what it would mean if my healthy three-year-old grandchild had this problem—and I prayed my heart out. The power of her plea bonded the community, who offered a resounding, "Lord, hear our prayer."

We believe the words of the psalmist; God "does not forget the cry of the afflicted" (Ps 9:12). Imagine the angel in the Book of Revelation standing before the altar in heaven offering God golden bowls filled with incense that represents "the prayers of the saints" (Rev 8:4). The incense symbolizes our prayers lifted up to God. "Lord, let my prayer be counted as incense before thee" (Ps 141:2). As baptized Christians, we have a unique opportunity to lift up our prayers to God through the Mass and so to live out our calling as "a chosen race, a royal priesthood, a holy nation" (1 Pet 2:9). The laity have a "priestly vocation" (*CCC*, 784) through our union with Christ, our High Priest and Mediator, to pray for the salvation of the world. Such is the meaning of the *Prayer of the Faithful,* otherwise known as *The General Intercessions.*

## EXPLANATION

During the *Prayer of the Faithful,* we petition our Father in the name of Christ, thus opening ourselves to the infinite graces God wants to bestow on us through His Son. Jesus implored His apostles to ask the Father anything *in His name,* saying, "Truly, truly, I say to you, if you ask anything of the Father, he will give it to you in my name. Hitherto you have asked nothing in my name; ask, and you will receive, that your joy may be full" (Jn 16:23, 24).

Christ is our intercessor (from the Latin *inter-cedere,* to go between), who stands between God and His people to offer prayers to the Father—for us. St. Paul tells us that there is one mediator between God and the human race, Jesus Christ (1 Tim 2:5), whose eternal priesthood enables Him "to save those who draw near to God

> *The Eucharist is the prime source of intercessory power for the needs of our times because it reflects the intercession, i.e., the sacrifice Christ Himself offered for those needs 2,000 years ago, renewed now at each celebration of the Mass and participated in during our time spent in prayer before His Eucharistic presence outside of Mass. It is our faith in this profound truth that makes our prayers of intercession, united with Christ's intercession, bear so much fruit for others, for the Church and for the world.*
>
> —Fr. John Grigus, OFM Conv.
> *Immaculata Magazine*

through him, since he always lives to make intercession for them" (Heb 7:24, 25). Jesus prayed often, interceding for His loved ones. He told Peter that Satan wanted to sift His disciples like wheat, "but I have prayed for you that your faith may not fail" (Lk 22:32). After the Last Supper and just before His arrest, Jesus asked His Father to keep His disciples from the evil one, praying for them and "for those who believe in me through their word" (Jn 17:20).

We have Vatican II to thank for the restoration of the *Prayer of the Faithful* in the Sacred Liturgy. After a lapse of many centuries (since the sixth century), the bishops at Vatican II reinstated the *Prayer of the Faithful,* saying that it had "suffered injury through their accidents of history" (*Constitution on the Sacred Liturgy,* 50). Today, it is included in all Masses, Sundays, holydays of obligation, and weekdays, immediately after the *Gospel* and *Homily.*

Although the celebrant introduces and concludes the prayers from the altar, a deacon or lector stands at the ambo where he or she places the hopes and needs of the community before God in a litany of petitions. It is really an invitation to prayer made up of a series of invocations, together with a congregational response such as "Lord, hear our prayer." For whom do we intercede? We pray for the whole Church, for government leaders, for those oppressed by various needs, for all of humanity and for the salvation of the entire world. The intercessions are described as "universal," because our concerns reach out to the farthest corners of the world. We also pray for the sick, the needy, the dying in our local parishes and for those who have died.

Although the intentions of the *Prayer of the Faithful* are standardized, they are flexible enough to include the special intentions of a given parish from Sunday to Sunday, as well as specific current events that are uppermost in peoples' minds and hearts. For weddings and funerals and other special liturgies, the intentions may be personalized to suit the occasion. In our parish on Sundays, when the lector reads the petitions, he or she reserves the final petition for the personal needs and intentions of the congregation, followed by a silent pause. This gesture allows us to silently include our heartfelt requests; it personalizes and individualizes the laity's involvement and heightens our active participation in the Mass, one of the primary goals of the Vatican II reforms of the Sacred Liturgy.

My former pastor encouraged the daily Mass-goers to verbalize their petitions. People named all kinds of pressing needs—for friends, family and the world at large. For months after September 11, not a day went by that we didn't pray for someone involved in the horrific tragedy. The same happened with the war in Iraq. This is one of my favorite moments in the Mass. Every day and hour of the week in cities and countries all around the world, Masses are being said for people and situations that are in need of God's help.

Imagine the universe as one giant electrical grid and the Mass as the main electrical outlet that plugs us into God's infinite love and power. When prayer taps His heart, currents of grace descend upon us and upon our world. Jesus stated very clearly that when we come together in His name, He is present and listening to us (Mt 18:20), and we can count on His promise: "if two of you agree on earth about anything they ask, it will be done for them by my Father in heaven" (Mt 18:19). Although God knows our needs before we say them, and certainly hears our requests even when we don't express them, when I'm able to state a petition out loud I feel more assured that I've connected to God—and to others.

What about our prayers that seemingly go unanswered? For over a year we prayed for a young man named Jimmy, a classmate of my son, Danny, who was battling cancer. He wasn't even from our parish, yet people who knew him would often mention his name during the *Prayer of the Faithful* at daily Mass. It seemed like the whole world was praying for Jimmy with great faith that God would heal him. He was an outstanding young man who collected lots of athletic trophies in school, married a classmate and had two small children. He came from a big family who was devoted to one another and their faith. Jimmy showed a lot of courage in the way he fought his disease, which overtook him after only two years. The painful reality of his death was, and is, hard to accept. Why, Lord? That is something we won't ever know, this side of heaven. God, of course, has His reasons, His will, which we believe is for Jimmy's greater good, his perfect joy.

When I pressed my good friend, Fr. Bill Byron, S.J., about prayer that doesn't "work," he gave an analogy that I will paraphrase. Imagine yourself on a boat on a lake, he said. As you approach the dock, you throw a line over and catch it on a cleat so that you can pull yourself into the dock. When we petition God in prayer, we are throwing our line over to catch it on the cleat. This draws us closer to God and aligns our will to God's, but it doesn't bend God's will to ours. We pull the boat to the dock; we don't pull the dock to the boat. Every prayer should be conditioned on "Not my will, but yours"(Lk 22:42).

In one way or another, we are always asking for more time. Inevitably, time runs out, for some sooner than others. When that happens, faith tells us that we will have arrived at the dock—our eternal reward—that is really the ultimate answer to all our prayers.

## HISTORY

The Church had been without the *Prayer of the Faithful* since the time of St. Gregory the Great in the sixth century when the lengthy prayer intentions were omitted, leaving only the litanic *Kyrie eleison.* Good Friday was an exception, when, in most parts of the world—

up to the present— the Church kept the ancient tradition of reciting or singing the ten *General Intercessions* following the reading of the Passion on Good Friday.

Intercessory prayer is very biblical. Abraham interceded for the inhabitants of Sodom and Gomorrah trying to save them from God's wrath (it didn't work) (Gn 18: 32). When Moses came down Mt. Sinai from his encounter with God and saw the Israelites breaking the new covenant by worshiping the golden calf, he prevented their destruction by interceding for them (Ex 32:11-14).

The early Christians knew the power of intercessory prayer. After all, the Lord had been in their midst for three years answering their prayers and healing the sick. On different occasions, Jesus urged them to pray without ceasing, saying, "Truly, truly, I say to you, if you ask anything of the Father, he will give it to you in my name" (Jn 16:24).

Undeterred by the impossibility of getting near Jesus because of the crowds surrounding Him, friends of a paralyzed man put him on a stretcher and lowered him through the roof of a house into the arms of Jesus. Instead of being angry at the intrusion, Jesus praised their faith, which moved Him to heal the sick man. When we pray in intercession, we are, in a sense, like the friends of the paralyzed man who bring our loved ones to Jesus. We bring them into God's presence so that He can touch and heal them just as he did the paralytic. The beloved St. John leaves no room for doubt, saying that when we ask Christ for anything according to His will, He hears us: "And if we know that he hears us in whatever we ask, we know that we have obtained the requests made of him" (1 Jn 5:15).

Liturgical intercessory prayer can be traced to the Jewish synagogue liturgies where prayers of blessing, thanksgiving

Palsied man let down through the roof/
James Tissot

and petition eventually found their way into the Christian Eucharist. St. Paul's letters reveal the use he made of intercessory prayer in his apostolate, in which he either offered prayers for his people or asked for them. In his letter to Timothy, St. Paul urges: "supplications, prayers, intercessions, and thanksgivings be made for all men, for kings and all who are in high positions " (1 Tim 2: 1).

King of Kings/Danny Hahlbohm

*[St. Paul's] meaning is that when we pray in church Christ does not stand aloof from our prayers. They find and echo, as it were, in his very soul. Christ the Lord knows of our prayer. He joins us in praying it—provided it is a worthy prayer—and presents it to His heavenly Father. It is thus that our prayers reach the Father's throne.*

—Fr. Josef Jungmann
*The Liturgy of the Word*

The term *Prayer of the Faithful* denotes its ancient heritage. In the infant Church, these prayers took place during Mass after the catechumens were dismissed, when only the faithful (the baptized) were allowed take part in the *Liturgy of the Eucharist*. These prayers actually introduced what was then known as the Mass of the Faithful, thus their name. In Acts we read that the early Christians "devoted themselves to the apostles' teaching and fellowship, to the breaking of bread and the prayers" (Acts 2:42). It is likely that the prayers referred to are what we now call the *Prayers of the Faithful*.

The Church Fathers and martyrs often mentioned these prayers in their letters and sermons, beginning with St. Clement of Rome (c. 96), who refers to prayers of intercession used during the Eucharistic Liturgies. Justin Martyr (c. 150) spoke of them in connection with the newly baptized, who, having just been received into the Church, were brought to the assembly after the *Liturgy of the Word* where they "make common prayers earnestly for ourselves and for [those

Sts. Peter and John at the Beautiful Gate/G. Dore

*Now Peter and John were going up to the temple at the hour of prayer, the ninth hour. And a man lame from birth was being carried, whom they laid daily at that gate of the temple which is called Beautiful to ask alms of those who entered the temple. . . . Peter said, "I have no silver and gold, but I give you what I have; in the name of Jesus Christ of Nazareth, walk." And he took him by the right hand and raised him up; and immediately his feet and ankles were made strong. And leaping up he stood and walked and entered the temple with them, walking and leaping and praising God.*

Acts 3:1, 2; 6–8

who have] been enlightened and for all others everywhere." He again alluded to the *Prayer of the Faithful,* saying, "We all stand up together and send up prayers."

Prayer was uppermost in the mind of second century bishop and martyr, St. Polycarp (*c.* 155), who wrote to the Church at Philippi while enroute to his certain martyrdom in Smyrna: "Keep all the saints in your prayers. Pray, too, for our rulers, for our leaders, and for all those in power, even for those who persecute and hate you." Speaking to the members of his vast diocese in Milan in the fourth century, St. Ambrose encouraged his listeners with these words:

You are told to pray especially for the people, that is, for the whole body, for all its members, the family of your Mother the Church; the badge of membership in this body is love for each other. If each one prays for himself, he receives less of God's goodness than the one who prays on behalf of others. But as it is, because each prays for all, all are in fact praying for each one. In this way there is a great recompense; through the prayers of each individual, the intercession of the whole people is gained for each individual. (*On Cain and Abel*)

## REFLECTION

The late retreat director and popular author, Fr. Anthony DeMello, S.J., would agree with St. Ambrose. In one of his many talks, he encourages us to "Pour the treasures of Christ over others, for they are infinite. The more you share with others," says Father Tony, "the more will you nourish your own heart"(Gabriel Galache, S.J., *Praying Body and Soul, Methods and Practices of Anthony De Mello*, 120). It is a widely accepted belief that when we pray for others, we ourselves are converted and healed. Another priest who writes about the value of praying for others is Fr. Michael Kwatera, who teaches theology at St. John's University in Collegeville, Minnesota. He reinforces the idea that our concern for others expands our hearts and directs our love outside of ourselves and into the lives of others. He suggests that we seek God's will in our intercessory prayer, not our own. "Intercessory prayer is not our means to coax something out of God," he says. "Rather, such prayer can change our sometimes self-centered and narrow attitudes, so that there is more room in our hearts for those in need" (*Preparing the General Intercessions,* 10). Thus do we follow Christ's command to "Bear one another's burdens" (Gal 6:2).

Caring for the needs of others and bearing one another's burdens is what intercessory prayer is all about. When we invite the Lord to live and pray in us, He will use us to help Him carry His cross, to share in His work of ongoing redemption. Someone eminently qualified to comment on this is Mother Nadine Brown, whose intercessory prayer ministry we cited in the *Opening Prayer*. She explains that when we really love and identify deeply with someone or something, whether it is with other people, our nation or our Church, these are "love burdens" from God. He has placed His deep level of love and concern within us. God is love, and as we come closer to the heart of God, Mother Nadine says, we're picking up the burdens in His heart and the people He wants to love (*Interceding with Jesus*, 34).

God's grace is there for the asking. Fr. Joseph Champlin, rector of the Cathedral of the Immaculate Conception in Syracuse, New York, received a letter from a young man in his late twenties who asked that his sister's name be added to the weekly prayer intentions. Recently diagnosed with advanced breast cancer, he wrote that "the outlook for her recovery was not good . . . she endured chemotherapy and radiation treatments and even underwent a bone marrow transplant." The young man acknowledged what a great comfort it was to know that the members of the Cathedral family were remembering his sister in their prayers.

A year later, Father Champlin received another letter from the young man, which said: *I am pleased to inform you that my sister has been classified as cancer free. Her outlook is good and her spirits have rebounded. Please remove her name from the prayer list. My heartfelt thanks to you and all of those who included Mary Kay in their prayers. My sister's recovery is a wonderful reminder of God's love for all of us and the true power of prayer* (*The Mystery and Meaning of the Mass*, 76).

When I hear a story like this, it inspires me to pray more earnestly and with greater trust that God hears, and answers, every prayer. When Francis MacNutt, the founder, along with his wife, Judith, of *Christian Healing Ministries,* was doing research for a new book, he discovered that "everyone in the early Church was encouraged to pray to heal the sick—and even to cast out evil spirits. For the first three centuries after Jesus' Resurrection, Christians boasted that any ordinary Christian could heal the sick." After about the year 350, MacNutt said things began to change. People began to think that they had to be unusually holy, a "saint," to expect that the sick would get well. Priests were called upon to minister the sacrament of the "Anointing of the Sick," which eventually became the *Last* Anointing (Extreme Unction); its primary purpose was no longer physical healing, but to prepare the Christian for death (Francis MacNutt, *The Healing Line*, 1).

Perhaps there is a relationship between God answering the prayers of ordinary people and the expectant faith of the early Christians. In the *Gospels*, deep faith always results in healing. When Jesus healed blind Bartimaeus, he said, "Go your way, your faith has made you well" (Mk 10:52). To the two blind men who followed Jesus and begged for mercy, He asked them, "Do you believe that I am able to

Two blind men healed at Capernaum/James Tissot

do this?" (Mt 9:27). When they said, "Yes," Jesus gave them their sight, saying, "According to your faith be it done to you" (Mt 9:29). The *Gospels* are filled with people who ask and receive, who search and find, who knock and have the door opened for them. Jesus "marveled" (Mt 8:10) at the faith of the centurion who believed that his paralyzed servant would be healed if only Jesus would just say a word. The Lord had high words of praise for the faith of this man: "Not even in Israel have I found such faith" (Mt 8:5-11).

We do not need to pray in order to remind God of what we need, writes Father Kwatera, "we need to pray in order to remind ourselves of who alone provides for our needs" (10).

True faith, it seems to me, is to act as if we have already received what we have asked for. We abandon ourselves to the heart of Christ, and trust in His response. It may not always be what *we* want, but it most certainly will be what *He* wants for us. And therein lies our peace and joy.

# The Liturgy of the Eucharist

*Preparation of the Gifts*

*Eucharistic Prayer*
*Preface, Acclamation, Epiclesis, Institution Narrative and Consecration, Anamnesis, Offering, Intercessions, Final Doxology*

*Communion Rite*
*The Lords Prayer, Rite of Peace, Fraction Rite, Communion*

*Introduction*

We have arrived at the climax of our celebration—the *Liturgy of the Eucharist*. If we look upon the Mass as a pilgrimage outside ordinary time and space which leads us—through Christ—to an encounter with the eternal Father, then we could say we are now approaching the Throne Room of God. The *Introductory Rites* drew us together as a community, opening us to receive God's Word and preparing us to meet Christ face-to-face in the Eucharist. In the *Liturgy of the Word*, God spoke to us through the *Readings* which we then reflected upon in the *Homily*, after which we affirmed our adherence to His Word in the *Profession of Faith*. Lastly, in the *Prayer of the Faithful*, we petitioned God for the needs of the Church and for the salvation of the world.

The celebrant now comes to the altar—the center of the celebration—where he will remain for the rest of Mass. We call this part of the Mass the *Liturgy of the Eucharist*, differentiating it from the *Liturgy of the Word*. In the *Liturgy of the Eucharist*, the gifts of bread and wine become the Body and Blood of Christ. The whole

Fr. Laurence Dunn begins the Liturgy of the Eucharist.

point of our preparation is to ready us for the act of offering which is expressed in the upcoming *Eucharistic Prayer.* Three rites comprise the *Liturgy of the Eucharist:* the *Preparation of the Altar and the Gifts,* the *Eucharistic Prayer* and the *Communion Rite.*

We call the Mass a "Liturgy" (from the Greek *leitourgia,* meaning public work or service on behalf of the people) because, in Christian tradition, it is the participation of faithful Christians in the "work of God." Liturgy is capitalized when it refers to a specific rite, such as the *Liturgy of the Hours* or the *Liturgy of the Eucharist.* But "liturgy" also may refer to other rites such as a funeral or baptismal liturgy. Regarding the Mass, the *Catechism* explains it clearly: "through the Liturgy, Christ, our redeemer and high priest, continues the work of our redemption in, with, and through his Church" (*CCC*, 1069).

This "work" is nothing less than our salvation—that, from all eternity, God planned to effect through His Son's sacrifice on the Cross—and which He made sacramentally available to us through the Sacred Liturgy. To really appreciate this gift, it is necessary to see the liturgy through the eyes of Jesus. This entails looking at it as He instituted it, both as sacrifice and meal.

In the aftermath of the Council of Trent in the sixteenth century, the sacrificial aspect of the Mass tended to be emphasized at the expense of the communal meal, so that a majority of Catholics did not regularly receive Communion because of an exaggerated sense of unworthiness. After Vatican II, the pendulum has tended to swing the other way, since the bishops highlighted the meal aspect of the Mass, seeing it as a completion of the sacrifice. They hoped to encourage a more frequent reception of the Sacrament. In fact, meal and sacrifice are intricately woven together: "In the Mass, therefore, the sacrifice and sacred meal belong to the same mystery—so much so, that they are linked by the closest bond" (*Constitution on the Sacred Liturgy*, 9, 3).

We will look first at the Eucharist as meal. Jesus often dined with His disciples and friends. Sitting around the dinner table with family and friends is one of life's greatest and most cherished pleasures. When it comes to Thanksgiving or Christmas, families gather in a spirit of celebration. The table is prepared with fine linens and china, flowers are arranged, the turkey or ham is cooked, and wine is served in crystal goblets. When everyone comes to the table, we say a prayer of blessing. What joy there is in the gathering of loved ones around the table who share a meal—and their lives—with one another!

This is the venue Jesus chose for His Passover celebration with

His apostles. They gathered in special room chosen for the occasion, in a spirit of thanksgiving and joy that Jesus expressed, saying: "I have earnestly desired to eat this passover with you before I suffer" (Lk 22:15). Then He gave thanks to God for the food (bread and wine) that He expressly designated as Himself—

The "Upper Room" in Jeruselum which tradition cites as the place where Jesus celebrated the Last Supper with His apostles.

His Body and Blood—His Body surrendered and His Blood poured out, which He actually fulfilled the next day in the sacrifice of the Cross. Jesus identified the bread that He blessed with His Body, and the wine that He offered with His Blood. He wanted His apostles and all future disciples to be able to participate in His sacrifice on Calvary, so He made it available *sacramentally*. Thus do we say, *when we eat this bread and drink this cup, we proclaim your death, Lord Jesus, until you come in glory.*

Jesus gave us a way to unite ourselves to Him in a ritual of eating and drinking, which would not only nourish us with His divine life, but allow us to enter deeply into the paschal mystery—His dying and rising—the great "mystery of our faith": *Dying your destroyed our death, rising you restored our life. Lord Jesus, come in glory.* We pray that just as the bread and wine become the Body and Blood of Christ, so will we—and the whole world—be transformed into the Body of Christ on earth. It is a great mystery how, when we eat regular food, it is changed into us; but when we eat and drink the Body and Blood of Christ, we are changed into Him.

In other words, we become what we eat and drink: we *become* the body of Christ. In doing so we *participate* in His Sacrifice. The word "sacrifice" comes from the Latin *sacrum facere,* to make holy, to consecrate. At Mass, we enter into the heart of Christ's consecration to the Father; joined to Him, we are consecrated to serve Him by laying down our lives for one another. United to His Passion by the "dying" in our daily lives, our suffering, our love, our life, like His, becomes redemptive. This is what Jesus asked us to do in memory of Him. This is the heart of the Eucharist—and our salvation—to become the Body and Blood of Christ on earth. As the English writer Margaret Silf says so beautifully,

> Like the Eucharistic bread, we are consecrated in order to be broken and given to others. Like the Eucharistic wine, we are consecrated in order to be poured out for others. Consecration is always a community matter . . . a vocation for all believers, and it has sacrifice at its heart. (*Inner Compass, An Invitation to Ignatian Spirituality,* 168)

St. John the Evangelist gives extensive coverage to Jesus' teaching on the Eucharist in chapter 6 of his Gospel. This contains Jesus' Bread of Life discourse in which He prepares His followers to accept *Him* as their food; Jesus spoke literally, saying, "For my flesh is food indeed, and my blood is drink indeed. He who eats my flesh and drinks my blood abides in me, and I in him" (Jn 6: 55). Yet of the four New Testament accounts of the Last Supper, St. John is the only evangelist who did not include the words Jesus spoke over the bread and wine, the words of consecration; he chose to stress the washing of the feet.

How can we relate to the ritual of the washing of the feet? Perhaps Fr. Bob Sears, S.J., a theologian who teaches at Loyola University in Chicago and who is in the healing ministry, can help us apply it to our lives. In a paper he wrote on the Eucharist for a regional meeting of the Association of Christian Therapists, Father Bob explores the meaning of the washing of the feet, saying: "Jesus interprets the essence of Eucharist by washing his disciples' feet (Jn 13:1-15). The Eucharist is not just a "static presence," he writes, "but a participation in an action of Jesus, an action of humble service of one another and of self giving love." Father Bob then elaborates on the meaning of "sacrifice":

> [The Eucharist} is, first of all a sacrifice, a letting go of personal prestige and ego-centered life, to receive God's service and serve the needs of others. Peter recoiled at Jesus' doing the work of a servant by washing his feet. Yet Jesus says that unless we accept His gift we can have no part with Him. Or as Jesus later explains in Luke 22:26, "let the greatest among you be as the youngest, and the leader as the servant." Eucharist begins by sacrificing our self-sufficiency and letting ourselves be "washed" by God, healed and transformed by God's resurrection power.
> (*Christ's Eucharistic Body and Healing*, 1)

Eucharist is really about self-giving love, in imitation of God who is "self-emptying and serving love" (2). That love is expressed when we give gifts, and especially when we give *ourselves* in the gift. This is the way God gives to us. In the Mass, the meal is a sign of the gift Christ makes of Himself as the Bread of Life.

The Washing of the Feet/Jacopo Tintoretto

*Jesus, knowing that the Father had given all things into his hands, and that he had come from God and was going to God, rose from supper, laid aside his garments, and girded himself with a towel. Then he poured water into a basin, and began to wash the disciples' feet, and to wipe them with the towel with which he was girded. (Jn 13:3–5)*

*John made the Footwashing an analogical presentation of the Eucharist to teach us about the true meaning of the celebration of the Eucharist. He teaches that the Eucharist is a true sacrifice, really making present the death of Jesus on the cross of Calvary. And that it was by means of the Eucharist of the Last Supper, which made Calvary* pre-exist *as the Mass makes it* post-exist, *that his Church was born. The Church thus depends upon the Eucharist not only for her sustenance and continual growth but, most importantly, because Our Lord willed that she have her very origin from His Eucharistic celebration of the first Holy Thursday. John thus teaches us that we, by our very origin, are a Eucharistic People and that the Eucharist must be the center of our lives if we are true disciples of Jesus, our Messiah king who reigns from the cross through the Eucharist, his greatest gift to us.*

—Rev. Msgr. Anthony La Femina, Iconographer

To "do this in remembrance of me" (Lk 22:19) is to lay down our lives for others. When we "take, bless, break and share" our lives with one another, we imitate the actions of Jesus at the Last Supper. When we consecrate our lives to His service, Jesus sanctifies all our actions. It is a paradox that when we empty ourselves, we are filled; when we give ourselves away, we find ourselves. This was Christ's prayer to the Father before His arrest, that His disciples would know the truth that would set us free (see Jn 17:17; 8:31). United to Christ, we will experience new life and freedom, not after we die, but now in the little and big things of our everyday lives and in the lives of all those for whom we pray.

The Church invites us to come to the Table. It is the Lord who bids us dine with Him; He presides at the Table through the priest who stands in His place at this celebration. The priest and the people now prepare for the arrival of our Divine Guest, the Risen Lord Jesus, who bids us share His celebration by uniting ourselves to Him and to one another around the Table of the Lord.

# The Preparation of the Gifts

I f we look at the *Liturgy of the Word* and the *Liturgy of the Eucharist* as the two pillars which support the edifice of the Mass, then we can view the *Preparation of the Gifts* as a bridge that leads us from one to the other, into the heart of the Sacred Liturgy: the *Eucharistic Prayer.* For centuries prior to Vatican II, these preparatory rites were called the *Offertory*. It was a *priestly* rite in which the celebrant said and did almost everything on his own. The priest prayed silently and the faithful participated by singing an *Offertory Antiphon*, period. The bishops at Vatican II renamed this part of the Mass the *Preparation of the Altar and the Gifts,* which more accurately describes what is transpiring. Now the congregation, by virtue of their royal priesthood, plays a more active part in the offering about to take place.

What takes place in these preparatory rites is a ritual "setting apart" of gifts that represent ourselves: bread and wine, "which earth has given and human hands have made" (for the bread), and, "fruit of the vine and the work of human hands" (for the wine). Like the ancient farmers and shepherds who presented the first cut of their crops or the first lambs of their flocks to the priest, so do we offer all that is dear to us, all that we are and have, the "first-fruits" of our lives, to God. The wheat and grapes are symbols of our body and blood—our suffering and tears, our joys and sorrows, our anxieties and fears, our hopes, our prayers and our love. While these are of small value in themselves, united to Christ's gift of Himself to the Father, they are consecrated and divinized, transformed from bread and wine into the Body and Blood of Christ.

Vatican II made it quite clear that the real offering of the Mass is that of Christ, represented by the gifts of bread and wine. We cannot bring some sacrifice of our own to the altar and add it to Christ's Cross. "Nothing," says Fr. Louis Bouyer, "can be added to the Cross: we are only to leave our lives and ourselves in the hands of Christ so as to be taken into His Cross." He adds that we should look upon our offerings as an "abandonment of ourselves through faith into the hands of Christ, so that we may be presented to the Father not only with Him, but also by Him and in Him" (*Life and Liturgy,* 170, 171).

"O wonderful exchange!" we pray in the Christmas liturgy. Yet even if we give our entire self—it is so little compared to what we receive through Christ's sacrifice.

### Preparation of the Altar

If the Church is the meeting place between God and His people, the altar is the meeting point. It is the centerpiece of our celebration where our Eucharistic Jesus comes to us, His majesty and splendor veiled under the appearance of bread and wine. The church and the altar should be conspicuous by their splendor and beauty, reverently prepared and adorned to receive our divine Guest.

Up to this point in the Sacred Liturgy, the altar has been bare except perhaps for candles. In our parish, the cross that the altar-server carries in procession is placed next to the altar facing the people so that we can see Christ crucified. The altar is to be covered with at least one linen cloth, and there should be a minimum of two lighted candles, either on or near the altar. Now the deacon or acolyte places the corporal, purificator, chalice and the *Sacramentary* on the altar. The corporal is a small folded linen cloth that is placed over the altar cloth. It is called "corporal" because the body ("corpus") of the Lord will rest on it. The purificator is a small cloth used for cleaning the chalice. The *Sacramentary* (missal) containing the prayers of the Mass is placed on the altar, as is the chalice that will hold the wine mixed with water, soon to be changed into the Precious Blood of Jesus.

According to the latest directives of the Catholic bishops regarding the liturgy, the altar "should be freestanding to allow the ministers to walk around it easily and Mass to be celebrated facing the people. It should be so placed as to be a focal point on which the attention of the whole congregation centers naturally" (*General Instruction of the Roman Missal*, 299).

### Presentation of the Gifts

For centuries, the faithful attended Mass as if they were an audience in a theatrical production, watching the action of the priest from a distance. Vatican II reinstated the ritual participation of the faithful at Mass that had flourished in the early Church and all but disappeared throughout the Middle Ages. The bishops made the "active participation" by the people a priority by bringing back the practice of the faithful presenting the gifts, saying: "Even though the faithful no longer, as in the past, bring the bread and wine for the liturgy from their homes, the rite of carrying up the gifts retains the same spiritual value and meaning" (*General Instruction of the Roman Missal*, 49).

Dr. and Mrs. Ron and Marge Galiene, members of St. Patrick Parish, in Lake Forest, Illinois, present the gifts of bread and wine with their grandchildren.

I've always felt it a special privilege to bring up the gifts. This procession becomes more meaningful when we realize that the gifts represent us. Instead of just watching our fellow parishioners process to the altar, we can enter into the spirit of the procession and add *ourselves* to the offering. The Church recommends that the faithful present the bread and wine at every liturgy, including weekday Masses. In our parish at daily Mass when there is no formal procession, someone in the front pews acts on behalf of the congregation and presents the gifts to the celebrant—a cruet of wine and a dish of unconsecrated hosts—that have been set aside on a small table.

In reality, we have nothing to "give" to God except ourselves— our own poverty and neediness. Jesuit Fathers Paul Cioffi and William Sampson reiterate the thinking of Fr. Louis Bouyer and other theologians who urge us to surrender or abandon ourselves to Christ. The only thing we can "give" God is our emptiness, they say, which they illustrate with a story from the life of St. Jerome, who once asked Jesus: "'What more can I give you, Lord, that you do not already have?' The answer he received: 'Give me your emptiness that I may fill it'" (*Gospel Spirituality and Catholic Worship,* 79).

The heart of our preparation is our ability—and willingness—to get in touch with our own emptiness, say the authors, to honestly come to terms with our negative feelings, our lack of love, our alienation. They share a profound insight which I have intuited for a long time: "If we wish to hear God in the Eucharist, and to receive His Spirit, we must first come face to face with our real selves" (79). I have often wondered if the lack of belief in the Real Presence of Christ in the Eucharist is due to a lack of our own self-awareness. If we are not in touch with our own inner reality, how can we be in touch with God? Moreover, if we are not aware of our sin and brokenness, we are living in illusion and don't even know our need for God. We are like the rich young man in Scripture (Luke 18:18-23), who was so caught up in the material world that he surpressed his need for what Christ was offering.

At Sunday Mass, the preparation of the altar and the presentation of the gifts is usually accompanied by a song. When the collection (money for the poor and the support of the parish) is taken up, it is usually laid in a fitting location near (but not on) the altar. Our gift of money also represents us—our labor, sacrifices, our human efforts—our very lives. In fact, our monetary donations show our willingness to lay down our lives financially, for our brothers and sisters in need. Sharing the Eucharistic bread means giving generously of ourselves in imitation of Christ.

The priest, standing at the altar, now takes the paten with the bread and, raising it slightly above the altar, says inaudibly: *Blessed are you, Lord, God of all creation. Through your goodness we have this bread to offer which earth has given and human hands have made. It will become for us the bread of life.* (If there is no presentation song, which there usually isn't at daily Mass, the priest says these prayers in an audible voice, to which the people respond: *Blessed be God forever).* These prayers over the bread and wine are patterned on the ancient Jewish prayers of praise that the father of a family says over the bread at the beginning of a Sabbath meal. It is likely that Jesus said prayers like these at the Last Supper. The same form of words is used in the prayer for the wine, inspired by the ancient Jewish blessing that Jesus pronounced over the cup: *Blessed are you, Lord, God of all creation. Through your goodness we have this wine to offer, fruit of the vine and work of human hands. It will become our spiritual drink.*

Fr. Laurence Dunn adds water to the wine.

## Mingling of Water and Wine

Before blessing the wine, the deacon or the priest pours wine and a few drops of water into the chalice, saying inaudibly: *By the mystery of this water and wine may we come to share in the divinity of Christ, who humbled himself to share in our humanity.* This prayer of St. Athanasius derives from an ancient liturgical practice symbolizing the union of Christ's two natures and the union of Christ with the faithful. At the Last Supper when Jesus instituted the Eucharist, He poured a little water into the wine according to the Jewish custom. The diluting of wine was necessary in the early Church because the wine was so strong. Of the Church Fathers who testify to this practice, St. Cyprian of Carthage has the most to say. A letter he wrote around 253 explains the significance of this rite: "When the wine is mixed with water in the chalice, the people are joined to Christ. If someone offers only wine, the blood of Christ remains without us; if someone offers only water, the people are without Christ." In other words, the droplet of water must be mingled with the wine, which inseparably unites us to Christ.

If we are not attentive, we can miss this ritual because it takes less than a minute for the priest to pour the wine mixed with water into the chalice while saying the prayer. I look forward to this moment because I can attach myself and all my intentions for this Mass to the little drop of water being poured into the wine; I imagine them being absorbed into the heart of Christ. St. Gertrude used to imagine her whole life as a drop of water which, when mingled with the wine, was transformed into Christ at the Consecration.

The late Thomas Merton, a convert to Catholicism, became a

Trappist monk and a priest at the Abbey of Gethsemane in Kentucky. Although he was hidden away in his hermitage at the abbey, his spiritual books and poems made him known the world over. His autobiography, *The Seven Story Mountain,* is considered one of the most influential works of the twentieth century.

When Merton became an acolyte, he wrote about the special meaning that the ritual of mixing water with the wine held for him:

> More than anything else, more than ever before I beg you, my God, to kindle in my heart the love of Christ and teach me how to give myself to You in union with His sacrifice. It will not be the first time I have reflected on the marvelous prayer the priest says when mingling a drop of water with the wine in the chalice. But I want that prayer to symbolize all that I live for. I want my whole life to be an expression of those words and of that rite. (*Sign of Jonas,* 35)

At this point in the Mass, the priest may incense the gifts and the altar. If a deacon is present, the celebrant and the people are also incensed. In this way he honors the offerings that will be transformed into the Body and Blood of Christ, and the people who participate in the celebration. Incense symbolizes the Church's prayer going up to God, while the fragrance represents His grace enveloping us.

## Washing of Hands

The washing of hands in the early Church was a necessary ritual because the priest handled so many gifts that the people brought from their homes, including animals. When the procession with the gifts disappeared in the Middle Ages (replaced by monetary collections), the hand washing was no longer a practical necessity. Nevertheless, the rite was retained as a symbolic gesture, through which the priest expressed his desire for inner purification. "The water that flows over the tips of the fingers," St. Augustine said, "washes away the last traces of our impurities." While he or an acolyte pours water over his fingers, the celebrant quietly recites a verse from Psalm 51: *Lord wash away my iniquity. Cleanse me from my sins.*

The celebrant goes to the center of the altar where he says a short prayer: "Pray, brethren, that our sacrifice may be acceptable to God, the almighty Father." The congregation responds saying: "May the Lord accept the sacrifice at your hands for the praise and glory of his name, for our good, and the good of all his Church."

### The Prayer over the Gifts

The congregation now stands and the priest, with hands extended, sings or says the prayer over the gifts. Similar in style and beauty to the *Opening Prayer* (Collect) that concludes the *Introductory Rites,* this short prayer, which is special to each day's celebration, liturgical season, and saint's feast, concludes the *Preparation of the Gifts.* Once known as the "Secret," because it was whispered *sotto voce,* this was the only prayer of offering in the early Church. "Secret" is from the Latin verb *secernere,* which means "to set apart." The celebrant now prays audibly over the gifts of bread and wine which have been "set apart" for the consecration, asking the Lord to look with favor on our sacrifice and accept our gifts. For example, the Prayer over the Gifts for Trinity Sunday illustrates their brevity and focus: "Lord, our God, make these gifts holy, and through them make us a perfect offering to you. We ask this in the name of Jesus the Lord." This is a final plea to the Lord to look with mercy on our offerings before we cross the bridge into the center and heart of the Sacred Liturgy—the coming of Christ in His Eucharistic Sacrifice. The Table of the Lord has been set and the gifts prepared. Everything is ready for the feast to begin. The celebrant will introduce the *Eucharistic Prayer* with an invitation to the faithful: "Lift up your hearts!"

## HISTORY

In the early Church, the catechumens were permitted to hear the Word of God and participate in the *Prayer of the Faithful,* but only the baptized were allowed to be present for the celebration of the Eucharist. Thus, the *Liturgy of the Eucharist* was known as "The Mass of the Faithful," to distinguish it from the "Mass of the Catechumens." Christ offered His sacrifice for the redemption of all, and gave us the Eucharist as the fullest expression of our unity and salvation. Those who do not believe what Christ taught us by His words and actions at the Last Supper separate themselves from full ecclesial union with the Church that He founded.

In the first description of the Mass (circa 150), St. Justin Martyr notes that after the *Prayers* and the *Kiss of Peace*, "one brought bread and a cup of wine to the one who presided over the assembly of the faithful." Only those who were baptized were allowed to offer gifts. St. Hippolytus (circa 215) said that people who brought gifts were the only ones who could receive Communion. St. Cyprian was critical of those "who come without alms and (in communion) receive part of the sacrifice that a poor person has brought." St. Augustine relates that his mother, St. Monica, "did not let a day go by without bringing her offering to the altar" (*Confessions*, 5, 9, 17).

What were these offerings? They brought bread and wine from their homes and other items such as wax, silver, wheat, grapes and even animals. St. Hippolytus mentions the offering of oil, cheese, olives, diverse fruits and even flowers. The early Christians looked upon their offering as a gift of self, which intimately associated them with the Sacrifice of the Mass and secured for them a share in the fruit of the Sacrifice. In the words of St. Gregory the Great, "It is necessary that when we accomplish the Sacrificial Act, we do immolate our own selves to God through the contrition of our hearts. Then, in fact, the host represents us before God, as if we ourselves have been made hosts."

In some areas, the

St. Augustine and his mother St. Monica/Ary Scheffer

*Could You, O God of mercy (2 Cor 1:3), despise the contrite and humbled heart (Ps 51:19) of so chaste and prudent a widow, generous in giving frequent alms, faithful in her help to Your holy ones, never failing even one day to attend the sacrifice at Your altar, coming to your church without fail twice a day, morning and evening, not for vain gossiping and idle talk, but so that she might hear You in Your admonitions and You might hear her in her prayers?*

—Confessions of St. Augustine, (Book 5, Ch 9)

people deposited their gifts near the door of the church. As communities grew larger, the gift giving soon turned into a long procession. In the East, it became known as the "great entrance," accompanied by the chanting of psalms and prayers acclaiming the King of Glory. This ritual survives today in our liturgy as an offertory antiphon either sung by the choir or read by the celebrant. The early Christians processed to the presiding bishop, who received what was necessary for the celebration; the remainder was set aside for later distribution to the needy.

Their desire to symbolically offer their lives to God in the *Offertory* led to "touching excesses," writes Fr. Lucien Deiss in *The Mass:*

> On the feast of Saint Fiacre, the patron of market-gardeners, the people brought bushels of vegetables into the sanctuary. On the feast of Saint Barbara, they brought bunches of safety lamps. On the feast of veterans, they brought a forest of flags. At canonizations, people offered the Pope two small casks of wine, candles, pigeons and turtledoves in pretty cages. (58)

The bread used in the Latin Church is unleavened, as was the bread Jesus used at the Last Supper according to the Passover ritual. Known as *matzoh*, the "bread of tears," it was the bread of itinerant and homeless people. Fr. Johannes Emminghaus says that in the first millennium of the Church's history, both in the east and west, the bread normally used for Eucharist was ordinary "daily bread," that is, leavened. The early Christians baked round or braided loaves of bread in their homes that they brought for the Eucharist. St. Gregory the Great relates the story of a woman who laughed during Mass, because, at Communion, she was given the very loaf she had presented at the *Offertory* (Dom Ernest Graf, *The Priest at the Altar*, 132).

When the use of unleavened bread (prepared with flour and water without leaven or yeast) became the norm in the western Church during the ninth century, the procession disappeared because people no longer brought bread from their homes. Also, the reception of communion declined. The presentation of bread and wine by the faithful was, from the eleventh century, gradually replaced by the giving of money. By the twelfth century, the round hosts that we still use today for Communion appeared, cut from unleavened dough in the shape of coins.

## REFLECTION

When we present the bread and wine to the celebrant during Mass, it represents the gift of *ourselves,* which the priest offers to God for us. I feel so blessed to have understood this at a young age, thanks in great measure to the nuns who taught me for twelve years, the Religious of the Sacred Heart. Perhaps the promise of God's intervention in my life is what motivated me to seek out God at Mass. I always knew, deep down, that it was God who could answer my needs and solve my problems. This *knowing* has grown up alongside of me.

Today the needs and problems have grown considerably, especially my recent trials with illness, namely scleroderma and three types of cancer. After a particularly grueling week of tests, I was at Mass one morning when the words of Isaiah fortified me and gave me hope in the Lord: "Thus says the Lord, your redeemer, the Holy One of Israel: I am the Lord your God, who teaches you to profit, who leads you in the way you should go" (Is 48:17). Since I was always in the dark as to where this illness was taking me, Isaiah helped put my life in perspective. He gave me the courage to offer my trials to the Lord and to let Him lead me. I share the following entry from my journal, hoping that the Holy Spirit will encourage you to offer every bit of your life to God.

*Today I feel grateful to actually have something to give to God. I can offer Him any physical suffering, the uncertainly, the fear, the anxiety—and hardest of all, the un-*

Isaiah/Louis S. Glanzman

*known. I want Him to lead me on the way I should go! This week has been proof that I am being carried on wings of grace, cared for by a wonderful doctor, kindly nurses and a husband who suffers more than I do over my condition. I passed the three tests with flying colors (biopsies of breast, stomach and bone marrow), hiding my fears as best I could. I offered any pain and anxiety to Jesus, which was really nothing compared to the torture He experienced for us. But I enjoy the ability to offer Him something—anything—however little it is.*

Perhaps now it is not so little. Dr. Cunningham just phoned with the latest report. The breast biopsy showed a small cancer that needs to be removed. He said not to worry, it is perfectly curable, but he was surprised—and sorry—to find it. He suggests that I schedule surgery for early January at which time he will also remove some of the surrounding lymph nodes. The bone marrow test is still inconclusive, which means they might have to do another one when I go in for the breast surgery. There is a small population of lymphocytes in the bone marrow but not enough evidence to suggest lymphoma. But there is no question about the stomach: the entire lower half contains malt lymphoma. So we are still in a holding pattern regarding treatment until the bone marrow issue gets settled.

I asked the doctor how it is that I have so many cancers: stomach, breast, thymus (which was removed last December) and possibly bone marrow. He said that I somehow inherited a faulty immune system, which I'm sure paved the way for me to get scleroderma, and all of this could have something to do with abnormal genes.

The idea that I can offer Jesus my pain and unite it to His Cross gives me hope, not only that I will be restored and made whole, but that the world and everyone in it will be—and already is—redeemed by His Precious Blood. *I offer You my suffering, Lord, and unite it to Your infinite sacrifice of Love. Let me die with You in order to rise with You to new life. Free me, Lord, from all that keeps me from good health emotionally, physically and spiritually. Unbind me, like Lazarus, from these bands of sickness and death. Thank you for already accomplishing this. Amen.*

We have the privilege and the power to bring the whole world to the altar with us. The wonder of the Mass is that we are able to lift up the world and everyone in it to the Father, through Christ. Jesus told His disciples that His Father knows what we need before we ask

Him (cf. Mt 6: 8), yet He respects our freedom and doesn't force us to come to Him. It is a grace to realize *that God is the answer*, and that He already paid the price for our freedom and salvation. Our redemption is not a one-time moment, it is ongoing. It is up to us to avail ourselves of the graces God wants to shower on us, especially when we kneel at the foot of the Cross at Mass, and offer our lives and problems to Him. When we do that, I believe God lifts us up to the Father who unites us to Himself and one another, transforming our lives with His love and glory (see John 17: 20-26).

# The Eucharistic Prayer

While every prayer in the Mass is important to the Liturgy, the *Eucharistic Prayer* is *the* prayer without which there would be no Mass. It is the reason we have come together: to share in the liturgical representation of Christ's sacrificial death that won our salvation. It is, according to my friend and mentor, Fr. Patrick Greenough, OFM Conv., provincial of the St. Bonaventure Province of the Conventual Franciscans, "the prayer to the Father that saves the world. It takes us to the stable, the Last Supper, the Cross, the tomb and into the heavenly Jerusalem." In other words, it is a total incorporation into Christ's life, death and resurrection.

This prayer is the high point of the Sacred Liturgy. The gifts have been presented and the altar prepared. Now begins the *Eucharistic Prayer,* which our Roman missal describes as "the center and summit of the entire celebration . . . the prayer of thanksgiving and sanctification" (*General Instruction*, 78). Praise and thanksgiving is its heart and soul. It is also referred to as the *anaphora* (from the Greek *anaphorein*, meaning "to offer up") and *Canon* (from the Latin/Greek for "rule" or "law"), a name derived from the earliest description of this prayer, the *Roman Canon.*

For centuries, there was only one *Eucharistic Prayer*, which remained relatively unchanged since the time of St. Gregory the Great, who died in 604. After Vatican II, Pope Paul VI commissioned the addition of three new *Eucharistic Prayers* and eight *Prefaces* that were officially published in 1968. Thus, the new Roman Missal of 1970 contains four *Eucharistic Prayers.* In addition, there are several new *Eucharistic Prayers* for Masses with Children and for Masses of Reconciliation.

In the name of the whole Church, the celebrant thanks almighty God for His transforming and unifying power in our lives, made present in Christ His Son, who gifts the world with His presence. The entire Mass, and the *Eucharistic Prayer* in particular, consists of the past, present and future saving actions of God among us. *The Eucharistic Prayer* is comprised of many elements which form one unified whole: *Thanksgiving* (called the *Preface*), *Acclamation,*

*Epiclesis, Institution Narrative and Consecration, Anamnesis, Offering, Intercessions* and *Final Doxology.* We will look at each part individually, explain its meaning, give a bit of its history, and reflect on how we can make it more personally meaningful to us.

## *Preface/Thanksgiving*

### EXPLANATION

The *Preface* or *Thanksgiving* is like a prologue which disposes our hearts for the proper praise of God. It begins with an opening dialogue which sets the tone for the entire *Eucharistic Prayer.* The body of the prayer is said by the celebrant and reads like beautiful poetry which praises and thanks God for His work of creation, redemption and sanctification. Strictly speaking, the *Preface* is not so much an "introduction" as it is a "proclamation"— a "speaking out"— before God and the people, which the celebrant does on behalf of the faithful. The *Preface* concludes with the *Acclamation,* "Holy Holy Holy," which is said or sung by the priest and the congregation. He calls each of us to stand with him and unite as one body— chanting a hymn of glory that the Church in heaven, the angels and all the saints sing to the thrice-holy God (*CCC,* 1352).

With hands extended, the celebrant says or sings the opening dialogue, to which the people respond in kind:

*The Lord be with you.*
*And also with you.* (response)
*Lift up your hearts.*
*We lift them up to the Lord.* (response)
*Let us give thanks to the Lord our God.*
*It is right to give him thanks and praise.* (response)

In this opening dialogue, we are invited to put aside our preoccupations and distractions, to *lift up our hearts* and thank our God for the gift salvation. The older I get, the more thankful I become, especially for the gift of faith, but also for the people and circum-

*At the 'Lift up your hearts,' the Son of God arose and through his*
*powerful attraction drew to himself the desires of all those present.*
*Then, turning toward the east, surrounded by the countless angels*
*who were ministering to him, he stood with raised hands and of-*
*fered to God the Father, through the words of the Preface, the words*
*of all the faithful.*

—St. Gertrude the Great

stances in my life; indeed, for life itself. Some days, I feel it more
than others; but the truth is—all is gift. Now we have an opportunity to stand before God and, in a spirit of humility and gratitude,
tell Him how we feel by raising our voices and our hearts to Him in
these prayers.

But do we really lift up our hearts? Do we prayerfully engage in
this dialogue, or has the familiarity of this ritual lulled us into a mind-
less repetition of words? Are we excited to witness the miracle of
transformation about to take place when the priest will speak the
words of Jesus and change our bread into His Body and our wine
into His Blood? If we really knew the gift of God in our midst, the
*living Bread come down from heaven* (Jn 6:51), might we not be able
to stand still, or quiet, or composed for that matter? Would we, like
Peter, James and John at the Transfiguration, want to set up a tent
and never leave?

All of the *Eucharistic Prayers* start off with a blessing or praising
of God. For example, this is how the *Preface* of *Eucharistic Prayer II*
begins: "Father, it is our duty and our salvation, always and everywhere to give you thanks through your beloved Son, Jesus Christ"
(*Sacramentary,* 548). The Roman Missal today contains eighty-four
individual *Prefaces*. While the opening dialogue always remains the
same, the main body of the *Preface* changes according to feast days,
liturgical seasons, votive Masses and special occasions.

The *Preface* is an explanation of the words: "Let us give thanks
to the Lord our God." We have so much for which to thank God!
This is our "moment" in the Mass to thank God for the mystery of
our Redemption about to be re-enacted in our midst. We lift up not
only our hearts—but the whole world— to God as we prepare for
the arrival of our Divine Guest.

## HISTORY

The origins of the *Eucharistic Prayer* appear to be rooted in the ancient Jewish custom of reciting table prayers at meals. During the meal, the father of the family, or leader of the community, said a prayer of blessing over the bread and later over the wine. Known as the *berakah*, it was a prayer of praise and thanks to the Father for the benefits bestowed on God's people, especially for the gifts of creation and redemption: "Blessed are you, Lord, our God, king of the world, who has brought bread from heaven." After this, the bread was broken and distributed to those present. Later in the meal, before partaking of the wine, he prayed, "Blessed are you Creator of the fruit of the vine."

The Last Supper/Denys Calvaert

We do not know the exact words Jesus used at the Last Supper, but He most likely thanked His Father for His great love, reflected in His own life and death. We know from St. John's account of the Last Supper that Jesus prayed for His Father's will to be done in the world—and for Him to bring to fruition the work He had begun in Jesus.

We know that the *Preface* existed in the earliest days of the Church; not a single ancient liturgy can be found without one. The early Christians imitated Jesus' example by using Jewish blessing prayers of thanksgiving in their celebrations of Eucharist. Until the third century, the celebrant improvised these consecratory prayers; then they were written down. The spontaneity of the prayer is alluded to by St. Justin Martyr in the second century: "The one who presides offers similarly prayers of thanksgiving, as much as he is able, and all the people answer with the acclamation: Amen." The most ancient *Eucharistic Prayer* is reflected in a model given in the *Apostolic Tradition* (c. 215) attributed to St. Hippolytus of Rome, which we still pray today in *Eucharistic Prayer II.* It contains its own *Preface*, which reads like poetry: "For our sake He opened his arms on the cross; he put and end to death and revealed the resurrection. In this he fulfilled your will and won for you a holy people" (*Sacramentary,* 548).

In the Western Church, the number of *Prefaces* increased to such a degree that, before the time of St. Gregory the Great, almost every formula of Mass contained a separate *Preface.* The *Leonine Sacramentary* attributed to Pope St. Leo the Great included as many as 267 prefaces. It is believed that St. Gregory revised the rite and reduced the number of *Prefaces* to ten.

We know from the writings of St. Cyprian that the introductory dialogue existed in the liturgy of the West as early as the third century. St. Cyprian's words apply as much to us today as they did to the newly baptized in third century Carthage:

> Let every carnal and earthly thought be left behind. Only things of God and things of prayer should fill the soul. To this end the priest, before the Prayer, prepares the people through an invitatory. He says: 'Let us lift our hearts.' And the people, answering 'We lift them to the Lord,' are reminded to think only of the Lord. (in Lucien Deiss, *The Mass*, 69, 70)

## REFLECTION

Fr. Lucien Deiss asks us to consider how wholehearted and spontaneous are the cheers of a crowd at a football or baseball game: "Let's go!" "Go, team!" "Hurray!" "Charge!" He notes that in the liturgy, there are similar acclamations: "Hosanna!" "Glory to you, Lord!" "Thanks be to God !" The Sacred Liturgy, of course, is much more than a sports event, and, he says, the participation of the congregation should be infinitely more intense and profound (and reverent) than that of fans "attending" a game:

> In the Mass it is the 'crowd' itself that 'plays'; *the entire*

*congregation is celebrating.* Their acclamations should, therefore, be much more convincing and humanly authentic (emphasis added). (*Spirit and Song of the New Liturgy,* 64)

Would that we could muster enough spirit during Mass to thank our God with such spontaneous praise. The *Preface* is a call to give thanks. Like the overture of a symphony or a keynote of an important address, it stirs our spirit of gratitude for the awesome gift of the Paschal Mystery enacted before our eyes, and invites the faithful to fill their hearts with praise to God for His wonderful work of creation and redemption. When it is sung, it is one of the most sublime chants of the Church. The Gregorian melody of the *Preface,* sober and majestic, is a work of art. Mozart is reputed to have said that he would gladly have sacrificed all of his accomplishments in exchange for the honor of having composed it himself.

The *Preface* is the first movement of the *Eucharistic Prayer*—a great thanksgiving that Christ offers to His Father, and which reaches its zenith in the hymn of the angels, the *Sanctus.* We are about to enter into the divine presence of Almighty God. This is the cause of our rejoicing, our praising, our thanksgiving. Emmanuel—God with us— is indeed coming into our midst! Although the priest says the words on the altar, the faithful echo his intention to give praise and thanks to God for all His gifts—especially the gift of Himself—which is Eucharist.

## *"Holy, Holy, Holy Lord"*

Although God is always spiritually present to us, we are about to enter into the actual physical presence of Almighty God. Filled with wonder and thanksgiving, the celebrant and the faithful join the angels in singing His praises in the *Sanctus.*

The angels are always in adoration before the holiness of God. In the pre-Vatican II liturgy, the *Preface* listed different ways in which the angelic choirs praise almighty God: "The Angels are praising, the Dominations adore, the Powers tremble, and the Seraphim are jubilant." That they are present now and fill the sanctuary we know from the eye witness account of St. Padre Pio

St. Padre Pio.

(1887–1968), who, when celebrating Mass, was blessed with mystical powers and "saw the heavens open, the splendor of God, and the glory of the angels and the saints." When asked if the angels attend Mass, he responded, "The whole celestial court is present" (Alberto D'Apolito, *Padre Pio of Pietrelcina*, 167). Into such exalted company we are now called to add our voices to sing God's praises.

## EXPLANATION

*The Sanctus* is a powerful and poetic cry from the heart by which we offer praise to our Father for His infinite goodness and holiness. A solemn and majestic chant of adoration and thanksgiving, it has been used in the Eucharistic liturgies of the Church since the fourth century.

"There is none holy like the Lord" (1 Sm 2:2), cried the once-sterile Hannah when she dedicated her son Samuel to God in the temple. She sings a hymn of praise, thanking God for this miracle, for His awesome power and majesty. So do we, like Hannah, come to our own temple, the Church, to dedicate our lives to God in the Mass. There, united to Christ, we offer "a sacrifice of praise," holy and pleasing to God the Father. Not only is the Church of Christ holy, said St. Thomas Aquinas, but "the temple of God is holy and that temple is you!" We are holy, says St. Cyril of Jerusalem (315–386), "not by nature but by participation, by fasting and by prayer." We are about to pray the prayer of all prayers. Giving glory to our heavenly Father is an action which "sets us apart" as His beloved children—sanctifying us in the name of Jesus.

*Holy, holy, holy Lord, God of power and might,*
*heaven and earth are full of your glory.*
*Hosanna in the highest.*

*Blessed is he who comes in the name of the Lord.*
*Hosanna in the highest.*

Those who grew up in the pre-Vatican II Church will remember the ringing of bells which introduced the *Sanctus,* a sign for the congregation to pay attention and rejoice, because Christ was coming. This custom has mostly fallen into disuse, no doubt because it has outlived its original purpose. For centuries prior to Vatican II, the priest said Mass with his back to the people. When it came time for the *Consecration,* a majority of the people wouldn't know it was happening, save for the sound of the bells. They still ring bells in some churches today, especially where Tridentine Masses are celebrated. I still like those bells; they signal that something important is about to happen, which indeed it is. Jesus is coming into our midst, not humbly riding on a donkey as on Palm Sunday, but in His sacramental presence, His flesh and blood disguised under the appearance of bread and wine. The *Sanctus* is our way of preparing our hearts and minds for the arrival of the "King of Kings, and Lord of Lords" (Rev 19:16), our Creator and Redeemer, who "humbles Himself to come on our altars."

While the celebrant alone says the *Preface*, the Church invites the faithful to participate in the *Eucharistic Prayer* by singing these beautiful acclamations. In a two-fold exclamation of praise, we acclaim God's divine holiness as we anticipate Christ's coming to our altar: First is the *Sanctus* ("Holy, holy, holy"), followed immediately by the *Benedictus* ("Blessed is he"), the triumphant acclamation of praise the crowds showered on Jesus when He entered Jerusalem on Palm Sunday.

Situated in the heart of the *Eucharistic Prayer*—close to the Consecration—the *Sanctus*, says Fr. Lucien Deiss, "is the most important acclamation in the Eucharistic liturgy." While the *Gloria* celebrates the magnitude of God's glory, it does not, according to Father Deiss, have the same dignity as the *Sanctus*. "If the congregation could sing only one song, it would be the *Sanctus*. It could even be said that the *Sanctus* is the one hymn that should be sung at every Mass." He explains why: "God's holiness represents the most profound quality of divine nature in an infinitely luminous purity . . . it is the holiness of His love" (*Spirit and Song of the New*

*Liturgy*, 82). The *Holy, holy, holy*, is our heartfelt attempt to respond to this Love.

## HISTORY

The *Sanctus* is taken almost word for word from Sacred Scripture, recalling the visions of two great evangelist-prophets: Isaiah and St. John the Evangelist. It is the beginning of his ministry, and Isaiah is in the Temple; the heavens open before him and God appears to him in glory and majesty. He is seated on a raised throne. The train of his royal robes is spread on the long staircase that reaches down to the Holy of Holies and fills the entire sanctuary. The Seraphim, beings of fire and light, serve as acolytes to the divine throne. Deep in ecstasy, Isaiah hears the six-winged Seraphim calling to each other chanting the praise of God: "Holy, holy, holy is the Lord God of hosts; the whole earth is full of his glory" (Is 6:2, 3).

We also find these angelic creatures in St. John's Book of Revelation, the last book of the New Testament, where he records similar words: "And the four living creatures, each of them with six wings . . . and day and night they never cease to sing, 'Holy, holy, holy, is the Lord God Almighty, who was and is and is to come!'" (Rev 4:8).

Jesus Enters Jeruselum/James Tissot

The *Benedictus* ("Blessed is he") follows immediately after the *Sanctus* and belongs to the second part of the acclamation. The disciples first chanted it when our Lord entered Jerusalem on Palm Sunday. "Hosanna" is a Hebrew word that comes to us from the early Church. It means "O Lord, grant salvation." It is a joyous exclamation, much like the English *God save the King!* or the French, *Vive la France!* It was also used in the Old Testament, where the people who were yearning for their redemption cried out, "Hosanna," "Save us!" The acclamation, "Blessed is he who comes in the name of the Lord"(Ps 118:26) was from the same Psalm, a part of the Hallel (Psalms 113–118), which means it was sung by Jesus at the Last Supper.

In the early Church, the "Holy, holy, holy Lord" was first sung as part of the morning office of the synagogue. In about the year 96, St. Clement of Rome quotes from the "Holy, holy, holy" text in a letter he wrote to the Corinthians, implying that they sang these words together, but he didn't specifically mention the Mass. Tertullian refers to the liturgical *Sanctus* as do many of the Church Fathers down to St. Athanasius, St. Cyril of Jerusalem and others of the fourth century. The *Sanctus* was also included in the *Apostolic Tradition* of St. Hippolytus around the year 200. It is rich in imagery and sentiment:

> A countless multitude of Angels adore you with the Archangels, Thrones, Dominations, Principalities, Powers, Virtues, and eternal armies such as Cherubim and Seraphim. With thousands upon thousands of Archangels and myriads upon myriads of Angels, they never cease to sing in one unending voice. May the people say with them:
> Holy, Holy, Holy, Lord Sabaoth!
> Heaven and earth are filled with his glory!
> Blessed is he forever. Amen.
>             (in Deiss, *Spirit and Song of the New Liturgy*, 89).

By the middle of the fifth century, these chants were incorporated into the Roman *Eucharistic Prayers.*

## REFLECTION

Thus have these chants echoed the praise of God throughout sacred history. Today, the communion of saints, living and deceased, gathers around the altar where with one voice we sing the praises of our almighty God and Father whom we worship and adore at every Mass celebrated in Catholic churches throughout the world. "No other song can rightfully even pretend to its magnificence" exclaims

Fr. Lucien Deiss, because when we sing the *Sanctus,* "we are at the heart of the Eucharist, in union with heaven and earth and their entire army," which of course means all the angels and saints (*Spirit and Song of the New Liturgy*, 91).

It is wonderful to picture all the angels and saints gathered around the altar during the celebration of Eucharist. We are meant to adore God just like they do. The Mass is the greatest means we have on earth of worshiping God, which we do through the sacrifice of Jesus, our High Priest, who alone gives His Father the honor and glory He deserves. "You shall be holy, for I, the Lord, your God, am holy" (Lev 19:1), the Lord said to Moses. When he came down from Mount Sinai after his encounter with the Lord, the skin of Moses's face was radiant, because he glowed with God's glory.

We, too, are meant to become radiant, to reflect the glory and holiness of God. How do we do that? First I think it is not so much something that we do, but something that Christ does in us when we fall in love with Him. When that happens, when we say "Yes" to God and establish a personal relationship with Him, we will start to think the way He thinks and love the way He loves. We will become like Him as we imitate Him in His poverty, His humility, His obedience—even to the Cross. Then we will begin to see reality through the eyes of Jesus; and His reflection will grow in us, so that others will recognize Christ's Spirit in us. Deeply aware of God's goodness, we will overflow with gratitude, which will spill over in a constant chorus of praise and thanksgiving to our Lord and Savior—a prayer which reaches its culmination in the Eucharist as we sing, *"Holy, Holy, Holy . . ."*

## Epiclesis

We are approaching the moment when the celebrant will repeat the words Christ said at the Last Supper over the bread and wine, changing them into His Body and Blood. The Church deems the *Consecration* the center and high point of the Mass, and just before it, inserts a special prayer known as the *Epiclesis*. During Mass, we will miss this important prayer if we are not careful. It is short; and although the priest says it audibly, we tend to see it as a prologue to the words of *Consecration* that follow, rather than as an essential and powerful prayer in its own right. It is integral to the *Eucharistic Prayer* because it calls down the Holy Spirit, who will change the bread and wine into Our Lord's Body and Blood.

Known as the Sanctifier, the Holy Spirit not only changes the bread and wine into the Body and Blood of Christ, but He also changes us, conse-crating us "in Spirit and truth" (Jn 4:24). The next time you are at Mass and the priest is about to say the *Epiclesis,* put your heart and soul into the prayer and ask that the transformation about to take place in the bread and wine also be accomplished in you. When the Holy Spirit came upon Christ's apos-tles and His mother, Mary, at Pentecost, He filled them with divine life, trans-forming and uniting them as one apostolic community.

Pentecost/Louis Galloche

The Church was born, gifted for all time, with the fullness of the Spirit of God. We are now the living temples of the Holy Spirit (cf. 1 Cor 3:16), and, says esteemed French theologian Fr. Henri de Lubac, "our churches are the 'upper room' where not only is the Last Supper renewed but Pentecost also" (*Catholicism,* 111).

## EXPLANATION

*Epiclesis* is a Greek liturgical term meaning "invocation," or "calling down/upon." Our *Catechism* defines it best:

> The *Epiclesis* ("invocation upon") is the intercession in which the priest begs the Father to send the Holy Spirit, the Sanctifier, so that the offerings may become the body and blood of Christ and that the faithful, by receiving them, may themselves become a living offering to God. (*CCC*, 1105)

"Let your Spirit come upon these gifts."
Fr. Lawrence Hennessey

There are two parts of the *Epiclesis* prayer in the Mass that the celebrant says on behalf of the community, in which He asks the Father to send the Holy Spirit to sanctify and transform our gifts and ourselves. He says the first part at the end of the *Sanctus* and just before the *Institution Narrative* (which includes the words of consecration). The priest joins his hands and, holding them outstretched over the offering of bread and wine, prays audibly: *"Let your Spirit come upon these gifts to make them holy, so that they may become for us the body and blood of our Lord, Jesus Christ."* After the consecration, the celebrant again "calls down" the Spirit, praying: *"Grant that we . . . may be filled with his Holy Spirit and become one body, one spirit in Christ. May He (the Holy Spirit) make us an everlasting gift to you."* We're asking to be *eucharistified*—to be drawn into the Living Body of Christ.

Perhaps a word about this Third Person of the Blessed Trinity will inspire our prayer. Who really *is* the Holy Spirit? We know Him as the Sanctifier, the One who is always at work in the world creating and saving. In the Book of Genesis, God's Spirit hovered over the waters of chaos and brought out life and order. "All life, all holiness comes from you, through your Son, Jesus Christ our Lord, by the working of the Holy Spirit," we pray in *Eucharistic Prayer III.*

The word for "spirit" in Hebrew is *ruah,* and in Greek, *pneuma.* Both words denote wind, storm or gentle breeze that brought rain to the fields from the Mediterranean, thus giving life to field and flock. The words also means breath, a gift of God that brings life and, at death, returns to God. We think of the Holy Spirit as God's breath in us. Even though we are seldom aware of our breath, we cannot live without it. Nor can we live without God's spirit, who empowers us to live a "spiritual" life. The very word "spirituality" reflects the realization that the Christian life is led in the power and under the guidance of the Holy Spirit. He is our guiding light, indispensable to our growth in wholeness and holiness. When we pray, it is God's Spirit praying in us, gifting us with His love, joy, forgiveness, kindness, goodness, gentleness and peace.

In the Old Testament, the Spirit of God is a symbol of divine dynamism. It was "the spirit of the Lord" who empowered Sampson to defend Israel with super-human strength, and who brought life back into the dry bones of the people of Israel (see Ezek 37:1-14):

> And I will put my spirit within you, and you shall live, and
> I will place you in your own land; then you shall know that
> I, the Lord, have spoken, and I have done it, says the Lord.
> (Ezek 37:14)

## HISTORY

When Jesus came to earth, He left us a precious legacy, the Eucharist and the Holy Spirit. St. Luke describes the outpouring of the Spirit at Jesus' conception and infancy, and how He received God's spirit at His baptism:

> Now when all the people were baptized, and when Jesus
> also had been baptized and was praying, the heaven was
> opened, and the Holy Spirit descended upon him in bodily
> form, as a dove, and a voice came from heaven, "You are
> my beloved Son; with you I am well pleased" (Lk 3:21, 22).

The Holy Spirit *anoints* Jesus for His mission, baptizing Him with power and authority to establish God's kingdom on earth. "It is the Spirit that gives life" (Jn 6:63), said Jesus; and it is through Him that we are able to call God our Father (Rom 8:15). He told His disciples to wait until the Spirit comes, to be imbued with power. At Pentecost, Jesus poured out that same Spirit He received from the Father at His baptism, which gave birth to the one, holy, catholic and apostolic Church. The Holy Spirit is our Advocate who will lead His disciples to all truth (Jn 16:13).

The early Christians were extremely aware of the Holy Spirit's power. The *epiclesis*, that is the formal petition that the Holy Spirit come upon the bread and wine, dates back to the earliest Christian liturgies, when bishops would invoke the Holy Spirit in two ways. First, they would use a consecratory formula invoking the Holy Spirit to change the elements into the Body and Blood of Christ, and, second, after the *Consecration*, they would ask the Holy Spirit to sanctify the faithful through their reception of the Eucharist. In the early Church, there was a profound awareness that the Holy Spirit effected the transformation of bread and wine into the Body and Blood of the Lord.

> *It is the Holy Spirit who makes our prayer and worship possible at all. To experience God is to experience the Holy Spirit, Who is the effective power of God in the world—the effective energy of Love in our lives.*
>
> —Fr. Lawrence Hennessey

*Eucharistic Prayer II*, which we say today is the oldest, and is based on a *Eucharistic Prayer* attributed to St. Hippolytus, who some regard as the most important witness to the liturgical practice of the early Church. The prayer has an explicit *Epiclesis*. These prayers were more varied in the Eastern liturgies, such as those of Sts. Basil and John Chrysostom in the fourth century, whose eloquence earned the latter the accolade "golden tongue":

> The priest stands. What he is going to pray to come down is not fire from heaven but the Holy Spirit himself. He prays with determination, not that fire fall from heaven on the victim and consume it, but that divine grace come down over the offering and through it lay hold of the soul of the participants, set it aglow, make it more glittering than silver purified by fire. (in Guy Oury, *The Mass*, 101)

In the Eastern liturgies, the *epiclesis* usually followed the Lord's words of Institution; and to this day, Eastern churches believe that this is the moment when the bread and wine is changed into the Body and Blood of Christ. We, in the Western Church, believe that transubstantiaton occurs during the *Institution Narrative,* which is embraced by the *epiclesis.*

St. Paul encourages us to yield our lives to the Spirit, saying: "Our Gospel came to you not only in word, but also in power and in the Holy Spirit" (1 Thess 1:5). That power is evidenced in His gifts and talents that strengthen and sanctify us. St. Paul lists the spiritual gifts as wisdom, knowledge, faith, healing, the working of miracles, prophecy, discernment of spirits, tongues and the interpretation of tongues (cf: 1 Cor 12). These charismatic gifts are "special graces," said the bishops at Vatican II, which the Holy Spirit gives to individuals or groups as a source of holiness in the Church (*Lumen Gentium,* 12). It is through the power of the Holy Spirit that we will be "witnesses in Jerusalem, throughout Judea and Samaria, and to the ends of the earth" (Acts 1:8).

## REFLECTION

One of the ways I like to pray is to dialogue with the Lord. At an Intensive Journal Workshop at Loyola University in Chicago, I learned how to journal as a tool of personal growth and self-discovery. I also used it for prayer. Fr. George Maloney, S.J., who has written numerous books on contemplative prayer, encourages us to dialogue with God to help us open our inner selves and surrender to the Lord at a deep level. It is a way for heart to speak to heart, so to speak. Father Maloney reminds us of St. Augustine's teaching: that God is more intimate to you than you are to yourself. Our task is to lovingly surrender ourselves to Him as we would to our best friend. "This," Father Maloney says, "is contemplation in the form of dialogue, but one on the level of being" (*Journey Into Contemplation,* 131).

After Christmas one year, I felt the need to get away for a few days of quiet and rest. I drove up to Our Lady Help of Christians Monastery (Holy Hill) in Hubertus, Wisconsin, not realizing that I was headed into a blizzard. When I finally got there, I was a captive of the weather, unable to go anywhere for the next four days except the chapel, the bookstore and the dining room. It was heaven!

There was a private chapel in the building where I stayed, and where I spent long hours in front of the Blessed Sacrament. With notebook in hand, I spoke to Jesus about anything and everything that was on my mind and heart. When I do this, I do not hear a voice or have inner locutions. I follow the lead of St. Teresa of Avila, who tells us that "Mental prayer is nothing else than an intimate friendship, a frequent heart-to-heart conversation with Him by whom we know ourselves to be loved." Conversation implies a mutual exchange of words and sentiments. Does Christ respond to our conversation? Does He converse with us in prayer? St. Teresa assures us in *The Way of Perfection* that He most definitely does: meditation is not a monologue, but rather a dialogue:

> Do you suppose that because we cannot hear Him, He is silent? He speaks clearly to the heart when we beg Him from our heart to do so . . . Soon after we have begun to force ourselves to remain near the Lord, He will give us indications that . . . He heard us. (169, 193)

St. Teresa does not intend to infer that this communication from Christ implies any supernatural vision or revelation. Christ speaks to our souls in simple, ordinary ways; and He speaks to all souls who pray to Him!

I share my prayer/dialogue with my readers in the hope that it will encourage your own prayer and help you grow in awareness of the nearness and love of the Holy Spirit.

> **Joan:** Jesus, I have such a desire to know the Holy Spirit better. Will you open me more to His gifts and His presence? Jesus, who is He?
>
> **Jesus:** Joan, the Holy Spirit is My Spirit living inside of you. Yes, it is a real mystery! It is a God mystery. It is My Spirit of love, joy, peace, understanding, fortitude, knowledge and fear of the Lord. When you have Me you have everything! I live inside of you. I walk with you, eat with you, sleep with you, pray with you. Joan, I never leave you unless you leave Me.
>
> **Joan:** Jesus, how can I get to know You—or recognize You—more easily? For instance, now while praying to You in front of the

Blessed Sacrament, it is Your Spirit speaking to me, having this conversation with me. Is that correct?

**Jesus:** Yes, child, it is. You are beginning to understand.

**Joan:** So, when people talk about a fullness of the Spirit, what does that really mean?

**Jesus:** Picture a glass of water. You are the glass and I (Holy Spirit) am the water. Even if there is only a small amount of water in the glass, I am still there, living and loving in you. The more you look to Me, pray to Me, ask Me for your needs, in short, the more you surrender your life to Me and let Me be your Lord and Savior, the more I fill you (the glass) with Myself. The more water there is the more My gifts can operate in your life because you have a deeper bond with Me.

**Joan:** Jesus, I like this imagery because I can understand it. But one question is bothering me. What about empty glasses with no water in them. Don't You choose to live in each person? Or, is Your life in us dependant on our opening to You through prayer?

**Jesus:** Joan, your question is a good one. Yes, I am present in each soul through the waters of Baptism. In Baptism, each child becomes mine. We have a special bond, like an umbilical cord, through which My love flows into you. Through the gift of faith that is offered (continually) to every soul, I seek to enter hearts more deeply, to be one with them. When, through faith, they respond to Me, My spirit fills the glass, drop by drop. If I filled the glass all at once, it would be too overwhelming. Growth is necessary. Growth in love is slow. If I didn't let you grow at your own pace I would be taking away your free will. And so, when you pray and open your heart to Me and ask Me for your needs, My Spirit of love responds inside of you, answering your call. My love, the water, rises in the glass in proportion to the depth of your surrender to Me.

**Joan:** Jesus, this is so wonderful. It is too good to be true! Why does this awesome truth escape most of us and we live on our own so to speak, sort of detached from Your Spirit?

**Jesus:** Another good question! Many souls have not developed their gift of faith. In fact, faith for most people is the least desirable gift of all that I have given them. They want a full share of talents that the world recognizes. The gifts of the Spirit that they receive through faith do not give any recompense in the world;

and so they think, what real good are they to me? Most people do not have any clue as to their real purpose in life—their spiritual journey to grow into oneness and union with their God. They flit about outside the castle—to use St. Teresa's image of the interior castle—caught up with the worms and vipers and serpents of Satan. Their lives are a continuous struggle against the forces of darkness that seek to overcome them every minute of every day. Many are overcome and living in sin and darkness. They have no awareness of the precious diamond that is their soul, and of the many rooms in the interior through which they will find graces and spiritual riches to delight and fill them with love and joy.

**Joan**: And so, for souls that have the gift of faith and develop it by growing closer to You in prayer, they enter the castle of their soul where Your Spirit dwells and invites them to receive more of a share of Your life?

**Jesus**: Yes, daughter, this is a rudimentary explanation, but it will do. I live deep in the heart of each soul. As you enter more deeply inside yourself and begin exploring the rooms of self knowledge, the veil of the world lifts, as it were, and opens your mind and heart to knowledge, understanding, love and so forth, always leading you closer and closer to Truth. My Spirit is your guide on the inner journey, gifting you at every turn, giving you what you need (not always what you want) to progress.

**Joan:** So, Lord, how then should we get to know and love Your Spirit better, so that He can lead us to You?

**Jesus**: There are many ways. The primary way is by daily attendance at My Holy Sacrifice, where I, Your Jesus, become present to you, fully and completely, Body, Blood, Soul and Divinity. I come to reside with you and in you. My presence is a substantial, sacramental one. I leave behind an imprint of My grace and My presence. I leave behind My spirit to dwell inside of you. Often throughout the day, talk to Me in you heart. Seek Me for all problems and decisions. Quiet yourself often to commune with Your Lord and then listen for My promptings and inspirations. Come often to be with me in adoration,  and our love will grow deeper with each visit. Joan, I have so much to give souls, if only they will look to Me, consult Me, listen to Me. Come before the Tabernacle and ask for all your needs. Trust Me completely,  and I will act in your life and care for you with the love of a mother and father.

**Joan**: What is Our Lady's role?

**Jesus:** Our Lady is the one who called you to come away so you could find the healing that your soul craves! She is always interceding for the needs of her children, bringing them to Me and asking for My intervention in their lives. She cares so deeply for each soul, tending to them like a mother hovers over her infant child. She is the spouse of My Holy Spirit. Together they make quite a team, caring for My flock with tenderest love and con-

Mother of God Rejoicing/Fr. William McNichols

cern! Ask her always Joan for whatever you need. My mother will never disappoint you.

**Joan:** Jesus, I feel so blessed and full. We are like children of a King who have the run of Your estate, which is our estate, and no matter what we do or where we run, we'll be safe and blessed and gifted at every turn! Baptism is the key that gains us entry into this vast estate. Once we're in it, we have the run of the place with Your Holy Spirit as our personal guide. We have access to You at all times but especially through the Mass and the Eucharist, which gives us an audience with You, so to speak. We can come into Your presence in adoration and be with you in Person for as long as we want. Then, when we go about our daily lives, Your Spirit intercedes for us to guide us, protect us, inform us, heal us, comfort us. Jesus, Your love is outrageous and wonderful. It is too good to be true! You have planned this so that we can live our heaven on earth. All this and heaven too!

Fr. Bob DeGrandis tells the story of a friend of his who was poor until oil was discoverd on her property. She had been wealthy all along only she didn't know it! He compares our spiritual heritage to her treasure, saying that the kingdom of God is within and as we surrender our lives to Christ, we have a priceless inheritance as sons and daughters of the King of Kings. We gain access to our inheritance through a prayerful study of the word of God says Father Bob, under the guidance of the Holy Spirit. It is through a deep, intimate relationshiip with the Holy Spirit that we will begin to enter into our inheritance (*Healing Through the Mass,* 69).

The Holy Spirit dwells in us through Jesus. And where Jesus is, so are the Father and the Holy Spirit. He will put life and love back into our dried-up prayers, just as he did to the dry bones of the Israelites. "Love is His greatest gift," says French theologian Fr. A.M. Roguet, O.P., He is "the soul of the Church" (*Holy Mass, Approaches to the Mystery,* 125). The Holy Spirit is to our spiritual life, what our soul is to our body: its life-giving principle. We cannot live without the Holy Spirit.

## *The Institution Narrative*

About a month before my dad died, I visited him every afternoon at St. Vincent's Hospital in New York City. One day, the compassion I felt for him came pouring out in words of gratitude for all the love and gifts he had lavished on me throughout my life. I'll never forget his response: "I haven't even started yet." What I heard in those five words was, "Even though I'm gone, I will always watch over and protect you."

My dad died fifteen years ago, and I still carry his words in my heart, trusting that he is caring for me just as he did in life. Now I know exactly how he felt. As a mother of four grown children whom I love more than life itself, and a grandmother of five (with two and, hopefully, many more on the way), I pray for the same opportunity before I die: to tell them how deeply I love them, and that I will watch over them—always.

If human beings love one another so much, how much more intense and passionate must be God's divine love for His children? The Bible is replete with references to God's spousal love for His people; God Himself likens His commitment to a marriage covenant between two people, sacred and eternal. Our human love is a faint reflection of the kind of love our Father lavishes on us, going so far as to send His own Son to die for us as a pledge of His unconditional love.

Jesus described Himself as the bridegroom to His people (see Mt 9:15). Before Jesus died, He invited those closest to Him to share a last meal together. He wanted to gift His followers with a memorial of His love, the Eucharist. What a gift! He instituted a ritual of eating and drinking in which bread is changed into His Body and wine is changed into His Blood, so that whenever His disciples would repeat these actions in memory of Him, Jesus would become present as truly and really as He had been when He walked among them in Judea and Galilee. The offering of bread and wine, which Jesus began in the Upper Room the night before, was completed the next day on Calvary, where He sacrificed His Body and Blood on the Cross—for the redemption of the world.

Temptation of Christ/Titian

*As the bridegroom rejoices over the bride, so shall your God rejoice over you* (Is 62:5).

Our Lord not only promises His continuing care for us after His death, He gifts us with new and eternal life— *Himself*—His real and abiding presence in the Eucharist.

The *Consecration,* now referred to as the *Institution Narrative,* is the heart of the Sacred Liturgy because the celebrant re-presents the words and actions of Our Lord at the Last Supper—thus changing the bread and wine into the Body and Blood of Christ. In obedience to Jesus, Catholic priests have, for two thousand years, repeated those sacred words on behalf of the faithful in every Mass in every Catholic Church all over the world: "This is My Body, which will be given for you; do this in memory of me. . . . This cup is the new covenant in my blood, which will be shed for you" (Lk 22:19).

Our God loves us so much that He gave us a way of never being separated from Him—on earth as well as in heaven. We are not able to fathom the magnitude of the gift of the Eucharist—because its benefits are of infinite value.

## EXPLANATION

While the ordained priest is the only one to say the sacred words of *Consecration*, he does so on behalf of the whole community. The gifts of bread and wine on the altar represent us. Today, the Church purposely includes a liturgical silence during the *Eucharistic Prayer*, not to exclude the faithful from participating, but to help them enter more deeply into the sacredness of the celebration. Fr. Josef Jungmann comments on the sacred stillness that pervades the atmosphere:

> Silence is a worthy preparation for God's approach. Like the High-priest of the Old Testament, who once a year was permitted to enter the Holy of Holies with the blood of a sacrificial animal (Heb 9:7), the priest separates from the people and makes his way before the all-holy God in order to offer up the sacrifice to Him. (*The Mass of the Roman Rite,* 138, 139)

Just before the Consecration, the celebrant places his hands over the offering and asks the Father to "Bless and approve our offering. . . . Let it become for us the body and blood of Jesus Christ, your only Son, our Lord." He takes the bread in his hands, and, raising his eyes to heaven, the celebrant speaks the same words Christ spoke at the Last Supper, pronouncing them in the person of Christ.

Fr. Patrick Greenough, OFM Conv.

> *The day before he suffered*
> *He took bread in his sacred hands*
> *and looking up to heaven,*
> *to you, his almighty Father,*
> *he gave you thanks and praise.*
> *He broke the bread,*
> *gave it to his disciples, and said:*

Bowing slightly he says:

*Take this, all of you, and eat it:*
*This is my body which will be given up for you.*

He elevates the sacred Host, places it on the paten and genuflects in adoration.

Then he takes the chalice, raises it slightly above the altar and continues:

Fr. Ted Keating

*When supper was ended,*
*he took the cup.*
*Again he gave you*
*thanks and praise,*
*gave the cup to his disciples*
*and said:*

*Take this, all of you, and*
*drink from it:*
*This is the cup of my blood,*
*the blood of the new and*
*everlasting covenant.*
*It will be shed for you and for all*
*so that sins may be forgiven.*
*Do this in memory of me.*

The celebrant lifts up the chalice above the altar, then places it on the corporal and genuflects in adoration.

Catholics have always believed that the words of *Consecration* effect a substantial change of the bread and wine into the Body and Blood of Christ. The technical word is *transubstantiation*, which designates the conversion of the whole substance of the bread into the Body of Christ, and the whole substance of the wine into His Blood. The concept has its roots in early Christian writings; centuries later, it was formulated as doctrine at the Fourth Lateran Council in 1215. St. Thomas Aquinas developed the concept of transubstantiation in greater depth.

By this sacramental action, Christ acts through his priest and transforms our bread into the living Flesh of the Son of God, and our wine into His precious Blood, so that Christ is truly, really and sub-stantially contained under the appearance of bread and wine. The "accidents" (color, shape, taste) of bread and wine remain. This is a great miracle that we will never be able to explain or prove. It re-mains the central mystery of our faith.

In his profound and beautifully written book on the Sacred Lit-urgy, Pope Benedict XVI (formerly Joseph Cardinal Ratzinger), sums

The Last Supper/Nicolas Poussin

up, with some emotion, the meaning of the *Consecration*:

> The moment when the Lord comes down and transforms bread and wine to become his Body and Blood cannot fail to stun, to the very core of their being, those who partici-pate in the Eucharist by faith and prayer. When this hap-pens, we cannot do other than fall to our knees and greet Him. The Consecration is the moment of God's great *actio* in the world for us. It draws our eyes and hearts on high. For a moment the world is silent, everything is silent, and in that silence we touch the eternal—for one beat of the heart we step out of time into God's being-with-us. (*The Spirit of the Liturgy*, 212)

The Holy Father sees the silence at the elevation of the consecrated species as, "an invitation to direct our eyes toward Christ, to look at Him from within, in a gaze that is at once gratitude, adoration and petition for our own transformation" (211).

## HISTORY

The first Eucharist took place in the Upper Room on the day before Jesus was crucified. Their Passover dinner was the culmination of a long series of meals that the Apostles and Jesus had enjoyed together. When they were at table, Jesus told them how eagerly He "desired to eat this Passover with you before I suffer" (Lk 22:15). The question of whether the Last Supper was truly a Passover meal is still debated by theologians. Sts. Matthew, Mark and Luke agree that it was, while St. John notes that the Passover took place on the evening of Jesus' death (see Jn 18:28, 19:31). Scripture scholar Fr. Raymond Brown suggests that the Last Supper was not a Passover meal in the strict sense, but a meal that had "Passover characteristics" (*The Gospel According to John,* 556*).* Whichever it was, we are quite sure that none of the apostles had an inkling of the great mystery that was about to unfold.

Jesus reinterprets the significance of the Passover by setting it in the context of the kingdom of God, saying: "I shall not eat it until it is fulfilled in the kingdom of God" (Lk 22:16). The "deliverance" associated with the Passover finds new meaning in Christ's blood that will be shed: "This cup which is poured out for you is the new covenant in my blood" (Lk 22:20).

Biblical scholars generally agree that St. Paul's narrative was written first, followed by the accounts of Sts. Luke, Matthew and Mark, and finally St. John. Although St. Paul wasn't at the Last Supper, he is intimately acquainted with it:

> For I received from the Lord what I also handed on to you, that the Lord Jesus, on the night he was handed over, took bread, and, after he had given thanks, broke it and said, "This is my body that is for you. Do this in remembrance of me." In the same way also the cup, after supper, saying, "This cup is the new covenant in my blood. Do this, as often as you drink it, in remembrance of me." For as often

as you eat this bread and drink the cup, you proclaim the death of the Lord until he comes. (1 Cor 11: 23-26)

The Gospel was preached for some years before Jesus' words were written down. The text of the *Institution Narrative* is not taken word for word from one Evangelist, but is a combination of the texts of Matthew, Mark, Luke and St. Paul (1 Cor 11:23-25). Although not uniform, they bear no contradictions, a testimony to their veracity according to St. John Chrysostom: "If the Evangelists agreed together exactly as to times and even words, enemies would never believe that they had written without an entirely human agreement: such agreement would not be a sign of genuineness."

The Acts of the Apostles and the Epistles of St. Paul describe the primitive community as "steadfast in the teaching of the Apostles and in the communion of the breaking of the bread and in prayers" (Acts 2:42). The "Prayers and the breaking of the bread" describe the Liturgy of the primitive Church.

Theologians generally agree that the words Jesus spoke at the Last Supper did occur in the Eucharistic Liturgy of the early Church when the entire *Eucharistic Prayer* was considered consecratory. In the Latin west, at what precise moment the *Consecration* took place was never a matter of concern until about the thirteenth century, when the *Consecration* was linked to the words Christ spoke during the *Institution Narrative*, an understanding held today. Pope John Paul II writes that it is the priest, who, "by the authority given him in the sacrament of priestly ordination, effects the consecration" (*On the Eucharist in its Relationship to the Church*, 11). When he says these words, "*he puts his voice at the disposal of the One who spoke these words in the Upper Room* and who desires that they should be repeated in every generation by all those who in the Church ministerially share in his priesthood."(11)

The writings of the Church Fathers contain deeply respectful references to the *Eucharistic Prayer* in the early Church. Speaking to an audience of newly baptized, St. Athanasius said:

> You will see the Levites bring forth loaves and a chalice of wine and place them on the altar. As long as the invocations and prayers have not begun, they are but bread and wine. But when *the great and wonderful prayers* have been

said, the bread becomes the Body and the wine the Blood of our Lord Jesus Christ.

Even more explicit are the words of St. Ambrose (340-397), who carefully explained that the bread which he brought to church (in those days the people brought the bread from their homes) is ordinary bread, but "before the sacramental words; but as soon as the Consecration takes place, that bread becomes Christ's Flesh." He asked his listeners, "Of what words is Consecration made up, and whose words are they?"

> *Jesus allowed me to enter the Cenacle, and I was a witness to what happened there. However, I was most deeply moved when, before the Consecration, Jesus raised his eyes to heaven and entered into a mysterious conversation with His Father. It is only in eternity that we shall really understand that moment. His eyes were like two flames; His face was radiant, white as snow; His whole personage full of majesty, His soul full of longing. At the moment of Consecration, love rested satiated—the sacrifice was fully consummated. Now only the external ceremony of death will be carried out—external destruction; the essence of the sacrifice is in the Cenacle. Never in my whole life had I understood this mystery so profoundly as during that hour of adoration. Oh how ardently I desire that the whole world would come to know this unfathomable mystery!*
> —St. Faustina Kowalska, *Diary, 684*

to which he answered, "Those of the Lord Jesus." He speaks of all the other prayers the priest says during the liturgy, "But as soon as the moment at which the venerable Sacrament comes into being is reached, the priest no longer speaks of himself, but uses the words of Christ. It is thus Christ's word which makes this Sacrament."

Enrico Mazza, a theologian who writes extensively on the Eucharist, goes so far as to say that St. Ambrose "gave birth to the doctrine of consecration"—which we understand to mean the words of Our Lord ("This is my body, This is the cup of my Blood") that are cited during the *Eucharistic Prayer*. Mazza explains Ambrose's belief: "It is the heavenly words, that is, which Christ speaks as God, that work the miracle of consecration" (*The Celebration of the Eucharist*, 154).

Some words have been added by the Church, for example, "He took bread in his sacred hands," "looking up to heaven," and "the mystery of faith." The latter phrase appeared in the Roman Mass towards the end of the eighth century, when, before the existence of the elevation or the ringing of the bells, the faithful were in danger of missing the *Consecration* because the churches were so large. A minister or deacon would cry out during the *Consecration*: "The mystery of faith is being fulfilled." Later, even when this addition became unnecessary, the ancient cry was incorporated into the text read by the celebrant.

## REFLECTION

Woman, Behold Thy Son/James Tissot

Of the seeds of faith that the Lord planted in my adolescent heart, one has born more fruit in my life than all the others: the teaching that the Mass is the most perfect of prayers, because it is God (Jesus Christ) who sacrifices Himself to God (the Father) for us. The Mass is a sacramental representation of Calvary. Our task is to bring ourselves—and the whole world—to the foot of the Cross at the altar, where we mystically participate in this ongoing act of our redemption.

This teaching deeply rooted itself in my being and became the cornerstone of my faith. The tattered, out-of-print booklet that contained these pearls of wisdom, authored by Frs. John McCormick, CSSR, and John Treinen, CSSR, sits on a bookshelf behind my desk reserved for *special* books. The book follows a close second behind the excellent teaching of the Religious of the Sacred Heart. I treasure both for being so instrumental in helping me to appreciate the relevance and spiritual significance of the Mass.

The Mass is the high road to sanctity. The Sacred Liturgy is not so much about us, as it is about God, who draws us to Himself in the Eucharist. It is a means by which God makes us holy—transforming us into Himself. How? When the priest changes the bread and wine into Christ's Body and Blood, we pray that He will also change us—consecrate us—making us holy and acceptable to Him, an offering in spirit and truth. During the *Consecration*, we pray that it will also become our sacrifice as we offer our bodies and our blood to the Father through Jesus. By "body" we mean everything to do with our physical lives—our time, our talents, our health, our energies, our affections. By "blood" (which we understand in its biblical meaning as the seat of life), we offer our suffering or "deaths," such as sickness, failures, problems and hurts. In the words of St. Augustine:

> Christ sacrificed His life for us not out of any need of His to be a sacrifice, but to show us that God wanted us to *become His sacrifice*. Through the Mass, Christ's Body and Blood are placed on the altar. As members of His body, we are also placed there by our gifts of bread and wine, making ourselves the sacrifice of God. (St. Augustine's *Sermons*)

In other words, to be holy (from the Latin, *sacrum facere;* persons are made sacred when they are consecrated to the divinity, or offered to God) is to become God's sacrifice. Consecration and sacrifice are like two sides of the same coin.

Our transformation begins when we *will* to become part of Christ's sacrifice. When Jesus says, "Thy will be done," His pain becomes redemptive. To the extent that our suffering is connected to His, it becomes, like His, redemptive. When we surrender our egos and agendas, our selfish motives and narcissistic wills, we will experience the same darkness that Jesus struggled with in the Garden of Gethsemane—even unto death." Author Margaret Silf explains it this way:

> We can't share in the consecration that was first enacted at the Last Supper and is reenacted in every Eucharist unless we are willing to become part of that sacrifice. Jesus draws us into His own consecration in order to consecrate

us for His service. Consecration is always a community matter.... Like the Eucharistic bread, we are consecrated in order to be broken and given to others. Like the Eucharistic wine, we are consecrated in order to be poured out for others. (*Inner Compass*, 168)

The bottom line is redemption, not just within the confines of our own story, but for our friends and family, for everyone we carry personally in our prayer.

"Our sharing of the Lord's Passion opens up a whole new freedom within us," Silf says, "which in turn becomes the source of an energy that is potentially the very energy of resurrection" (*Inner Compass*, 167, 168).

This is the real meaning of the Mass. It is the covenant feast of God's people. It is a wedding feast in which Christ, the Bridegroom, consummates the marriage with His Bride, the Church, in a union of intimate belonging. And it is through our union with Christ that we are made new, resurrected, transformed, and made whole—and holy.

## Anamnesis

The *Institution Narrative* ends with Jesus' request, "Do this in memory of me." The Church responds with the *anamnesis* (Greek for "calling to mind"), a prayer of remembrance (*amnesia*, on the other hand, means loss of memory). When the priest, in the name of the faithful, imitates the words and actions of Jesus at the Last Supper, he recalls Christ's death: "As often as you eat this bread and drink the cup, you proclaim the Lord's death until he comes" (1 Cor 26). Jesus asked the Twelve to imitate His actions at the Last Supper to bring back His presence to the celebrating community.

Usually, the words "memorial" or "remembrance" suggest that the person or deed commemorated is past and absent. *Anamnesis* signifies exactly the opposite: it is an objective reality, in and by which the person or event commemorated is actually made present, is brought into the realm of the here and now.

In this sense, the entire Mass is an *anamnesis*, because it is a memorial and a re-presentation of the passion, death, resurrection and ascension of Jesus Christ. The *memorial acclamation*, which the

Church now invites us to proclaim, sums up this central "mystery of faith," enabling the community to celebrate its victory in the resurrection of Christ. Like the Jewish people who, when they retell the story of their deliverance from bondage, relive their liberation every time they celebrate Passover, so do Catholic Christians actually take part in Christ's saving acts in the Mass. The past is made present, enabling us to enter into the Paschal Mystery—the dying and rising of Jesus; we acknowledge the actual, real presence of Jesus in a victorious acclamation of our faith. By this living memorial, we participate *now* in the wondrous reality of our Redemption, drawing its power into our lives.

## EXPLANATION

Following the words of consecration, the celebrant says or sings the *memorial acclamation*: "Let us proclaim the mystery of faith," to which the people respond in one of four ways, the most oft-repeated and popular being: "Christ has died, Christ is risen, Christ will come again." Or the celebrant may choose to lead the faithful in one of the following verses:

*Dying you destroyed our death,*
*rising you restored our life.*
*Lord Jesus, come in glory.*

*When we eat this bread and drink this cup,*
*We proclaim your death, Lord Jesus,*
*until you come in glory.*

*Lord, by your cross and resurrection*
*you have set us free.*
*You are the Savior of the world.*

While the role of the priest is to speak the words of Christ in the *Institution Narrative*, the people now participate in the Eucharistic Prayer by singing or saying these acclamations. The actual words date back to the ancient Roman Canon when they were part of the consecration of the wine. Now, they follow it.

For centuries, the faithful remained silent during the entire *Eucharistic Prayer.* The bishops at Vatican II changed that, giving the laity an opportunity to add their voices to the *Eucharistic Prayer* by proclaiming their belief in the paschal mystery—in the mystery of Christ dying, rising and present now among His people. It is really an invitation for the community to exercise their royal priesthood conferred on them at baptism, by expressing their faith in their Risen Lord, present and active in the Eucharistic Liturgy.

Just after the *Memorial Acclamation,* the priest extends his hands and continues the prayer of remembrance:

> *Father, calling to mind the death your Son endured for*
> *our salvation, his glorious resurrection and ascension into*
> *heaven, and ready to greet him when he comes again,*
> *we offer you in thanksgiving this holy and living sacrifice.*

Each Eucharistic Prayer has a different *anamnesis.* When Jesus said those words to the Apostles, "Do this in memory of Me" (*eis ten emen anamnesin*) (Lk 22:19), He was not only asking them to remember Him, but He was also teaching them to imitate His actions which, when repeated, would continue His Sacrifice. This we do in the Mass, the liturgical celebration by which the apostles and their successors memorialize Christ's Passion, resurrection and the glorious return of our Lord and Savior, Jesus Christ.

At this moment in the Mass, we recall to God the sacrifice of Christ, so that its benefits may be made available to the faithful here and now. We remember (subjectively) the whole work of redemption—Christ's sacrifice on the Cross and His resurrection and ascension—which becomes present (objectively) on the altar. In other words, we are standing at the foot of the Cross on Calvary, and we are witnessing the empty tomb on Easter Sunday. We also look forward to Christ's future coming in glory.

The commemoration of Christ's life and death in the Eucharistic Liturgy is a sacramental and objective reality—connected to the offering of bread and wine—and through which the benefits of Christ's sacrifice will be received in Holy Communion. The Mass is an invitation to enter into the Paschal Mystery by joining Jesus in offering His sacrifice to the Father— while also experiencing His Risen Presence. As one theologian noted, "Christ's love which led him to the cross, to the grave and to resurrection, is reality *now,* just as it happened in the historical uniqueness of the event in Jerusalem within the historicity of this world" (Michael Kunzler, *The Church's Liturgy,* 229).

The Jews' Passover/James Tissot

*In this manner you shall eat it: your loins girded, your sandals on your feet, and your staff in your hand; and you shall eat it in haste. It is the Lord's Passover.*

*—Ex 12:11*

# HISTORY

What Jesus was asking the apostles to do—to say prayers of blessing over the bread and wine—was already practiced by the Jews at their religious meals. In the Old Testament, God asked the Chosen People to remember their deliverance from their bondage to the Egyptians by celebrating a Passover dinner in which they would sacrifice and eat the paschal lamb. God told Moses and Aaron that, on that same night, He would go through the land of Egypt and kill the firstborn and the animals. He would pass over the houses where they had marked the doorposts with the blood of the lamb. Then He asked them to observe a memorial feast to the Lord, as a perpetual institution for all generations of God's people (see Ex 12:12-14). The Jewish people, to this day, faithfully observe the Passover dinner in which they celebrate how God freed them from the clutches of the Pharaoh and led them to a new life of freedom. To the Jews, the remembrance of past events actually made them present. At each memorial celebration, they relived their deliverance as if it was happening in the present moment.

What is different about the Last Supper, says noted theologian Fr. Clifford Howell, S.J., is that Jesus changed the *meaning* of their remembering. Whereas formerly they celebrated the memory of

God's liberation of the Chosen People, from now on their ritual would memorialize what God had done for the new chosen people—the Church. It is no longer about deliverance from the slavery of the Egyptians; it is now about redemption from sin and death through the Blood of Christ. "And whereas what had been shared in the past had been bread and wine," says Father Howell, "in the future what would be shared would be His own body and blood." Father Howell adds: "the important point to remember is the 'this' which Our Lord said, was to be done in memory of *Him*; so 'this' is the very heart of the Mass" *(Mean What You Say,* 49). He is speaking of the Eucharistic Prayer—in which we relive and celebrate our salvation story—our sharing in the death and resurrection of Christ.

The *anamnesis* is one of the most ancient parts of the liturgy, probably dating to apostolic times. We find it in every extant Eucharistic Prayer, including the Canons of Sts. Hippolytus and Ambrose. It is always associated with the words Our Lord said at the Last Supper. The *anamnesis* in the *Apostolic Tradition* of Hippolytus reads as follows:

> . . . *When you do this,*
> *do this in memory of me.*
>
> *We commemorate, then, your death*
> *and your resurrection,*
> *We offer you bread and wine,*
> *We give you thanks for finding us worthy*
> *to stand before you and serve you.*

## REFLECTION

My husband gave a magnificent eulogy for my dad. He almost brought him back to life by recounting a few of the stories that my dad loved to tell. He was an excellent raconteur, Tommy said, and no one laughed louder at the punch lines than he did!

I will retell one of the stories because I was a part of it. It was a frigid snowy Christmas day in the late fifties. I was fifteen and thrilled that my dad often sought my company. (Usually he asked me to accompany him as a co-pilot to fly somewhere in his single engine Cessna. One day, we flew to Bangor, Maine, where he had played baseball as a rookie. It brought back so many memories that he recounted over lunch).

Carl Schurz Park, 2005, New York City/Rich McHugh

But on this snowy Christmas day, we just went out for a walk together. We walked two blocks to the East River, to Carl Schurz Park, where the mayor of New York had his home. There was a big grassy area that was fenced off right in the middle of the park. It was covered with snow, but that didn't deter a bunch of neighborhood kids from a rough and tumble game of touch football. My dad lit a cigarette and leaned on the fence to watch. He started to coach them, which they appreciated, and before long, they came over to talk.

My dad had an audience; and for the next hour he regaled these kids with stories of Babe Ruth and Lou Gehrig, both of whom had been his friends. Lou Gehrig and dad were classmates at the High School of Commerce in New York City. He reminisced about the time in 1920 when they took the train to Chicago (President Herbert Hoover was on the train) to play in the national high school championships. Gehrig hit a grand slam out of Wrigley Field to win the game and the series.

Dad had met Babe Ruth on a ball field somewhere (my dad had somewhat of a baseball career, was drafted by the Cincinnati Reds, and then quit after three months because they didn't play him). He befriended "the Babe," and he and my mom ended up socializing with this larger-than-life hero and his wife.

The neighborhood kids were *fascinated* and didn't want my dad to leave. His stories brought these heroes and their experiences to life, and made these kids feel as if they had been a part of the story. They showed their enthusiasm and appreciation with loud exclamations, saying, "No Way!" while giving each other high-fives.

My dad told them how they, too, could be heroes; how they could make a success of their lives if they applied themselves in school, worked hard, made intelligent decisions and obeyed their parents. It was now dark. My dad invited all of them to our apartment for turkey sandwiches. They accepted immediately, phoned their mothers (at my dad's request), ate heartily, and listened to my mother play Chopin for them.

The kids never forgot this encounter. It probably changed their lives. Over the years, they kept in touch with my dad, reporting on how they were doing in life. One boy later brought his wife and child back to meet the man who had been so generous and kind that Christmas day.

What my dad did for these kids was to bring them back to the days of Ruth and Gehrig, so that they actually felt a part of the scene. History came to life for them, making them more alive and grateful for the experience. Perhaps they would become heroes in their own world, because of their personal encounter with greatness.

The Church invites us to experience even more during the *Eucharistic Prayer,* when we fulfill the command of Our Lord and celebrate a *living* memorial of His death, resurrection and ascension in the *anamnesis.* In this way, we participate *now* in the wondrous reality of our Redemption, drawing its power into our lives.

## *Offering*

Following the *anamnesis,* and very closely related to it, is the prayer of *offering.* It is another part of the Eucharistic Prayer in which the celebrant, in the name of all, offers God the sacrifice of His Son, then asks that He accept it. The Church defines its purpose:

> In this very memorial, the Church—and in particular the Church here and now gathered—offers in the Holy Spirit the spotless Victim to the Father. The Church's intention, however, is that the faithful not only offer this spotless Victim but also learn to offer themselves, and so day by day to be consummated, through Christ the Mediator, into unity with God and with each other, so that at last God may be all in all. (*General Instruction of the Roman Missal,* 79)

This prayer of *offering* which follows the *Consecration* is the essential act of offering in the Mass; it is through this prayer that the Church makes Christ's offering its own.

While the *offering* is really one prayer, in Eucharistic Prayer I, it is divided into three parts. (The prayer of *offering* in Eucharistic Prayers II, III and IV is shorter and includes an *epiclesis,* an invocation of the Holy Spirit on the assembly). In the first part of the prayer, we recall the offering of Christ's Sacrifice which has sacramentally taken place on the altar; in the second, we mention examples of Old Testament figures

Fr. Patrick Greenough, OFM Conv.

whose sacrifice foreshadowed Christ's; and finally, we ask God's holy angel to carry our Sacrifice to God's altar in heaven.

In the first prayer, we call to mind Christ's Passion, but we also reflect on His Resurrection and Ascension. The priest, in the name of the faithful, proclaims that we (the Church) offer "this life-giving bread, this saving cup" (Eucharistic Prayer II), or, "this holy and living sacrifice" (Eucharistic Prayer III).

With hands extended, the priest says:

*In memory of his death and resurrection,*
*we offer you, Father, this life-giving bread,*
*this saving cup.*
*We thank you for counting us worthy*
*to stand in your presence and serve you.*
*May all of us who share in the body and blood of Christ*
*Be brought together in unity by the Holy Spirit.*
(Eucharistic Prayer II)

Each Eucharistic Prayer has a unique prayer of *offering.* Only in Eucharistic Prayer I does the celebrant include the names of Abel, Abraham and Melchisedek, Old Testament types who were figures of Christ. Our concern is that God will "look with favor on these offerings" and accept our Sacrifice as He did theirs. We know that God will accept the Sacrifice of His Son; but insofar as we are associated with the offering, we want to be sure that our intentions are as pure as those of Abel, Abraham and Melchisedech, so that it will be pleasing to God. This, no doubt, is the meaning behind the instruction cited above, that "the faithful not only offer this spotless Victim, but also learn to offer themselves . . ." Theology professor Michael Kunzler explains:

> The Church enters into Christ's movement of offering, in which he raised human nature to the Father's glory, by presenting to the Father his unique sacrifice of the cross, now an actual presence in the liturgical celebration, and so through her Head arrives at "an ever more perfect union with God and with each other, so that finally God may be all in all." (*General Instruction*, 55) (*The Church's Liturgy*, 229)

## HISTORY

The Church holds up three examples from sacred history as models of selfless giving—of sanctity. Abel, a shepherd, offered the first fruits of his flock; Abraham offered a sacrifice of faith and obedience in willingly being ready to sacrifice his only son to God, and Melchisedech offered a sacrifice in the form of bread and  wine in thanksgiving for Abraham's military victory. Melchisidech was an ancient priest and king of Salem (Jerusalem) (Gn 14:18-20), who offered Abraham a share in bread and wine as a sacrifice of thanks, blessing him as Christ blesses us in the Eucharist.

But it is not so much what they offered, as the spirit in which they offered it. Their sacrifice represented the gift of *themselves*. The Church now asks us to do the same, to give our all to Christ, to become "a living sacrifice, holy and pleasing to God" (Rom 12:1). We pray that our offering may be as worthy as

Abraham/Louis S. Glanzman

theirs, pleasing to God and, therefore, accepted by Him.

In the context of our Eucharistic celebration, one theologian explains this act of offering as an "inner reshaping of our lives . . . the inner change of the participants that must follow the change of the bread and wine" (Adolf Adam, *The Eucharistic Celebration*, 87). This conversion happens, Adam says, by:

> Submitting to God's will without reservation; growing in love of God and of neighbor; walking the way of the cross in our own lives and offering up this life under the cross not only for the salvation of our own souls but also for the temporal and eternal welfare of all. All this is part of being conformed to Christ's redeeming offering of himself. (87)

And so we pray:

> *Look with favor on these offerings and accept them as you once accepted the gifts of your servant Abel, the sacrifice of Abraham, our father in faith and the bread and wine offered by your priest Melchisedech.*

In the third prayer, we ask God's angel to take this sacrifice to His altar in heaven: *Almighty God, we pray that your angel may take this sacrifice to your altar in heaven.*

Our earthly Mass is linked with the liturgy celebrated in heaven. There, the angel offers incense along with the prayers of the saints on the golden altar before the throne of God (Rev 8:3,4). St. Thomas Aquinas notes that we ask that the angel may bear to the altar of heaven, not the body of Christ, which abides there continually, but the act of offering which we make on our earthly altar (A. Croegart, *The Mass, a Litugical Commentary*, 236, 237). We pray that the gifts that we are offering, our own desires and prayers, be united to Christ's sacrifice and be carried up to heaven.

We don't really know who the angel is. Suggestions have included everyone from Jesus Himself, to the Holy Spirit, to the angel who guards the church or altar, or the priest's guardian angel. Others think it might be St. Michael, the great defender of the Church and protector of the Blessed Sacrament.

## Reflection

At a Jesuit retreat house in the hills of the Frascati wine region near Rome, Fr. Joseph Champlin was directing a group of seminarian retreatants. One evening they gathered for informal prayer and reflection. Following the reading of a Scripture passage, some of the students placed objects on the table symbolizing special experiences of the day. Each presenter said a spontaneous prayer to the Father explaining the significance of the gift being offered:

> A pair of glasses that helped me see the beauty of your creation in this gorgeous spot. An apple, which symbolizes all the good things of nature, you have given to me. A prayer book that has been my constant aid and companion in talking with you today. A pillow representing the great sleep I had today made possible because of the deep peace and contentment I found here. (*The New Yet Old Mass*, 64)

The objects the seminarians offered to the Lord in prayer represented a part of *themselves*.

We have the same opportunity as the seminarians: to offer *ourselves* to the Father through Christ. This is where all things come together, where our life finds meaning and hope, where our past, present and future all merge into one giant heartfelt prayer of *thanksgiving*. This is the heart of Eucharist. To join ourselves to Christ's sacrifice in such a way, says the *Catechism*, "the lives of the faithful, their praise, sufferings, prayer and work, are united with those of Christ and with his total offering, and so acquire a new value" (1368).

We are at the meeting point between heaven and earth, command central, where we unite ourselves to Our Lord, asking Him to carry us and all those we love to the Father on the wings of grace. During the *Offering* at Mass, we have the extraordinary privilege of praying for the redemption and consecration of the entire world.

One who has captured the essence of this spiritual reality in prose is Bishop Vincent Nichols, author of *The Gift of the Mass*, who I cited in the *Opening Prayer*. He is a Bishop in North London in the

Archdiocese of Westminster, and was previously General Secretary of the Bishops' Conference of England and Wales. In this treasured little volume on the Mass, Bishop Nichols offers us food for thought and prayer:

> When we lift up again the Body and Blood of Christ, be it in the smallest chapel or greatest cathedral, we lift up all human striving, all humanity's attempts to "get it right." Our efforts at human loving, at good government, at industrial or academic excellence, all are included. And in that moment, in our total incorporation into Christ, all finds its fulfillment. In him it is achieved, accomplished. In us it is, as yet, still a promise. (87)

## Intercessions

We might wonder why we are again saying intercessory prayers when we already said the *Prayer of the Faithful* that concluded the *Liturgy of the Word*. In a broad sense, the entire Mass is a prayer of intercession, a memorial of the Paschal Mystery, through which Jesus leads us to the Father through His Passion, death, resurrection and ascension. He is a bridge, says Pope Benedict XVI, who takes us to the Father. "He has opened a way that we ourselves could not have pioneered," he writes, "because we are not able to build a bridge to God." Jesus Christ "became that bridge," says the pope, who challenges us "to allow ourselves to be taken up into His being for all people, to let ourselves be embraced by His opened arms, which draw us to Himself" (*The Spirit of the Liturgy*, 59).

When we celebrate Mass and allow ourselves to be taken up into His being for all people, we are praying in intercession. Imagine the Cross as a bridge. When we unite ourselves to Christ on the Cross, we step onto that bridge and, if we choose, we can bring the whole world with us.

Where does the bridge lead us? To the other side of life—life eternal—into the presence of almighty God our Father in heaven.

## EXPLANATION

This segment of the Eucharistic Prayer the Church calls *Intercessions*, another form of memorial in which we pray for all of humanity, both the living and the dead. It is important to realize that Mass is celebrated in communion with the whole Church, both living and dead—a communion whose bonds transcend our earthly life. We present a list of names to God, asking that the people we pray for benefit from the fruits of this celebration, a prayer that is the oldest form of intercession.

In the *Intercessions,* the celebrant remembers all the members of the Church on earth (Church Militant), the suffering souls in purgatory (Church Suffering) and the saints in heaven (Church Triumphant). In that way it is unlike the other prayer of intercession of the Mass, the *Prayer of the Faithful,* in which we pray for the specific and temporal needs of the Church.

The placement and wording of the *Intercessions* varies slightly in each Eucharistic Prayer. In Eucharistic Prayer I, which comes to us from the original Roman Canon of the early Church, we intercede for the living before the *Institution Narrative* and for the dead afterward. In Eucharistic Prayers II, III and IV, both the commemoration of the living and the dead follows the *Instititution Narrative.*

According to Enrico Mazza, the *Intercessions* are structured somewhat like a pyramid, at the base of which is a prayer asking the Father to watch over and guide His holy Catholic Church; then we pray by name for our Pope, for all the bishops and clergy, and "for all who hold and teach the catholic faith that comes to us from the apostles" (*Sacramentary*, 542). The theme of the *Intercessions* is the Church and redemption. Mazza writes that "God is being asked to grant the Church the salvation brought by Jesus" (*The Celebration of the Eucharist,* 294). We are asking Him for unification and entrance into the kingdom, a prayer as old as the Church itself, found in the *Didache* that was written around the same time as the four Gospels: "Bring your Church together from the ends of the earth into your kingdom" (*Didache,* 9.4).

Next comes one of my favorite moments in the Mass: an opportunity to pray for those special people in our life who need prayers. I appreciate the moment of silence our pastor gives us to recall their names. He then asks God to remember the celebrating community.

In Eucharistic Prayer I, these commemorative prayers lead into the *Institution Narrative*, after which the celebrant prays for the dead: "Remember, Lord, those who have died and have gone before us marked with the (baptismal) sign of faith, especially those for whom we now pray, N. and N." Although it is not prescribed in the rubrics, I am always grateful when our pastor again pauses long enough for us to reflect on who have died and who might need our prayers. My list is already made up. It includes my mother and father, my in-laws, my Aunt Helen, Gertrude (the nanny who was like a mother to me), Fr. Anselm Romb, OFM. Conv., and about six or seven other close friends, priests and relatives to whom I was especially close. If it happens to be a birthday or anniversary of one of these special people, my prayer takes on an emotional intensity because I feel very connected to that person. I also pray for people who have just died and who have no one to pray for them. I once read that the Lord told St. Gertrude that during Mass she could ask to have a personal visit with a deceased relative or friend. That always stuck with me, so that I actually look forward to these intercessory prayers, both for the living and the dead.

> *A comforting thought: in the Eucharist we not only pray for separated loved ones, living and deceased, but we are united with them in the Lord's body and blood.*
> —Fr. Joseph Champlin
> *The New Yet Old Mass*

Following the commemoration of the dead is a prayer in which we ask for "some share in the fellowship of your apostles and martyrs." At the top of the list is John the Baptist, followed by Stephen, Matthias, Barnabas, and other early men and women martyrs. They are the real spiritual heroes and heroines of our faith, who gave their all to Christ, physically, emotionally and spiritually. "Fellowship with the saints!" says the late author and theologian Fr. John T. McMahon, "is the greatest favor we can ask." While we really don't deserve their company, he urges us to pray to them because "those near the King have the King's ear, and they can ask for much" (*Live the Mass*, 184).

I think they especially "have His ear" on their feast days. When I go to Communion on the feast of a saint whom I love, I ask to be

Defenders of the Eucharist/Peter Paul Rubens

with them for a few minutes, so that I can bask in their closeness to the Lord. If I have a special prayer request, I give it to them and ask that they intercede with Jesus for me. If my dad said it once, he said it a hundred times: "In order to get ahead in life, it's not so much a matter of what you know as who you know." It's all about connections and networking. If we put this in a spiritual context, we have it made! I truly believe that the saints will do everything in their supernatural power to help us get ahead in the spiritual life by interceding for us and by leading us closer to Christ.

## HISTORY

The Eucharistic Prayer is modeled in part on the Jewish *Berakah,* prayers of praise and thanksgiving which were part of every Jewish meal. The father of the family, or the leader of the community, said prayers first over the bread, and later over the wine, in which he blessed or praised God. Toward the end of the meal over a cup of wine he asked God to have mercy on the people of Israel, to send the Messiah and restore the house of David. At some early point in the Christian liturgy, prayers of petition and intercession for the dead were added to this formula, thus making the *Intercessions* a permanent part of the liturgical tradition. While they are not part of the oldest Eucharistic Prayer, written by St. Hippolytus (which today is Eucharistic Prayer II), the intercessions found their way into the liturgy by the time of Innocent I (416), who testified that "the 'offerings' were 'recommended to God' by the prayer of the priest" (A.G. Martimort, *The Church at Prayer,*

*The Eucharist*, 149).

These "offerings" were known as *diptychs,* a name derived from a hinged board. On the two wings of the board were names of the living, and sometime later the deceased, people for whom the prayers of the Church were offered to God during the what used to be called the *Offertory* at the beginning of Mass. At first, around the middle of the third century, the names of those who had brought an offering of bread for the Eucharist were read by a deacon. Sometime later, names of the deceased were added, followed by people who were alive but not necessarily present at the Eucharist. Finally, saints and martyrs were added to the lists, singled out from the rest of the departed, to thank them for their sacrifice. The reading of the names became so lengthy that they divided them by mentioning the deceased before the Consecration, and the living after it.

The Church Fathers occasionally make mention of these commemorations. St. John Chrysostom recognizes that the practice of remembering the dead during the Eucharistic Liturgy is of apostolic institution: "Not in vain did the Apostles decree that during the awful mysteries a commemoration should be made of the departed." It is possible that the *Intercessions* go that far back, at least according to a fourth century papyrus fragment attributed to the anaphora of St. Mark:

> 1. Give peace to the souls of the deceased, 2. Remember those [for whom] we keep a memorial on this day, 3. And those whose names we speak and whose names we do not speak, 4. [Above all] our very faithful fathers and bishops everywhere, 5. And permit us to take part and lot, 6. With [the assembly] of the holy prophets, apostles and martyrs. (Josef Jungmann, *The Mass of the Roman Rite,* 449)

St. Augustine comments on the *Intercessions*:

> The whole church observes the tradition of the Fathers, according to which prayers are offered for those who have died in the communion of the Body and Blood of Christ, at the moment when their names are commemorated during the sacrifice, and the sacrifice itself is offered in their behalf.

St. Augustine surely must have offered prayers of intercession for his own mother, St. Monica, who on her deathbed requested that Augustine and his brother: "Lay this body wherever it may be. Let no care of it disturb you: this only I ask of you that you should remember me at the altar of the Lord wherever you may be" (F.J. Sheed, *Confessions*, Book 9, 11).

It was a custom in the Roman Church until about the tenth century to commemorate the dead only at daily Mass, whereas the names of the living were remembered on Sundays and Feasts. At first, notes Father Jungmann, the Church mentioned by name only those who remained in communion with her, who were "marked with the sign of faith." But then, he says, "the circle widened" to include "all who are waiting their final purification, since there is none among them who could have attained his salvation except 'in Christo'" (*The Mass of the Roman Rite*, 444).

## REFLECTION

The saints believed in the Mass as the most powerful intercessory prayer on earth. They understood that it is not the strength of their pleadings, but instead Christ's, which makes this prayer powerful. The greatest gift God gives us is the opportunity to unite ourselves and our intentions to His sacrifice, which is one of infinite reparation, thereby empowering us to empty purgatory and open the gates of heaven for our deceased loved ones. "When we want to deliver from purgatory a soul dear to us," said St. John Vianney, "let us offer to God, through the Holy Sacrifice, His Beloved Son with all the merits of His death and Passion. He will not be able to refuse us anything." This holy priest spoke from personal experience. He told his parishioners how he prayed for the repose of the soul of a good friend of his who had died:

> One day God let him know that his friend was suffering in purgatory. So the Cure offered Mass for him. During the Consecration, he held up the host and said: "Holy Eternal Father, let us make an exchange. You hold the soul of my friend who is in purgatory, and I hold the Body of Your Son in my hands. Well, good and merciful Father, deliver

my friend, and I offer you your Son with all the merits of His death and Passion." The request was answered. In fact, at the moment of the elevation, he saw the soul of his friend, shining in glory, rising to heaven; God had accepted the deal. (Sister Emmanuel of Medjugorge, *The Amazing Secrets of the Souls in Purgatory*, 18, 19)

Stories like this abound. Another great saint and Doctor of the Church is St. Teresa of Avila, who often saw Christ with her bodily eyes during Mass. She shares experiences of seeing the souls of her spiritual daughters, and those of others, rising from the ground and going up to heaven while Mass was offered for them:

Once I was in a college of the Company of Jesus (Jesuits). . . . On that night a brother of that house of the Company had died (this was Alonso de Henao, who had come from the Jesuit College at Alcala and died on April 11, 1557); and, while I was commending him to God as well as I was able, and hearing a Mass which was being said for him by another Father of the Company, I became deeply recollected and saw him ascending to Heaven in great glory, and the Lord ascending with him. I understood that it was by a special favor that His Majesty bore him company. (E. Allison Peers, *The Autobiography of St. Teresa of Avila*, 374)

St. Gregory the Great praised the sacrifice of the Mass for the great benefit it brings to souls both living and deceased. In his *Dialogues*, Gregory related a story about one of his monks, Justus, who broke his vow of poverty by hoarding three gold pieces before he died. Although he died repentant, the abbot ordered that Mass be offered for thirty days for the repose of his soul. We have St. Gregory's own testimony that when the last Mass was offered, the dead man's soul appeared to his natural brother, assuring him that he had been in torment but was now released. Gregory's teaching on the value of the Mass in releasing souls from purgatory is now a tradition in the Church known as "Gregorian Masses for the Dead."

Although we do not know to what degree the prayer of the Mass brings refreshment to any particular soul in purgatory, theologian Monsignor Chevrot encourages us, saying: "It is enough for us to

St. Gregory the Great/Rutilio Manetti

know that He who applies its fruits to them is Infinite Mercy. Jesus will doubtless take into consideration the merits acquired by the dead while they were on earth, but he will no less take into account the faith and dispositions of the living who now offer Jesus's Sacrifice to Him on their behalf." He concludes these thoughts with an admonition to "pray confidently at this moment which unites you to your dear departed" (*Our Mass Explained*, 181).

## *Final Doxology*

Even an untutored ear recognizes the ending of a classical symphony by the repetition of the dominant chords of the last movement, known as the *coda*, which marks the real finality of the piece. So, too, in the Mass: the final chord of the *Eucharistic Prayer* resounds with a burst of glorious praise to God Almighty—Father, Son and Holy Spirit. Known as the *Doxology* (from *doxa,* praise and *logos,* word or utterance), it is a short verse giving glory, praise and honor to the Father through the Son in the unity of the Holy Spirit. The Church praises God the Father *through* His Son, who is our Mediator and High Priest, *with* Christ who invites every member of His Church to join with Him in praising His Father, and *in* Christ, the Vine, who sustains every branch of His Mystical Body with the spiritual sap of sanctifying grace in Communion.

This prayer is the high point and conclusion of the *sacrificial* part of the Mass, when we "with confidence draw near to the throne of grace, that we may receive mercy and find grace to help in time of need" (Heb 4:16). In this way—by this complete offering of humanity redeemed in Christ—"all honor and glory" is given to the Father, in the unity of the Holy Spirit.

## EXPLANATION

Just before pronouncing the *doxology,* the celebrant recites a short prayer, saying, "Through him you give us all these gifts. You fill them with life and goodness, you bless them and make them holy" (*Sacramentary*, 547). This prayer is taken from Eucharistic Prayer I and has very ancient roots. It originally referred to the variety of gifts the people brought to the altar to be blessed for the Sacrifice and/or donated to the poor. Fortunately, the Church has kept this prayer in the liturgy. In a few profound words, it sums up all that has gone before and proclaims Christ as the Gift, who gives us His Body and Blood in the Eucharist which sanctifies all of life. All the gifts of God are brought into the context of the one great Gift, the first fruits of the new creation, Jesus Christ. It is one more opportunity for the faithful to participate in the *Eucharistic Prayer* (through the words of the priest), by thanking the Father for the mediation of His Son who blesses and makes all of creation holy.

"The beauty of this prayer of blessing is now evident," writes Fr. Pius Parsch (1884-1954), a German theologian and author, who was ahead of his time in attempting to engage Catholics in a more active participation in the liturgy. He is recognized as the "originator" of the lay liturgical movement by which the faithful, after centuries of little to no participation in the liturgy, once again became involved in the Mass. He writes about the blessing of the gifts people offer at Mass:

> Around the Eucharistic Sacrifice has been gathered the whole city of God—the Church militant, triumphant and suffering—unto the building up and nurturing of the Mystical Body of Christ. And now nature too is sanctified in the Eucharist, and the gifts of nature, which Christ has chosen to be the mantle of His real presence, are taken to represent the whole of inanimate creation, which 'groans and travails until now' for the blessings of Redemption."
> (*The Liturgy of the Mass*, 253)

All the *Eucharistic Prayers* conclude with praise of the Trinity in the form of the *doxology.* Theologian Aime Georges Martimort writes that the restoration of the doxology in the *Eucharistic Prayer* is "one of the most important reforms of recent years." After a lapse of six centuries, Vatican II restored it to its original beauty and importance, and, says Father Martimort, "much must be made of it" (*The Eucharist,* 170).

The celebrant lifts the paten with the hosts and the chalice in a gesture of offering and says or sings: "Through him, with him, in him, in the unity of the Holy Spirit, all glory and honor is yours, almighty Father, for ever and ever." Christ is present and the community unites behind this miracle with a resounding "Amen"—a response in word or song by which the assembly declares its faith in the mystery we celebrate—that Jesus has died, is risen, will come again, and is truly present in the appearance of Bread and Wine on our altar.

When the priest says the *doxology*, he takes the paten with the consecrated Host and the chalice and lifts them both shoulder high in a "little elevation," which, until the Middle Ages, was the only elevation in the liturgy (the elevation during the Consecration was not introduced until the thirteenth century). If a deacon is assisting the celebrant, he holds the chalice during the *doxology* and the priest holds the paten with the Host. This elevation is deemed even more important than the "major" elevation at the Consecration because we—priest and people— are offering the Body and Blood of the Lord to God the Father. Fr.

Fr. Lawrence Hennessey saying the doxology.

Lucien Deiss gives a compelling explanation of the meaning of the *doxology:*

While saying the doxology, the priest lifts up the bread and wine in a gesture of offering. In this gesture are signified the history of the world and its ultimate destiny. All of creation is born in the heart of the Father, fruit of his love. All of creation is established in existence through Christ, "the firstborn of all creation" (Col 1:15). All of creation is indwelt by the Spirit who fills it with his love. Having become the body of Christ in the bread and wine, changed into Eucharist, that is, into thanksgiving and praise, creation now goes up to the Father. It is this movement of the universe toward the eternity of God that the gesture of the doxology signifies." (*The Mass*, 88, 89)

Imagine lifting up the universe to God the Father! It is a wondrous task in which we are privileged to share. If a deacon is present, both he and the celebrant continue to hold up the paten and chalice until the people say the concluding "Amen," often referred to as the "Great Amen." "Amen" is a Hebrew word which means "Yes, that is so," which the early Christians borrowed from their Jewish brethren to incorporate into their worship. Christ frequently used "Amen" (or "Amen, amen") for solemn emphasis, such as the time He spoke about His Real Presence in the Eucharist to the crowd of Jews who followed Him across the Sea of Galilee (see Jn 6:53).

Said (or sung) by the congregation, the faithful now have the honor of putting their stamp of approval on all that the celebrant said and did in the *Eucharistic Prayer* by saying *Amen*. This *Amen* is considered to be the most solemn in the whole liturgy of the Church. Why? Because in all of human history, there is no event of greater magnitude and importance than the Lord's death and resurrection, which we witness on our altar and confirm with our "Amen."

St. Augustine refers to the *Amen* as the congregation's signature under the prayer of the priest. This prayer is so important that the rubrics of the Missal state that the celebrant must wait for the people to say *"Amen"* before he replaces the paten and chalice on the altar. If we could pull back the curtain sixteen centuries and look in on a Christian assembly gathered for Eucharist, we would be put to shame by the way those congregations prayed. According to St. Jerome, our Christian ancestors said the *"Amen"* with such enthusiasm and gusto that it echoed like a clap of thunder through the great basilicas.

## HISTORY

Theologians conjecture that the prayer of blessing before the final *doxology* originated in the liturgies of the early Church as a blessing of the fruits of the earth. In the Roman Mass, the celebrant prayed: "It is ever through him [Christ] that all good gifts, created by you, O Lord, are by you sanctified, endowed with life, blessed and bestowed upon us." People brought all manner of gifts to be offered in their Eucharistic liturgies: bread and wine, but also oil, wax, wool, flowers, silver and even animals. The bread and wine was taken for the holy Sacrifice, while the remaining gifts were set aside on an offertory table for later distribution to the poor. Testimony from St. Hippolytus suggests that the blessing of the gifts following the *Eucharistic Prayer* is ancient: "If anyone still has gifts to offer, he may have them blessed now." Evidence from the pontificates of Sts. Leo and Gregory indicates that water, honey and milk (to be drunk by the neophytes) were blessed, as were beans, grapes and, on the Sunday after Easter, the lambs of St. Agnes (which were led around the church during the singing of the *Agnus Dei*). Today one custom remains: the blessing of the holy oils (for the anointing of the sick and for baptisms, holy orders and special consecrations) which takes place at this point in the Mass on Holy Thursday.

It wasn't until the end of the *Eucharistic Prayer* in the Roman Mass of the early Church that the people were shown the consecrated elements. Until then, it was difficult to observe what the priest was saying or doing; the priest silently said the prayer of *Consecration*. Breaking the Host (today this Fraction rite takes place later), he lifted up the Sacred Species and, in a gesture of offering (the "little elevation"), said the *doxology*. As he did so, he touched the Host to the rim of the heavy two-handled chalice, which was raised by a deacon. This rite, says theologian Fr. A. Croegart, "would seem to have signified that Christ's Eucharistic Body and Blood constitute *one* sacrificial offering (*The Mass, A Liturgical Commentary*, 249). This was the only elevation the people saw up until the twelfth century. It was then, and is now, a ceremonial act of praise and adoration to the triune God, which forms the solemn conclusion to the thanksgiving of the *Eucharistic Prayer*. "To come before God with the offerings was the high point of the ancient oblation ritual," notes Fr. Raymond Moloney, S.J., in his book on the Eucharistic Prayer. "Such are the riches of this moment," he adds, "that the ancient Irish liturgy loved to delay over it, so that this *doxology* was sung no less than three times over" (*Our Eucharistic Prayers in Worship, Preaching and Study*, 26).

There is ample testimony from Scripture and the Apostolic Fathers to show us how important this *Great Amen* was in the early Church. In words similar to our *doxology,* St. Paul wrote to the early Christians: "For from him and through him and to him are all things. To him be glory forever" (Rom 11:36); and, "to him be glory in the church and in Christ Jesus to all generations, forever and ever. Amen" (Eph 3:21). In the middle of the second century, St. Justin Martyr wrote: "When the prayer of thanksgiving is ended, all the people present give their assent with an Amen." He also said that the Amen of the congregation is a meaningful expression of the priesthood of the baptized as they unite themselves to the Eucharistic action (in Martimort, *The Eucharist*, 106). St. Ambrose instructed his catechumans:

> "You reply 'amen' that is to say, 'it is true'. O that your soul might confess the truth that your mouth proclaims! That the word that sounds on your lips, might express the holy affections of your heart!"

## REFLECTION

One summer I spent a week at Stella Maris Retreat House on the ocean in Elberon, New Jersey. I will never forget a talk I had with Sister Madeleine, a nun up in years who was riddled with multiple sclerosis, but whose joy was contagious. Leaning close to me as if to share a great secret, she said, "Joan, the whole bottom line is for us to know how much God loves us and gifts us. The spiritual life is about recognizing our gifts, the love that is in us, and spreading that love to others." She gave me a great gift that day, a new way of looking at the spiritual life.

Praise and thanksgiving is the heart and soul of our life as a Christian. God has given us the world and everything in it, all our gifts and talents, and His own divine presence in the Eucharist—none of which we deserve or have a right to. What else is there to do in the face of the absolute seriousness of God's love for us? He lavishes His goodness on us, most especially through the Mass, the means by which Jesus gives glory to the Father and saves us. The Eucharist is our life, our thanksgiving, summed up in the words of the *doxology*. Lifting up the Body and Blood of Our Lord, the priest says, *Through him, with him, in him, in the unity of the Holy Spirit, all glory and honor is yours, almighty Father, forever and ever, Amen.*

We lift up Jesus—and ourselves—to the Father in a gesture of thanksgiving, in which we proclaim God's praise and throw ourselves on His mercy. Giving thanks was at the heart of Jesus' relationship with His Father. When Andrew found the little boy with five loaves and two fishes and brought them to Jesus, St. Mark records that Jesus first gave thanks to His Father; only then did He give the food to the disciples to distribute to the people. His thanksgiving led to an immediate miracle that provided food enough to feed five thousand people (see Mark 6:41-44). Another time, before Jesus raised Lazarus from the dead, He first said, "Father, I thank you for hearing me" (Jn 11: 41); then he called Lazarus out of the tomb. When Jesus healed the ten lepers and only one of them came back to give

The Feeding of the Five Thousand/Ambrosius Fracken

thanks, He recognized the leper's words of praise and gratitude, saying, "Rise and go your way, your faith has made you well" (Lk 17:19).

Even though all ten lepers were healed physically, Jesus did something extra for the one who returned and gave thanks. When

Jesus said, "Your faith has made you well," the word He used in Greek is *sozo,* which means salvation of the soul as well as the body. Jesus offers a salvation that embraces the whole person. He didn't come just to save souls. He is concerned with the total person, which means both the soul and the body.

This, I think, is the bottom line of Sister Madeleine's message. When we praise and thank God for His gifts, our praise takes us out of ourselves and releases His healing graces. It allows God to wrap His arms around us and fill us with whatever it is we most need. The best setting for this to happen is during the Sacred Liturgy, where we most perfectly and completely give thanks to God.

Healing the leper at Capernaum/
James Tissot

One who witnessed God's miracles during Mass is the late Fr. Emiliano Tardiff, a Missionary of the Sacred Heart who worked in the Dominican Republic for thirty years.

He was skeptical about miracles until he was healed of tuberculosis through charismatic prayer. Speaking about people being healed during Mass, he writes,

> You cannot imagine the physical and inner healings that have been achieved by an abandonment accompanied by prayers of praise. The prayer that best expresses abandonment and faith is not that of petition, but of praise. When we praise, we always receive what we don't necessarily receive when we ask. Many people who have begged, prayed and implored for their recovery have finally obtained it when they abandoned themselves, unconditionally, into the hands of their merciful Father. (*Jesus Lives Today,* 118)

Over a thirty-year period, he witnessed spiritual conversions, physical and inner healings, and miracles of all kinds. Many of them happened during Mass. One of my favorite stories involves a priest whose bishop in the Cameroons invited him to go on one of Father Emiliano's retreats. The priest didn't want to go because "we are only going to hear about more miracles." The bishop assured him that the theme of the retreat wasn't on healing, but prayer. So the priest went to the retreat. On the third day, he stood up and said:

> The chronic arthritis in my hands was so bad that I couldn't even tie my shoelaces. At the same time I would like to make it clear that I didn't want to come to this retreat, as I feared that we were only going to hear about miracles. But in Mass yesterday, I felt a great heat in my hands. Glory be to God, I am perfectly healed. I can move my hands now.

Father Emiliano laughed, saying that the priest didn't want to hear about miracles, and now he couldn't stop talking about them and announcing the wonders of the Lord! Everyone laughed and praised God as the priest showed them how he could now move his hands. Father Emiliano sums all of this up, saying, "Our attitude must be that of unconditionally placing ourselves in the hands of a loving Father. He has a wonderful plan for each of us" (*Jesus Lives Today*, 67). There is no better place to put ourselves in God's hands and seek His plan for our lives than in the Sacred Liturgy.

Thanks be to God.

# *The Communion Rite*

## *The Lord's Prayer*

Our belief that Jesus was sent by His Father in order to save the world from sin and lead us to our eternal salvation is what drives our Catholic faith. He came for *everyone*, which is why the Church Jesus founded is *Catholic*, or universal. The Son of God came to show us that *His* Father is also *our* Father, Whom we dare to call by name. In a touching discourse at the Last Supper, Jesus warned His apostles that the ruler of this world had no power over Him; and once again, He professed His love for His Father, saying, "I do as the Father has commanded me, so that the world may know that I love the Father" (Jn 14:30).

In response to the disciples asking Jesus to teach them how to pray, Jesus taught them the *Our Father*, which, according to Biblical scholar Joachim Jeremias, is "one of the most holy treasures of the Church" (*The Lord's Prayer*, 5). Situated just after the *Eucharistic Prayer* and before *Communion*, it was Pope St. Gregory the Great who set the *Our Father* in this place of honor: over the Body and Blood of Christ.

For hundreds of years, the celebrant prayed or sang the *Our Father* alone, the congregation only joining him at the end saying, "Amen." It wasn't until Vatican II that both priest and people began to say or sing the *Our Father* together. Now the *Our Father* clearly introduces the *Communion Rite*.

While the presiding priest extends his arms outward as if to encompass the whole world, the community often joins hands to signify their oneness in the Eucharist—the sacrament of our unity. Like brothers and sisters who gather around the family dinner table, we stand before the Table of the Lord and sing to our Father. (It may also be recited aloud). The *Our Father,* known also as *The Lord's Prayer* and the *Pater Noster,* is the family prayer of the Church through which the meaning of the Mass comes into sharp focus: it is both a prayer and an offering of Christ to the Father—which we now make our own.

## EXPLANATION

The *Catechism* calls the *Our Father* the "fundamental Christian prayer" (2773), while St. Thomas Aquinas describes it as "the most perfect of prayers," because "in it we ask, not only for all the things we can rightly desire, but also in the sequence that they should be desired" (2763). It is the premier prayer of the Christian, first, because it was uttered from the lips of Christ Himself, and second, because He invites us to share His own intimate way of speaking to His *Abba* Father.

We find the *Our Father* in the Gospels of Matthew and Luke. It is made up of an address followed by petitions and some concluding words of praise to God (doxology). The first three requests ("Thou petitions") are directed to God: "Hallowed be thy name," "Thy kingdom come" and "Thy will be done on earth as it is in heaven." The rest ("we petitions"), revolve around our need and desire for daily bread and for forgiveness. In Matthew's Gospel, the *Our Father* is part of the Sermon on the Mount, following an instruction on prayer and introduced by the words of Jesus: "Pray then like this" (Mt 6:9). It is composed of an address and six petitions. Luke's Gospel varies ever so slightly, having an address and five petitions. Jesus "was praying at a certain place, and when he ceased, one of his disciples said to him, 'Lord, teach us to pray, as John taught his disciples'" (Lk 11:1).

We visited the place on the Mount of Olives that, according to the diary of Egeria, is considered the spot where Jesus taught His disciples the *Our Father*. A Carmelite convent stands over the ruins of the Church of the Eleona (Olives), which Constantine's mother, St. Helena (d. 330), commissioned to commemorate Christ's instruction of His disciples. It is built around a cave not far from the place of the Ascension. The walls of the cloister walk are decorated with tiled panels that illustrate the *Lord's Prayer* in seventy-two languages. It was so moving to hear our local guide recite the *Our Father* in its original Aramaic.

We recite Matthew's version of the *Our Father* in the Liturgy. The celebrant  invites us to pray, saying, *Let us pray with confidence to the Father in the words our Savior gave us.* Or, he may choose one of three other verses to prepare our hearts for prayer: "Jesus taught

Carmelite convent built over the ruins of the Church of the Eleona.

us to call God our Father, and so we have the courage to say," or, "Let us ask our Father to forgive our sins and to bring us to forgive those who sin against us," and finally, "Let us pray for the coming of the kingdom as Jesus taught us."

In the Old Testament, God is seldom referred to as "Father." People hardly dared to mention His name or to approach Him. Joachim Jeremias says that "no good Jew would dare address God as father." But Jesus changed all that; He called God *Abba*, a privileged, familial term (similar to our "daddy") which Jewish children used to address their fathers. "This term *abba*," Jeremias says, "contains the ultimate mystery of Christ's mission and His authority. He, to whom the Father had granted full knowledge of God, had the messianic prerogative of addressing Him with the familiar address of a child." But what is really astonishing, he says, is that,

> Jesus authorizes His disciples to repeat the word *abba* after Him. He gives them a share in His sonship and empowers them, as His disciples, to speak with their heavenly Father in just such a familiar, trusting way as a child would with his father. (*The Lord's Prayer*, 20)

Jesus goes so far as to say, notes Jeremias, that "It is this new childlike relationship which first opens the door to God's reign" (20). Simple trust and dependence on God is our path to conversion and eternal life: "Truly, I say to you, unless you turn and become like children, you will never enter the kingdom of heaven" (Mt 18:3).

One of the most endearing qualities of children is their readiness to forgive. Forgiveness is the centerpiece of the *Our Father*. It is also one of the measuring rods of our Christian discipleship. We are to forgive those we have wronged or who have wronged us not seven times, but "seventy times seven" (Mt 18:21), Jesus told Peter. We who have been forgiven much, must do the same and forgive our brother and sister from our heart (see Mt 18:35). The words "Forgive us our trespasses as we forgive those who trespass against us," address this issue. We are not only expected to extend forgiveness, but to admit our share of the problem or hurt and ask God to forgive us.

There is a story in *Witness to Hope* of a parish community that modeled this kind of reconciliation. They belonged to a Catholic church in the heart of Poland, near Warsaw. In 1984, their pastor, Fr. Jerzy Popieluszko, was kidnapped, beaten, thrown into the trunk of a car and murdered by a group of secret police. For ten days, Masses were said every hour while tens of thousands of people packed the streets and surrounding area. During Mass one day, his friend, Fr. Antonin Lewek, announced that Father Jerzy's body had been dredged from the Vistula. The priest urged the congregation to remember Christ weeping over the death of his friend, Lazarus, and not to lash back in anger. Then, Father Lewek recalled:

Fr. Jerzy Popieluszko

> Something very moving happened. Three times they repeated after the priests, "And forgive us our trespasses as we forgive those who trespass against us. And forgive us our trespasses as we forgive . . ." It was the Christian answer to the un-Christian deed of the murderers. (479, 480)

Forgiveness and healing go hand in hand. We have an extraordinary opportunity before we meet the Lord in *Communion*, to admit our faults and sins and to ask forgiveness for all those whom we have offended. This is a ritual that I look forward to, thanks to a priest who shared a personal experience of forgiveness with me during a visit to New Melleray Abbey in Dubuque, Iowa. He had had a misunderstanding with a good friend which was difficult to resolve. At Mass everyday during the *Our Father,* he offered his friend to the Lord, mentioning her by name. After about three months, they resolved their differences and reinstated their relationship. Thanks to this wise priest (he was celebrating the sixty-fifth anniversary of his ordination), I never say the *Our Father* without telling the Lord of someone I'm having a problem with and need to forgive. Then I bring that person to Communion with me and ask the Lord Jesus to bless him or her. I've witnessed some deep resentments melt like a snowman on a warm sunny day and bring healing to a very difficult relationship.

The Lord's Prayer/James Tissot

At the end of the *Our Father,* the celebrant extends his hands and elaborates on the last petition, "Deliver us from evil." He adds a prayer known as an *embolism* (from the Greek *embolisma,* piece of cloth added to a garment):

> *Deliver us, Lord, from every evil, and grant us peace in our day. In your mercy keep us free from sin and protect us from all anxiety as we wait in joyful hope for the coming of our Savior, Jesus Christ.*

It is the Eucharist that will deliver us from sin and from the power of evil—and bring us true peace. We confidently proclaim our belief in the power of God's divine presence to break into every corner of our darkened war-torn world, bringing His light and peace.

The *embolism* concludes with a *doxology,* a short prayer of praise to God: "For the kingdom, the power and the glory are yours, now and forever."

## HISTORY

The roots of the *Our Father* are sacred because it is the prayer of Jesus Himself which two of the Evangelists, namely Matthew (Mt 6:9-13) and Luke (Lk 11:2-4), recorded in their Gospels. Also referred to as the *Lord's Prayer,* a similar form is found in the *Didache,* written around the same time as the four Gospels, somewhere between 70 and 100 AD. In the *Didache* (in Greek, "didache" means "teaching"), the *Our Father* was recited before the Breaking of the Bread in the Eucharistic Liturgy; and Christians were instructed to recite the *Our Father* three times daily. St. Hippolytus (170-235) also advocated its use as part of the daily prayer of Christians. The Father of Western Monasticism, St. Benedict (c. 480–550), recited it aloud at morning and evening offices (Lauds and Vespers). Called the "prayer of believers," the newly baptized, or those seeking admittance to the Church, learned the Lord's Prayer by heart (they also had to learn the Creed). In the ancient Church, the Lord's Prayer was so revered that it was kept secret from outsiders; it was a privilege reserved for the baptized.

> *Let us try to realize that we have within us a palace of ineffable splendor, built entirely of gold and precious gems; a dwelling worthy, in a word, of the Master to Whom it belongs. Represent to yourself the truth that within this palace dwells the great King Who has, in His bounty, deigned to become your Father and that He is seated on a throne of inestimable value, namely, your heart.*
>
> —St. Teresa of Avila

The early Christians were amazed that they were allowed to speak to God personally and say, "Abba, Father." In the Old Testament, the Name of God was so sacred that the high priest was only allowed to utter it on the Day of Atonement. Benedictine monk Fr. Dom David Bird adds that God's name was treated with such awe, that when the high priest entered the Holy of Holies, he filled the sanctuary with incense smoke so that, if pronouncing the sacred Name provoked God to reveal Himself, he would have some kind of protection, because "no man can see God and live" (*The Royal Road to Joy, The Beatitudes and the Eucharist,* 217, 218).

It is no wonder then that the early Christians felt such joy for the privilege of saying *Our Father.* They were no longer servants or slaves of a harsh, demanding God, but beloved sons and daughters of a loving, compassionate Father who offered His children comfort and eternal salvation (see Gal 4:6, 7). Christ is our High Priest who prays to His Father for us and with us, allowing us the privilege of addressing God with His own sentiments and words: *Our Father, who art in heaven, hallowed be thy name.*

The writings of Church Fathers, notably St. Cyril of Jerusalem in the East, and St. Ambrose in the West, reveal that the *Our Father* was incorporated into the Eucharistic Liturgy around the middle of the fourth century. Early in the fifth century, St. Augustine says that "almost the whole world now concludes" the *Eucharistic Prayer* with the *Our Father.* Sts. John Chrysostom, Ambrose and Augustine all reflect on its privileged place in the heart of the liturgy—close to Communion. Augustine likens it to a purification or cleansing, a washing of our face before receiving Communion.

He explains why it is spoken before the reception of Christ's Body and Blood:

> If perchance, in consequence of human frailty, our thought seized on something indecent, if our tongue spoke something unjust, if our eye was turned to something unseemly, if our ear listened complacently to something unnecessary . . . it is blotted out by the Lord's Prayer in the passage: Forgive us our debts, so that we may approach in peace and so that we may not eat or drink what we receive unto judgment. (in Josef Jungmann, *The Mass of the Roman Rite,* 465)

On Easter Sunday, St. Augustine taught the newly baptized adults that when they gathered around the altar during the Eucharistic Liturgy and prayed the *Lord's Prayer*, all their sins would be washed away and forgiven. We can assume the same.

## REFLECTION

Soon after seeing the film *The Passion of the Christ* by Mel Gibson, I was extolling its virtues to my son, Danny, over the phone. He hadn't seen it yet and asked me what impacted me the most. "Jesus' relationship with His Father," came tumbling out of my mouth. My response, I could tell, was different from other reactions he had received. The movie stunned me into a fresh awareness of the intimate relationship between Jesus and His Father. I thought that the actor, Jim Caviesel, brilliantly portrayed Jesus' childlike dependence on His Father's will, especially in the opening scene in the Garden of Gethsemane and later on the Cross. Jesus' blind trust in His *abba* (daddy) Father oozed out of every drop of sweat, allowing us a glimpse of the depth of Christ's love for His Father—and for us. His humility and obedience touched me deeply. Christ endured an extraordinary amount of suffering for every soul on earth, so that we would know that *nothing* could separate us from God's love for us (see Rom 8: 38, 39). This, for me, was the theological underpinning on which the movie stood.

Author Scott Hahn tells a remarkable story about a father who modeled the love of our heavenly Father. An earthquake in Armenia in 1989 killed more than thirty thousand people in less than four minutes. A young father who had dropped off his son at school earlier that morning ran through the twisted streets, desperate to find his boy alive. Finally locating the school now turned to rubble, he began to dig. He dug for hours. He kept thinking about the promise he had given to his son so many times:

> "No matter what happens, Armand, I'll always be there." When others tried to discourage him from digging anymore, he kept on. Thirty-eight hours later he heard a muffled groan from under a piece of wallboard. When he pulled back the board, he shouted "ARMAND!" His little son cried out, "Papa . . ." then other voices joined his. They found fourteen of the thirty-three students still alive. Weak as he was, Armand tried to help dig until all his surviving classmates were saved. Then he turned to his friends and said, "See, I told you my father wouldn't forget us." "That's the kind of faith we need," concludes Scott Hahn, "because that's the kind of Father we have." (*A Father Who Keeps His Promises*, 13, 14)

This is the father Jesus describes in the parable of the Prodigal Son and the Father we address when we recite the *Our Father*. In this Gospel story, Jesus portrays a Father who welcomes home a son—who has brought shame upon himself and the family— by killing the fatted calf and having a dinner in his honor. It is hard for us to imagine a God who cares for us with such unconditional love, compassion and forgiveness.

This is the God Fr. Henri Nouwen hungered to find:

> Here is the God I want to believe in: a Father who, from the beginning of creation, has stretched out his arms in merciful blessing, never forcing himself on anyone, but always waiting; never letting his arms drop down in despair, but always hoping that his children will return so that he can speak words of love to them and let his tired arms rest on their shoulders. His only desire is to bless.
> (*The Return of the Prodigal Son*, 95, 96)

A chance encounter with a reproduction of Rembrandt's *The Return of the Prodigal Son* catapulted him on a long spiritual adventure in which he questioned, "How am I to find God?" His search led him to realize that *God was looking for him* and the question became, "How am I to let myself be found by Him?"

To let himself be found by God was a long and painful task, as those of us who have traveled the inner journey know. Why? Because most of us have spent the better part of our lives erecting barriers that keep out God's love. We simply can't believe that we are worthy of God's love because we think of ourselves as worthless and unimportant. Father Nouwen shares that his core spiritual struggle was against the demons of self-rejection, self-contempt and self-loathing. He admits that he got things backwards and thought of his low self-esteem as some kind of a virtue. By the grace of God, he began to realize:

The Return of the Prodigal Son/Rembrandt

> The real sin is to deny God's first love for me, to ignore my original goodness. Because without claiming that first love and that original goodness for myself, I lost touch with my true self and embark on the destructive search among the wrong people and in the wrong places for what can only be found in the house of my Father. (107)

Rembrandt's painting was the catalyst God used to help him remove the barriers that kept him from loving himself—and God. He was desperately searching for that inner place where he could be held as safely as the young man in the painting. To get there, Father Nouwen admits that he had to undergo a lot of inner pain, the cost of letting go of his defenses and addictive behaviors that stood in the way of his transformation. A series of emotional and physical crises compelled him to let go, and ultimately to find God's presence deep within himself, in his own inner sanctuary where God promises to dwell: "If a man loves me, he will keep my word, and my Father will love him, and we will come to him and make our home with him" (Jn 14:23). Father Nouwen admitted that while he had "not arrived," he had taken a few steps closer to welcoming God into the home of his own heart.

Perhaps the next time we say the *Our Father*, the examples of our Father's love for us in these stories will inspire us to dwell on each word and really pray it with every fiber of our being. No matter what kind of a human father we have or how we have looked upon the eternal Father until now, the Church gives us an opportunity in the Sacred Liturgy to begin a relationship with Him by acknowledging His presence deep within the inn of our own souls where He dwells as our divine Guest. Like the little boy in Armenia whose father found him in the rubble after the earthquake, or the prodigal son who fell into his father's welcoming arms, so will we experience the consoling, forgiving, all-consuming love our Father wants to lavish on us—His chosen and beloved children—when we invite Him into our hearts and lives.

## *The Rite of Peace*

The word for peace in the Old Testament stems from the traditional Hebrew salutation: *shalom*. It is a peace that comes from God's indwelling presence. Jesus' *shalom* is the gift of salvation that He promised His disciples. In His Last Supper discourse, Jesus encouraged His apostles to have faith and believe in the Spirit whom the Father would send in His name to remind them how to live truthful and loving lives—and to live peacefully in union with one another:

> *Peace I leave with you; my peace I give to you; not as the world gives do I give to you. Let not your hearts be troubled, neither let them be afraid* (Jn 14: 27).

Peace, then, is Christ's legacy to us—His gift—not earned but freely given to all generations of disciples. It begins in our own hearts, and it is fitting that during Mass, which is the very act by which Christ reconciled the world to Himself, we pass on the gift He has given us to others. Peace is the fruit of our union with God, a union we prepare for now in the *Rite of Peace* by *showing* our unity with one another through His Body, the Church.

### EXPLANATION

The *Rite of Peace* follows the *Our Father,* the prayer which we say as brothers and sisters in faith. Gathered as one around the Table of the Lord, we now acknowledge our oneness as members of God's family. We exchange the peace of Christ just before the Eucharist, because to be in communion with Christ is also to be in communion with one another. The Sacrament of Unity that unites us to Christ incorporates us into His Body, the Church.

Following the *Doxology*, the priest extends his hands and says aloud:

> *"Lord Jesus Christ, you said to your apostles:*
> *'I leave you peace, my peace I give you.'*
> *Look not to our sins, but on the faith of your Church,*

*and grant us the peace and unity of your kingdom
where you live for ever and ever. Amen."*

The people answer, "Amen." Then the celebrant extends peace
to the assembly, saying, "The peace of the Lord be with you always,"
to which they respond, "And also with you." Then the deacon or
celebrant may add: "Let us offer each other the sign of peace." The
celebrant may invite the people to exchange the *Sign of Peace* (or
omit it, because it is optional), but he may not transfer this rite to
another part of the Mass.

The tradition of the priest coming down from the altar and extending peace to the congregation comes from the early Church. While
it is done today in most parishes and appears to be a good custom,
some theorize that it makes the priest the sole provider of the peace,
which he then
extends to those
nearby in the
congregation,
who in turn share it with each other. Fr. Dennis Smolarski, S.J., author
of a "how to" book on good liturgy, echoes the thinking of the bishops
(*The Sign of Peace,* 1977) and cautions against this "trickle-down" cleri-
cal practice because, he says, the presiding priest has already greeted
everyone by means of the liturgical greeting: "The peace of the Lord
be with you always." Exceptions are in order for more personal situations such as weddings, funerals or ordinations, when he may want
to offer the sign of peace to a few of the faithful near the sanctuary,
but in general, Father Smolarski cites the official word of the Church
that the presiding priest remain in the sanctuary "so as not to disturb
the celebration" (*General Instruction of the Roman Missal,* 154). He
adds that when the presiding priest greets large numbers of people
on a regular basis, it tends to prolong the liturgy unreasonably and
"obscure the fact that *taking* and *blessing* should soon be followed by
*breaking* and *giving*" (*How Not to Say Mass,* 88, 89). This being said,
most of the priests celebrating Masses that I have attended choose to
extend peace to the parishioners closest to the sanctuary.

*Greet one another with a holy kiss* (Rom 16:16).
—St. Paul

# HISTORY

In the Old Testament, the kiss was significantly more important than it is today. The Jewish people commonly exchanged a kiss of peace when they greeted one another, or when they said good-bye to family and friends. They also used a kiss to venerate holy objects. For instance, it was customary to reverence the temple by kissing the threshold or doorpost. Pagans blew kisses to their idols and kissed their altars and their dinner tables. They knelt to their gods and kissed divine images of them (see 1 Kings 19:18). When Samuel anointed Saul, he kissed him (1 Samuel 10:1).

The Betrayal of Christ/Giotto

In the time of Christ, the Jews kissed one another before a meal. It was also a common form of greeting, not unlike the one that Judas gave Christ in the garden to identify Him to the temple police. Theologian Fr. Dom Gregory Dix, author of an epic work on the formation of the liturgy, notes that the kiss may well have been in use at the Lord's Supper in the early days at Jerusalem, if not at the Last Supper itself. He reminds us that St. Paul refers to it more than once as a token of Christian communion, but without direct reference to the Eucharist, though its use at the liturgy in his day can hardly be doubted. Later, in the second century and beyond, the kiss became identified with the preparation for the Eucharist (*The Shape of the Liturgy*, 107).

Members of Christian communities greeted one another with a kiss. St. Paul urged the Romans to "greet one another with a holy kiss" (Rom 16:16). It was also used as a sign of initiation into a fraternity or society. When someone was initiated into the Christian community through Baptism, the bishop then confirmed the neophyte, after which he gave him a kiss. When the new Christians mingled among the faithful in church, they kissed them. (Until they were baptized and confirmed, catechumens were not allowed to exchange the kiss of peace with the faithful.) For years, the bishop kissed the newly confirmed, a tradition which changed into the bishop giving them a tap on the cheek.

Christians adopted the custom of kissing in their liturgies. There was a close connection between peace and communion, because they took Jesus' teaching on forgiveness to heart:

> "So if you are offering your gift at the altar, and there re-member that your brother has something against you, leave your gift there before the altar and to; first be recon-ciled to your brother, and then come and offer your gift"(Mt 5:23-25).

Father Dix notes, "in the second century and after, the kiss had its most frequent and significant Christian use as the immediate preparation for the Eucharist" (107). St. Cyril of Jerusalem instructed the newly baptized to look upon the kiss as something holy, because it is a sign of reconciliation that brings souls into union with each other—a pledge that all disagreements are healed.

In the early Christian liturgies, the priest kissed the altar at the beginning of Mass and, again, just before the final blessing. St. Justin Martyr is the first to refer to the placement of the kiss right after the *General Intercessions* and just before the *Offertory* (now *Prepara-tion of the Gifts*), where it stayed for several hundred years until its position shifted to before *Communion*. The gesture was an affirma-tion of the Scripture readings, and an enactment of the unity called for in the Gospels. (In the East, it remains there to this day.) Tertullian noted that the kiss of peace was looked upon as the "seal" put on prayer.

In fifth century Africa, St. Augustine records that the kiss of peace followed the *Our Father* as a preparation for communion:

> "After the Lord's Prayer there is said, 'Peace be with you'; and Christians give one another a holy kiss. This is a sign of peace; that to which your lips bear witness must be also in your conscience."

The custom spread to Rome in 416 when Pope Innocent I wrote a letter to the Bishop of Gubbio, advocating its present position as part of the *Communion Rite.*

By the tenth century, it was customary to spread the kiss of peace from the altar to the congregation. An interesting development took place in thirteenth century England, which Fr. Clifford Howell relates:

> The kiss of peace was passed on to all the congregation by means of a *Pax-brede* (originally 'pax-board'), a tablet of wood on which was engraved a figure of our Lord or a symbol of Him such as a lamb. It had a handle and was given to the priest, who kissed the altar and then the *Pax-brede.* The server likewise kissed the *Pax-brede* and then took it down from the altar to the people, who passed it from one to another, each kissing it as he did so. Slowly the practice of conveying the sign of peace fell into disuse among the faithful at Mass, although it was retained by the clergy. (*Mean What You Say,* 71)

This practice spread to the continent and found its way into the Missal of Pius V in 1570, where we also find the introduction to the sign of peace, "Lord Jesus Christ, you said to your apostles . . ." Then the *Rite of Peace* was usually considered the priest's private prayer in preparation for *Communion.* During the Middle Ages when reception of Communion declined, the kiss of peace was considered a kind of substitute for the Sacrament.

## REFLECTION

Soon after Vatican Council II ended, Fr. Joseph Champlin was a newly appointed pastor who traveled to many parishes throughout the United States and Canada to speak about the changes in the liturgy. He said the one that stirred the most controversy was the exchange of peace among the faithful that Vatican II had reinstated after a long absence. (For years it was limited to the clergy and ministers of the altar). Back in his home parish, he conducted listening sessions with his parishioners. There was such tension and opposition surrounding this gesture that he postponed implementing this rite in his own parish for two years! (*The Mystery and Meaning of the Mass*, 104).

Looking at this now, it is hard to fathom. Yet, some people still oppose it. Why has the *Rite of Peace* caused such opposition and division? Some priests cite it as one of the more commonly held reasons why people no longer come to Mass. Fr. Francis Randolph offers an interesting perspective. He suggests that, at a time when we need real peace and quiet, the noisy interruption breaks the mood of the Consecration. He also suggests that some people have a difficult time greeting strangers while others need privacy and find communication difficult. The "general melee," he says, "terrifies them" (*Know Him in the Breaking of the Bread*, 150, 151).

While this point of view may have some merit, there is another perspective that illustrates how a person can feel unwelcome and unwanted when the Sign of Peace is withheld. Fr. Ian Petit, a monk who runs a pastoral center in York, England, relates the story of an alcoholic who, after he stopped drinking through the great work of AA, decided to return to Church. Because he had been away for many years, he felt a certain apprehension. Vatican II had reinstated the *Rite of Peace* and when the time came for the kiss of peace during Mass, this person turned expectantly to the person next to him to extend peace and was told, 'I do not do that.' Sadly, he took the remark personally and never went back to that church again (*This is My Body*, 72, 73).

There is yet another option: to look at the *Sign of Peace* as a blessing that we can extend to others. My good friend, Fr. Tom McCarthy, now in his eighties and more active than most people in their fifties, shared a story about blessing in one of his homilies. He encouraged parents to develop some kind of liturgical celebration in the home. He suggested that they bless each other every night, as well as their children, before sending them off to bed. How? After

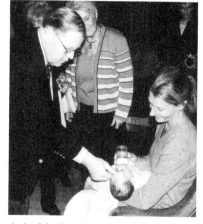

Author's husband, Tom McHugh, blesses his new granddaughter, Eleanor McHugh Ranke.

placing their hands on each other's head they could pray silently for awhile, then make the sign of the cross on the forehead while saying, "May God bless you and I bless you" (*Forever A Priest,* 132).

A few weeks after this homily, Father McCarthy received a letter from a parishioner who had heard his homily. That Sunday night she had gone into her baby's room and blessed her as Father Tom had instructed. Sometime in the night, the child died, a classic case of "crib death." The fact that she had given her baby a final blessing was a great source of comfort to her (133).

We could look upon the *Sign of Peace* at Mass as a "hands on" prayer if you will, a means to actualize our prayers and extend Christ's peace and love to the people next to us. St. Luke tells us that the Lord will honor our prayer and bless them, and He will also bless us:

> "Give, and it will be given to you; good measure, pressed down, shaken together, running over, will be put into your lap. For the measure you give will be the measure you get back" (Lk 6:38).

In fact, we could look upon this rite as a laying on of hands through which we ask the Holy Spirit to give that person whatever it is they need most. When we bless someone in the name of Jesus, we become Christ's hands, extending His healing touch to our brothers and sisters in faith. This is a moment of ministry, a chance to really connect with others with a friendly handshake or a smile, and bless one another from our hearts saying, *the peace of the Lord be with you.*

## The Fraction

Immediately following the *Rite of Peace,* the priest breaks the large consecrated Host either by himself or he may be assisted by a deacon or concelebrant. This breaking action is significant in its own right and thus has its own heading, but it is often hidden behind the chanting of the *Lamb of God,* which may occupy our attention. During the *Fraction Rite,* the celebrant imitates the actions of our Savior when He broke the Eucharistic bread before distributing it at the Last Supper. St. Paul speaks to the rite's meaning when he says that because we all share in the same loaf, we are united as one in the Body of Christ:

> "The cup of blessing which we bless, is it not a participation in the blood of Christ? The bread which we break, is it not a participation in the body of Christ? Because there is one bread, we who are many are one body, for we all partake of the one bread." (1 Cor 10:16, 17)

Not only does the Eucharist signify unity, it *effects* unity, something which Dorothy Day, the saintly founder of *The Catholic Worker,* personally observed when she began to attend daily Mass before she converted to Catholicism. She was moved by the inclusiveness of the congregation, the lack of distinction between classes of people who gathered for worship. Dorothy Day experienced the true spirit of the Catholic faith which St. Paul urged upon his pagan converts: "There is neither Jew nor Greek, there is neither slave nor free, there is neither male nor female; for you are all one in Christ Jesus" (Gal 3:28). This is the unity to which we are called and for which we now pray.

## EXPLANATION

Fr. Lawrence Hennessey

The *Breaking of the Bread* is one of the most ancient—and venerable—customs of our liturgy. For many years it was submerged in other rites but restored to its original importance in the Mass by the liturgical reforms of Vatican II. Really a two-fold ritual, the *Breaking of the Bread* and *Commingling* takes place while the *Lamb of God* is sung or recited aloud.

When the celebrant has finished giving the *Sign of Peace* to the deacon and/or extraordinary ministers, he takes a large host and breaks it in half over the paten. I always appreciate it if he waits until the *Sign of Peace* is finished, so the faithful can focus on the breaking of the consecrated Host.

The assembly then chants (or recites aloud) an ancient hymn:

*Lamb of God, you take away the sins of the world:*
  *have mercy on us.*
*Lamb of God, you take away the sins of the world:*
  *have mercy on us.*
*Lamb of God, you take away the sins of the world:*
  *grant us peace.*

"This prayer is an invocation to Christ that recalls His sacrificial death," says Fr. Josef Jungmann, S.J. "but at the same time it has something of the overtones of a hymn of victory offered to the triumphant Lamb of the Apocalypse." (*The Mass*, 211)

We kneel in honor of the Paschal Lamb whose feast we celebrate in the Eucharist. A figure of innocence and helplessness, Jesus is a Lamb without blemish whose Blood takes away the sins of the world. In the Book of Revelation, the title of "Lamb" is applied to Jesus twenty-eight times. In St. John's vision, the elect gather around God's throne and join the multitudes who come "from every nation, from all tribes and peoples and tongues" (Rev 7:9) to worship the Lamb. Gathered around the altar, we share in the eternal liturgy of heaven and add our voices to those of the angels as we sing our praises to the Lamb of God, who "was slain to receive power and wealth, and wisdom and might and honor and glory and blessing!" (Rev 5:12). Jesus is the sacrificial Lamb who has won for us the remission of our sins and the peace that the world cannot give—all of which He gives us in the Eucharist.

As the celebrant breaks the large consecrated Host in half, he places one half on the paten; then he breaks off a small piece from the other half and places it in the chalice, praying *sotto voce: May this mingling of the body and blood of our Lord Jesus Christ bring eternal life to us who receive it.* Our Roman Missal does not give an explanation for this rite, known as the *Commingling,* perhaps because its origins are somewhat obscure. But, according to Fr. Lucien Deiss, the Church has kept it in the liturgy through "faithfulness to tradition" (*The Mass*, 93).

What does the gesture signify? Theologians conjecture that it may have served to emphasize the unity and indivisibility of the Body and Blood of Jesus Christ. Because the bread and wine are consecrated separately, the Body and Blood *appear* to be separated. When the consecrated elements are mingled with each other, this symbolically expresses that the Body is not without the Blood, and the Blood not without the Body. Christ is wholly present under each species, so that if we only receive the Precious Blood we are receiving the Body and Blood of Christ. Some scholars add that just as the separate consecration of the Body and Blood of Christ represents Christ's death (the Body being in one place, the Blood in another), so does the union of His Body and Blood mingled on the altar symbolize His Resurrection (Chevrot, *Our Mass Explained*, 200).

If the celebrant uses an extra large host for the Consecration, he breaks it into many parts, placing most of them back in the ciborium for distribution to the faithful during Communion. This act is in accordance with the rubrics, which state that "the Eucharistic bread should be made in such a way that in a Mass with a congregation the priest is able actually to break the host into parts and distribute them to at least some of the faithful" (*General Instruction of the Roman Missal*, 321).

## HISTORY

In Scripture, there are a number of references that relate the "breaking the bread" to the celebration of the Eucharist, beginning with Our Lord's *taking, blessing, breaking* and *giving*, at the Last Supper (See Mt 26:26; Mk 14:22; Lk 22:19; 1 Cor 11:24). The bread that He broke at table with His disciples would become His Body in a new Christian rite that Jesus instituted to perpetuate the memorial of His sacrifice—broken and given on the Cross for our salvation. After the Resurrection, the eyes of the two disciples on the road to Emmaus were opened when Jesus went to their house and broke bread with them. As soon as He said the blessing and broke the bread, they recognized the Risen Christ (Lk 24:30). Henceforth people would know Jesus in the "breaking of the bread."

Among the Jews, the expression "to break bread" meant to eat or dine with someone. In the earliest days of the Church, the Mass was first called "The Breaking of the Bread." The custom of referring to the Eucharist as "the breaking of the bread" grew among the early Christian converts who "devoted themselves to the apostles' teaching and fellowship, to the breaking of the bread and the prayers" (Acts 2:42). "Breaking bread in their homes" (Acts 2:46) referred to the celebration of Mass. One time when St. Paul celebrated the Sunday liturgy at midnight in Troas, "they were gathered together to break bread" (Acts 20:7).

The actual *Fraction Rite* is one of the most ancient customs of our liturgy. In the third century, St. Hippolytus of Rome records that just before the *Fraction Rite*, the priest invited the faithful to Communion, saying: "Holy things for the holy!" to which the people replied, "One is holy, one is the Lord Jesus Christ in the glory of God the Father." One of the oldest prayers recited during the *Fraction Rite* is found in the *Didache:* "As grain once scattered on the hillside was in this broken bread made one, so we who are many are one body, for we all share in the same bread" *(Didache,* 12).

In the New Testament, we are introduced to Jesus through John the Baptist as "the Lamb of God, who takes away the sin of the world" (Jn 1:29), who proclaims that He is the *Lamb of God* who redeems us. The lamb was a familiar and beloved image to the Jews of both the Old and New Testaments. The early Christian community was familiar with this title for God because the Jewish understanding of the lamb was that of a sacrificial victim. The Passover (the Pasch) was a great national feast in Israel in which the people relived their deliverance from the slavery of the Egyptians. The Lord instructed Moses and Aaron to order every

The Lamb of God/Joel Tanis

Jewish family to mark their doorposts with the blood of a lamb to ward off the destroying angel that would "pass over" their houses and slay the firstborn of the Egyptians. Then God asked the Israelites to memorialize their deliverance with a sacred banquet in which they roasted and ate a lamb.

The early Christians understood that they had received the redemption prophesied by Isaiah through the blood of the spotless lamb, the Messiah, Jesus Christ:

> "The Lord laid on him the iniquity of us all. He was oppressed, and he was afflicted, yet he opened not his mouth; like a lamb that is led to the slaughter, and like a sheep that before its shearers is dumb, so he opened not his mouth" (Is 53:6, 7).

St. Peter addresses his listeners, reminding them that they were saved "not with perishable things such as silver or gold, but with the precious blood of Christ, like that of a lamb without blemish or spot" (1 Peter 18).

When Jesus instituted the Eucharist, He transformed the Jewish Passover into the *Pasch,* a new Christian rite in which Christ's faithful would celebrate their deliverance from sin and death. Jesus offered *Himself* at the Last Supper as the new and eternal *Paschal Lamb,* the supreme victim who would shed His blood for the salvation of the world. We therefore refer to the heart of the Christian liturgy as "the Paschal Mystery," symbolized by the lamb.

The *Commingling,* the dropping of a particle of the host into the consecrated wine, is ancient as well, dating back to the early Church when the faithful were allowed to take the Eucharist to their homes. Because the bread was leavened, it hardened quickly and had to be dipped in water or wine to soften it. In the ancient Church, the laity received the Body of our Lord mingled in the Precious Blood by means of a small spoon. In the Papal Mass at Rome, when the presiding Pontiff said, "The peace of the Lord be with you always," he dropped a piece of the *sancta* (the consecrated Eucharistic particle) into the chalice; it had been saved from a previous Sunday Mass and shown to the Pope on his entry so that he could adore it. At each Sunday's Mass, a part of the consecrated Host was reserved to be brought in solemn procession to the next "Station" church, a term designating the church where Mass was celebrated. The purpose of the *sancta* was to show the unity of the Church and the continuity of the Sacrifice. The Pope also sent a Eucharistic particle known as the *fermentum* (leaven) to priests of the churches of Rome who could not attend his Papal Mass. When the sacred particle arrived at a church, the celebrating priest would drop it into his chalice. In this way the faithful of Rome were symbolically united with their bishop and with one another.

The Jews baked round flat loaves of bread an inch or so thick and about the size of a dinner plate which the head of the house broke and distributed to the family and guests, saying, "Praised be Yahweh, our God, the king of the world, who brings the bread forth from the earth." Fr. Josef Jungmann notes that this ritual was a beau-

> *During Mass one day, at the elevation of the host, as she was offering this same sacred host to God the Father as a worthy reparation for all her sins and to make up for all her negligences, she understood that her soul, presented to the divine majesty, was as pleasing to him as was Christ Jesus, the splendor and image of his Father's glory (Heb 1:3), the spotless Lamb of God, who was offering himself to God the Father at the same moment on the altar for the salvation of the world.*
>
> —St. Gertrude the Great

tiful way of expressing the unity and fellowship that was to exist among the guests of the house (*The Early Liturgy*, 32).

After the persecution of the Christians in the early Church had ended, it became possible to celebrate the Eucharist in large public buildings (basilicas) instead of private homes. A great number of people received communion, which took a long time because enough consecrated bread had to be broken by the priest and deacons for the entire assembly.

By the seventh century, there was a long wait for Communion. Pope Sergius I (687-701), devised a way to fill the time while the priest and deacons were breaking the bread. He introduced a chant into the Mass, a litany to Christ, the *Lamb of God*. The faithful sang it as many times as might be required to occupy the time of the *Fraction Rite*.

By the ninth century, unleavened bread was introduced into the liturgies of the West. The people no longer brought bread baked in their homes. Instead, monks and nuns baked altar breads. In the twelfth century, wafer-thin hosts the size of small coins were used for communion. The profound symbolism of the "breaking of the bread" was lost, and there was no need of a chant during the *Fraction*. Even the *paten* (a plate held under the communicants chin to catch the crumbs), was rendered superfluous. But the chanting of the *Agnus Dei (Lamb of God)* had become so popular that it was retained in the liturgy. Moved closer to the *Rite of Peace*, it was now sung only three times. According to Pope Innocent III (1198-1216), the ending "Grant us peace" was substituted for "Have mercy on us" after the third *Lamb of God* during a time of great distress in the Church.

## REFLECTION

When Jesus dined with the two disciples at Emmaus, they were delighted to be in His company and didn't want Him to leave. They had an intimate encounter with the Risen Lord that culminated in a meal they shared together: "When he was at table with them, he took the bread and blessed and broke it, and gave it to them. And their eyes were opened and they recognized him; and he vanished out of their sight" (Lk 24:30). Jesus made His point: *Even though I no longer will be with you in my human body, I now will be in full communion with you in the Eucharist.* They realized that every time they imitated the actions of the Savior and "broke bread" together, Jesus would become one with them; His Body and Blood would merge with their body and blood so that He would live within them.

The lives of the disciples were transformed. They set out immediately for Jerusalem to tell the Apostles that the Lord showed Himself to be alive in the breaking of the bread. They were able to connect His suffering and death foretold by the prophets to His resurrection, and to His sacramental presence in the meal. From now on, they would never be alone again. Jesus would be with them, intimately, profoundly, permanently, participating in every detail of their lives. They were bonded in the Spirit of love, drawn together now by their love for Christ and for one another. This was the "kingdom" Jesus spoke about, a new way of living in commun-

The Supper at Emmaus/Girolamo Brusaferro

ion with God and in community with each other.

During the *Fraction Rite,* just after the commingling, the priest joins his hands and prays inaudibly:

*Lord Jesus Christ, Son of the living God, by the will of the Father and the work of the Holy Spirit your death brought life to the world. By your holy body and blood free me from all my sins, and from every evil. Keep me faithful to your teaching, and never let me be parted from you.* (*Sacramentary,* 563)

Or, he may choose a shorter prayer:

*Lord Jesus Christ, with faith in your love and mercy I eat your body and drink your blood. Let it not bring me condemnation, but health in mind and body.*

This time of prayer is known as the private preparation of the priest, a moment which my good friend and mentor, Fr. Patrick Greenough, OFM Conv., anticipates. "As a priest," he says, "you're on stage, so to speak, you don't have much time for your own personal prayers." Father Pat takes advantage of these few quiet moments to commune personally with the Lord. The silence is a welcome respite for the congregation as well, giving the faithful an opportunity to ready their hearts to receive Jesus in Communion.

Fr. Raniero Cantalamessa offers yet another perspective on the *Fraction Rite.* "It would be impossible to express in words the essence of the interior act that accompanies the action of the breaking of the bread," he writes in *The Eucharist, Our Sanctification.* "It might seem harsh and cruel whereas it is the most supreme act of love and tenderness that has ever been made, or can ever be made, on this earth." When Father Cantalamessa holds up the Host at the consecration and repeats the words, "He broke the bread," it is an emotional moment for this Capuchin Franciscan, preacher to the papal household:

> I can sense something of the sentiments that filled the heart of Jesus at that moment; how he completely gave his human will to the Father, overcoming every resistance and repeating to Himself: "Sacrifices and offerings thou hast not desired, but a body hast thou prepared for me; Lo, I have come to do thy will, O God" (cf. Heb 10:5-9). What Jesus gives His disciples to eat is the bread of His obedience and His love for the Father. (18)

Father Cantalamessa shares how this "breaking" action has an impact on him:

> Then I understand that to "do" what Jesus did that night, I must, first of all, "break" myself . . . Lay before God all hardness, all rebellion towards him or towards others, crush my pride, submit and say "yes," fully to all that God asks of me. I too must repeat the words: Lo, I have come to do they will, O God! You don't want many things from me; you want me and I say "yes." To be Eucharist like Jesus signifies being totally abandoned to the Father's will. (18)

These special priests offer deep food for thought, teaching us that we are not mere passive observers of a ritual that the celebrant "does." We are part of a Sacred Rite which draws us into union with Christ—in His dying and rising—this according to a Vatican II decree on the Mystery of the Church: "Really sharing in the body of the Lord in the breaking of the Eucharistic bread, we are taken up into communion with him and with one another " (*Dogmatic Constitution on the Church,* art. 7).

The Church gives us this moment in the Mass to unite our broken and fallen selves—and world—to the broken bread that is now Christ's Body. How? By surrendering our own hardness and rebellion to the Lord, by "breaking" our wills and allowing Christ to remake us in His own image. Jesus wants to bring redemption to the wounded and fragmented parts of our lives so that He can transform us and make us whole. He comes to live in us, to turn our weaknesses into strengths, our suffering into joy, our darkness into light. When we are in communion with Jesus, we become Christ to our brothers and sisters in faith, people like us who need forgiveness, love, compassion, food, clothes, freedom, understanding, justice and peace. How willing are we to break our wills and be remade into another Christ? Perhaps this is the perfect time to ask Our Lord how *He* would like to refashion us.

## Communion

It is a wondrous mystery that God gives us Himself in Holy Communion; that He desires to be in a personal and intimate relationship with us. In the language of the Church, the Eucharist is "a sacrament of love, a sign of unity, a bond of charity" (*Constitution on the Sacred Liturgy*, 47). We bond with Jesus not only in the flesh, but in spirit. Jesus told German mystic St. Anne Catherine Emmerich (1774-1824) that He pervades the soul of a communicant just as sugar is dissolved in water—and the union between the soul and Jesus is always in proportion to the soul's desire to receive Him. He will never force Himself on us, but waits, like a Bridegroom for the Bride to beckon Him. This is exactly where we are in the Sacred Liturgy—awaiting Our Lord's arrival in Holy Communion

I consider it a great grace that God gave me the faith to realize how much He loves me and to know deep down that I am the apple of His eye. The psalmist's prayer became mine: "Keep me as the apple of the eye; hide me in the shadow of thy wings" (Ps 17:8). At a young age, I discovered the gift of the Mass where I daily sought Christ's company in Communion. It was a sacred time of bonding, of closeness, of belonging to Jesus who loved me for myself, not for what or who He needed me to be. After Communion I poured out my heart to Him, sometimes with tears, asking for help with problems big and small. I *connected* with Him. He was present to me in every detail of my life and I could share in all the experiences of His life. His love was like liquid gold that sealed up the cracks in my sometimes broken heart. I always came away from church with a renewed sense of self-worth and inner peace because I trusted that God was with me; united to Him, life was an adventure with unlimited possibilities. Problems would be solved and I felt full and happy.

## EXPLANATION

The word "communion" comes from the Greek *koinonia,* meaning unity or sharing. The early Church adopted the phrase "Holy Communion" to describe the church community. The Eucharist evolved into the "Sacrament of Communion." Christ's sacrifice on Calvary is re-presented in the consecration of the bread and wine at Mass. Those who receive Him perpetuate His presence in their lives. The Sacrament challenges us to say, "Lord, this is my body, this is my blood for you," and to sacrifice ourselves to bring Jesus' risen presence to others. Communion is not a private act of devotion between "me and Jesus," but the action of a community who, as they draw closer to Christ, draw closer to one another.

After the *Breaking of the Bread* and the private preparation of the priest, there follow a few blessed moments of silence. It is a silence which one theologian describes as an integral to the Sacred Liturgy, "purposeful, pregnant, and controlled—the thunderous quiet of people communicating that which escapes being put into mere words" (Aidan Kavanagh, *Elements of Rite,* 51). What is so difficult to put into words is the nature of the gift we are about to receive— Jesus Christ in Holy Communion. The silence, however brief, allows us prayerfully to ponder this awesome mystery: we are about to be united with the Risen Christ and through Him with the Blessed Trinity.

Then the celebrant genuflects. Raising the Host slightly over the paten he faces the people and says: *This is the Lamb of God who takes away the sins of the world. Happy are those who are called to his supper (Sacramentary,* 564) He leads the faithful in an act of humility, using words from the Gospel: *Lord I am not worthy to receive you but only say the word and I shall be healed.*

These words are taken from the New Testament story of the centurion who approached Jesus asking for a cure for his paralyzed servant who was lying at home in a terrible state of suffering. When Jesus told him that He would come and cure him, the centurion responded: "Lord, I am not worthy to have you enter under my roof; but only say the word and my servant will be healed" (Mt 8: 5-9). His humility and faith amazed Jesus and caused Him to say, "Amen, I say to you, in no one in Israel have I found such faith" (Mt 8:10). Scripture records that "at that very moment" (Mt 8:13), his servant was healed. Jesus performed the miracle in response to the centurion's faith. We, too, pray for healing and for the faith of the centurion that makes us "worthy" to receive the Eucharist.

Lord I Am Not Worthy/James Tissot

The celebrant then receives Communion. Facing the altar, he says inaudibly: *May the body of Christ bring me to everlasting life.* Then he takes the chalice and says inaudibly: *May the blood of Christ bring me to everlasting life.* He reverently drinks the blood of Christ.

The gifts we presented earlier in the Mass—our lives symbolized by the bread and wine—which Christ accepted and offered to His Eternal Father, we now receive when the celebrant gives Communion to the assembly. Taking a host for each person, he raises it slightly, saying: *The body of Christ,* to which the communicant answers, *Amen,* and receives Communion. When we say "Amen" (from the *Hebrew*, "it is true"), we are affirming our belief that this truly is the Body and Blood of Christ. St. Augustine drew the analogy that our "Amen" is like putting our signature on a document. It is ours, we own it. It is the same when we drink from the cup containing the Precious Blood. The celebrant or minister says, "The Blood of Christ," to which we respond, "Amen."

When these gifts are changed into Christ's Body and Blood, we, too, are changed, transformed and renewed by His victory over death. In the words of St. Leo the Great, "the sharing in the Body and Blood of Christ has no other effect than to accomplish our transformation into that which we receive" (*Lumen Gentium*, 26).

### Receiving Communion Worthily

The early Church struggled with moral disorder and sin no less than we do today. St. Paul warned the Corinthians that their immoral behavior distorted the meaning of the Eucharist—the death of Jesus that is an act of pure love expressed in and through the shared drinking and eating. Their sinful behavior ruptured their communion with God—and with one another—and made them guilty of profaning the Body of Christ. In the Middle Ages, people refrained from receiving Communion out of a sense of unworthiness; they didn't feel they were good or holy enough to receive Our Lord. To receive Jesus worthily, the Church stipulates that we be in a state of grace and purified through sacramental confession, especially if we have committed serious sin.

To receive Communion is not our right, but our privilege, and to do so we must examine ourselves and confess our sin, because "anyone who eats and drinks without discerning the body eats and drinks judgment upon himself" (1 Cor 11:27-29).

In addition, we must believe that the consecrated Bread and Wine is changed into the Real Presence of Christ—His Body, Blood, Soul and Divinity—even though the appearance of bread and wine remain. The Church also asks us to observe a one-hour Eucharistic fast prior to Communion, and finally, one must not be under an ecclesiastical censure such as excommunication.

### Receiving Under Both species

During the thirteenth century, the practice of giving holy Communion only in the form of bread became dominant in the Western church. Only the celebrant communicated from the chalice, though this custom was contrary to the practice of earlier centuries. Even though the Council of Trent in 1545 taught that Christ is received whole and entire under each Species, there were very few exceptions to this rule until Vatican II, when the bishops reinstated Communion under both Species, saying, "As sign, Holy Communion assumes a more complete form when it is received under both species. Under this form, the sign of the Eucharistic banquet appears more perfectly" (*Instruction on Worship of the Eucharist,* 32). If we use the model of the meal Jesus shared with His apostles at the Last Supper, He offered them bread and wine, something to eat and drink. It makes perfect sense that communicants participate in the Lord's Supper in the manner in which Christ instituted it, by eating His Body and drinking His Blood.

The Church slowly introduced the practice of drinking from the cup, initially only offering it to priests, religious and laity at the discretion of the bishops. Extending the chalice to the laity at weekday and Sunday Masses slowly evolved into a more general practice and, in 1973, came into full use with the addition of Extraordinary Ministers of Communion. Today there is no reason why communion in both species should not be given in every church at every Mass.

Wine used for Mass must be grape wine only. It may be given directly from the chalice or by *intinction* (dipping the Host in the chalice). Regarding this practice, the Church instructs: "The option of administering Communion by intinction always remains," and "the communicant should receive the Sacrament from the priest only on the tongue" (*Redemptionis sacramentum,* 103). The priest or deacon dips the host in the chalice and then presents it with the words: "The Body and Blood of Christ." *One may never dip the Host himself.* This is to guard against what some refer to as "self-service liturgy." In this same document, the Church recommends using a Communion plate (or paten) in order to avoid the danger of the sacred host or some fragment of it falling.

According to the directives of the Catholic bishops, bread used for Mass must be made solely of wheat; it must be recently baked, and, according to the ancient tradition of the Latin Church, must be unleavened (*General Instruction of the Roman Missal,* 320). There are a small number of people who suffer from celiac disease which makes them intolerant to gluten, the protein in wheat. Some insist that the Church should make hosts out of rice which they could tolerate. But the Church has no power to change the elements that Jesus used which were wheat flour and grapes. There are two alternatives for people with this unfortunate disease: they can take a sip of the Precious Blood, which contains Christ whole and entire, and/or they can ask their pastor to order some low-gluten hosts approved by the U.S. Bishops and made by the Benedictine Sisters of Perpetual Adoration in Clyde, Missouri.

## Distribution of Communion

The manner of receiving Communion has changed over time and has been the subject of heated controversy. During Vatican II, a majority of bishops voted overwhelmingly in favor of retaining the traditional manner of receiving Communion on the tongue, opposing the practice of placing Holy Communion on the hand. They were concerned that Communion in the hand would open the door to disrespect for the Sacrament and possibly even profanation. Eventually, however, the pope permitted the practice with the approval of diocesan bishops. The Church stipulates that when the faithful do receive in the hand, they should consume the sacred Host *before* returning to their seat. Following the Council, many abuses resulted from the new practice, causing John Paul II to write an encyclical in which he stated: "Communion is a gift of the Lord, given to the faithful through the minister appointed for this purpose. It is not permitted that the faithful should themselves pick up the consecrated bread and the sacred chalice, still less that they should hand them from one to another" (*Instruction Concerning Worship of the Eucharistic Mystery*

Fr. Tom McCarthy distributes Communion.

, 9). Today we can receive Communion either on the tongue or in the hand. We no longer kneel, but stand, having come full circle from the earliest days of the Church, when standing for prayer and to receive the Eucharist was a sign of respect. The Church recommends that the communicants make a sign of reverence, such as a slight bow, before receiving the Sacrament.

As soon as the priest communicates, the congregation sings the *Communion Song,* similar in spirit to the *Entrance Song.* Its purpose is to unite us as a community and to enable us to express our joy in song. If there is no *Communion Song,* the faithful recite the antiphon in the Missal before the celebrant distributes Communion.

## Thanksgiving after Communion:

When the distribution of Communion is finished, the priest and faithful spend some time praying privately. I look to the saints to help me grasp the magnitude of this moment. The early Church Fathers used powerful images to describe the effects of Communion. They compared the intimacy of the soul's union with Christ to "two wax tapers melted into one, two intertwining flames, a fiery coal in a blazing furnace, the leaven that raises the dough, the heat that causes water to boil, or perfume that emanates from a cloth" (Francois Charmot, *The Mass, Source of Sanctity,* 169, 170). Meditating on any one of these inspires prayer.

The Church teaches that the living Christ is with us for as long as the Sacred Species remains, which means about ten or fifteen minutes. Sadly, some people walk out the door even before they consume the Host. If the mystic St. Philip Neri (1515-1595) were alive today, he would send two altar servers with lighted candles to accompany them, because he had such a profound awareness of the presence of Christ in the soul of the communicant. He himself would go into ecstacy for several hours after reciting the *Lamb of God* during Mass, yet people would have a hard time guessing that he was such a mystic. The humor and jokes of this down-to-earth saint drew the youth to him—and to church—in droves. Franciscan Fr. Stefano Manelli sums it up best, saying, for the sake of good manners, if for no other reason, when a person receives a guest he pauses to give his attention to him and takes interest in him. If this guest is Jesus, then we will only have reason to be sorry that His bodily presence within us scarcely lasts fifteen minutes (*Jesus Our Eucharistic Love*, 38).

Christ's presence is a source of deep consolation. A young father who lost his seven-year-old son, John Paul, in a freakish car accident in front of his own home, sought comfort in the Blessed Sacrament. He writes words that can only come from God's heart:

> In the Eucharist, both in Mass and in adoration of the Blessed Sacrament, he is as close as he will ever be until we meet again in heaven. I am one with my son in the Eucharist. I touch him, love him, and speak to him in adoring the Lord with whom he is perfectly one. Heaven and earth touch in Christ. Father and son touch in Christ. I kiss my son in the Eucharist. (Gregory Floyd, *A Grief Unveiled,* 164)

## Purification and Final Prayer

In the brief period of silence following the *Communion Song* and before the final "Let us pray," the deacon or celebrant consumes what remains of the Precious Blood. He or the ministers transfer any remaining consecrated hosts to the tabernacle, where they are reserved to bring to the sick and for adoration. Standing to the side of the altar, the celebrant cleanses the vessels (they may also be put on the *credence* table to be washed after Mass by Eucharistic ministers). The altar server pours a little water into the chalice which the priest drinks, then he wipes the sacred vessels dry with a purificator. Praying inaudibly, he says: *Lord, may I receive these gifts in purity of heart. May they bring me healing and strength, now and for ever.*

Then standing at his chair or at the altar, the celebrant says or sings: *Let us pray.* He says the *Prayer after Communion* which, like the *Opening Prayer* that concludes the *Introductory Rites,* focuses on the fruits of the mystery just celebrated. The faithful echo their agreement by saying, *Amen.*

## HISTORY

The words of Our Lord resounded in the ears and hearts of the early Christians: "I am the vine, you are the branches" (Jn 15:5), "My flesh is food indeed, and my blood is drink indeed" (Jn 6: 55), "As the living Father sent me, I live because of the Father, so he who eats me will live because of me" (Jn 6:57).

In the first thousand years of Christianity, belief in the Real Presence of Christ in the Eucharist was undisputed. Christians lived—and died—believing that the Eucharist was the Body, Blood, Soul and Divinity of Christ. Scores of true stories portray the courage of priests, deacons and everyday Christians who offered their lives rather than denounce the Eucharist. One story in particular involves a group of Christians who gathered at someone's home in Carthage in the year 304 to celebrate Mass, despite the prohibition under penalty of death. When the man who had offered his house for the *Dominicum* (early term for Mass) was asked by the pagan governor why he had done this, he answered quite simply: "These are my brothers. I could not keep them from it because without the holy Mass we cannot live." They all died for their faith.

In those days, everyone who assisted at the Sacrifice of the Mass received Communion. Before the *Fraction Rite,* the deacon dismissed those who were not communicating, saying: "Let him who does not communicate depart!" If they were not yet baptized, or for whatever reason had not remained faithful to their baptismal grace, people were "excommunicated." Then the deacon invited the people to Communion, saying, "Holy things to the holy,"

Jesus distributes His Body and Blood/Anonymous

recalling the purity necessary for the reception of the Sacrament.

The faithful received Communion under both species, but it was the deacon—not the priest—who presented the chalice.

The Church continued to offer the chalice to the faithful for many years in memory of its institution by Our Lord, but gradually the chalice was no longer given to the people. At the Council of Constance in 1415, the practice of presenting the chalice was discontinued in the West.

In the ancient Church, the faithful received Communion in hierarchical order. First was the celebrant, then those connected with the Church's ministry: lectors, singers, ascetics and, on the other side (men and women were separated), the women, deaconesses, virgins and widows. Then came the children followed by the faithful. When young mothers went to Communion, they brought their infants up to receive a drop of the Precious Blood. The communicants came up to a balustrade demarcating the sanctuary where they stood to receive Communion. The priest said, "The body of Christ," and they replied "Amen."

Several historical records of the *Communion Rite* in the early Church reveal an attitude of deep reverence among the faithful. St. Cyril of Jerusalem offers a telling description:

> When you approach Communion do not come with your
> hands outstretched or with your fingers open but make
> your left hand a throne for the right one, which is to re-

ceive the King. With your hand hollowed receive the body of Christ and answer Amen. After having, with every precaution, sanctified your eyes by contact with the holy body, consume it, making sure that not a particle is wasted, for that would be like losing one of your limbs. (in M. Chevrot, *Our Mass Explained*, 212)

Standing to receive Communion, the faithful took the Bread in their hand then drank from the cup, sometimes through a straw or metal pipe. The men presented their bare hand while the women covered their hand with a linen cloth called the *dominical* (to prevent the celebrant's hands from coming into contact with the female communicants). It wasn't until the ninth century that people began receiving Communion directly into the mouth, possibly due to a growing respect for the Sacred Species and/or for hygenic reasons. This custom coincided with the introduction of unleavened bread in the form of wafer-like hosts. Communion on the tongue may also have been driven by exaggerated feelings of unworthiness (due to heresies) among people receiving Communion. By the eleventh and twelfth centuries, there were so few communions that the Lateran Council of 1215 directed the faithful to receive Communion once a year. Later the Council of Trent encouraged frequent Communion, but it was St. Pius X (1835-1914) who helped reverse the trend of avoiding Communion and brought people back to the Eucharist. He issued a decree recommending frequent and even daily communion for anyone free from mortal sin and in the state of grace. This dealt a final death blow to Jansenism, a heresy which had the majority of Catholics believing that only the most worthy could receive Communion.

During the age of persecutions and beyond, the people took some of the consecrated bread to their homes so that they could receive Communion on succeeding days. St. Justin Martyr says that the deacons "carried the consecrated things to those absent," which probably means the sick and those awaiting martyrdom. They preserved the Eucharist in vases or boxes kept especially for that purpose. St. Jerome was concerned that people were abusing the privilege by communicating at home without going to Mass. St. Hippolytus addressed a different type of abuse in his *Apostolic Tradition:*

Let each one take care that no unbeliever, or mouse, or other animal taste the Eucharist and that no piece of the Eucharist fall on the ground or get lost. It is really the body of the Lord that the faithful eat, and it must not be scorned.

## REFLECTION

It is not too difficult to imagine why God, who loves us so much, chose bread and wine as the means of giving Himself to us. My friend and mentor, Fr. Larry Hennessey, said something unforgettable in one of his homilies on the Eucharist: "God desires to be as close to us as nourishment is to our bones."

This same realization was a turning point in St. Augustine's conversion:

> And I knew that I was far from You in the region of unlikeness, as if I heard Your voice from on high: "I am the food of grown men: grow and you shall eat Me. And you shall not change Me into yourself as bodily food, but into Me you shall be changed" (F.J. Sheed, *Confessions,* Book 7, 10).

When a person eats bread and wine, they assimilate it into themselves. But when we consume the glorified Body and Blood of Christ in Communion, *we are changed into Christ,* a belief central to our faith: *"It is no longer I who live, but Christ who lives in me"* (Gal 2:20).

In the Gospels, deep faith results in healing. Jesus was interested in the whole person, body and soul, and often healed people of their physical ailments and diseases. He frequently prefaced his miracles with: "Do you believe that I can do this?" (Mt 9:27), as He did before he restored the sight of the two blind men. He told His disciples that if they have faith in God, they can literally move mountains if they don't doubt and believe with all their hearts that it can be done (see Mk: 11:22-24). On several occasions, Jesus said, "whatever you ask in prayer, believe that you will receive it, and you will" (Mk 11:24). Imagine what could happen if we really lived this way and relied on our faith in God!

At Mass one Sunday, I was deeply touched by the Gospel story of the blind man sitting by the side of the road who cried out in a loud voice as Jesus passed by: "Jesus, Son of David, have mercy on me!" (Luke 18:35). Jesus asked him what he wanted and the man told Jesus that he wanted to see. Then Jesus healed him, saying, "Receive your sight; your faith has made you well" (Lk 18:42).

I had just received word that I had to have a thymectomy, radical surgery to remove a tumor in my chest. The doctor explained that he would have to saw my breast bone (just like open heart surgery) to get at it. I was terrified. During Communion, I begged Jesus for the grace to believe, to trust that He would heal me just like the blind man.

On Monday morning, I phoned Fr. Peter Rookey, "the healing priest," never expecting to talk to him. I just wanted to put my name on the list for prayers. Father Rookey took my call, and after I explained my upcoming operation, he prayed for me. Then he uttered what sounded like a prophecy: "Be at peace daughter. Your faith has made you well."

This is difficult to explain, but I felt as if Jesus was speaking to me. *He was confirming the word He spoke to the blind man in the Gospel, only now He was speaking it to me personally.* I was overjoyed and filled with a sense of wellbeing

The Healing of Blind Bartimaeus/Carl Bloch

and gratitude. The Lord seemed to be telling me through Father Rookey that He is watching over me and that I would be well.

This is exactly what happened. I was unusually calm when they wheeled me into the operating room. My fear was gone, replaced by a kind of euphoria. My doctor was a handsome young man whom I liked very much. He was Jesus to me. I put myself in his hands and surrendered my life to the Lord. The doctor removed a tumor the size of an egg; in fact he removed my entire thymus gland. The tumor was completely contained, meaning it hadn't spread to other organs. No chemo or radiation was necessary. Once again, it was God's perfect timing. I could see, and feel, His hand upon my life.

About a week later at Mass, I was thanking the Lord after Communion when He gifted me with an awareness of His closeness. I wrote in my journal:

*After Communion I was bursting with so much life. Gratitude for my clean bill of health. So much gratitude! Deep joy in all areas of my life fills me to overflowing. I feel like I'm riding a wave on the ocean, enjoying the ride so much. I thanked the Lord for being with me and was wondering how I could be closer to Him because I feel pulled in so many directions. Just then I had an interior impression—an image or a thought. Jesus was telling me how close He is to me by using examples: He is the song, and I am the music. He is the perfume, and I am the scent. He is the message, and I am the words. He is the flame, and I am the wick. These thoughts made me cry.*

Jesus is the same yesterday, today and forever. He is real and alive and comes to us in His risen presence in the Eucharist to bring us peace and healing. He is still fulfilling the promises He made when He walked in Galilee, answering people's needs and restoring health—physically, mentally and spiritually. It is up to us to approach Him with real faith, believing that we already have what we ask for, and it will be ours. *Now that is faith!*

# The Concluding Rites

*Announcements, Greeting and Blessing, Dismissal,
Veneration of the Altar, Recessional*

## Introduction

The *Concluding Rites* are similar to the *Introductory Rites* that
began the liturgy. In the beginning of Mass, they helped us cross
the threshold from the world to the sacred space of our parish
church, and united us as a worshipping community. Now, the *Concluding Rites* send us back out into the world to share the Good News
that we have experienced: a personal encounter with the living God.
Like the Emmaus disciples who "set out immediately" to tell their
brothers and sisters in Jerusalem about their meeting with the Risen
Lord, we go back to our homes, our offices, our everyday lives to
bring the hope and love and promise of Christ's nurturing real presence to a world spiritually starved for Love.

We are called to continue the Eucharistic celebration—our
thanksgiving—by the way we live our lives and minister to others,
by deed and example. Unless we translate our love into action for
our neighbor, the words of the Eucharist are empty of meaning. St.
Teresa of Avila liked to say that Christ has no hands on earth but
ours. It is up to us now to live the Gospel story in a way that will
bring Jesus to life in the world.

## EXPLANATION

### Announcements

Following the *Communion Rite*, the liturgical celebration moves to its conclusion. We know that the *Concluding Rite* is beginning when the celebrant (or a deacon) comes to the ambo to make some final announcements. These are usually brief and important to the life of the parish community.

## Greeting and Final Blessing

Then the rite of dismissal takes place. Similar to the *Greeting* at the beginning of Mass, the priest now faces the people, extends his hands and sings or says, "The Lord be with you," to which the people answer, "And also with you."

The celebrant then offers a final blessing to the congregation. While making the Sign of the Cross over the people, he says, "May almighty God bless you, the Father, and the Son, and the Holy Spirit." The faithful affirm this blessing by saying, "Amen." Or, he may say, "Bow your heads and pray for God's blessing. May almighty God bless you, the Father, and the Son, and the Holy Spirit," to which the people respond, "Amen." On Sundays and feast days, the celebrant may extend a more solemn blessing such as this one from Ordinary time:

> *May the Lord bless you and keep you.  R. Amen.*
>
> *May his face shine upon you*
> *And be gracious to you.  R. Amen.*
>
> *May he look upon you with kindness,*
> *And give you his peace. R. Amen.*
>
> *May almighty God bless you,*
> *the Father, the Son, and the Holy Spirit. R. Amen*

This tripartite blessing comes from the Old Testament; it is identical to the priestly blessing the Lord asked Moses to pass on to Aaron to bless the Israelites (see Num 6:22-27).

And, finally, on certain occasions, the final blessing may be replaced by yet another form, such as a bishop's blessing or a blessing given at weddings.

## The Meaning of Blessing

This blessing is not unlike the one Christ gave to His disciples before His ascension. To catch the spirit and significance of this blessing, let us look at Jesus' final moments on earth.

When the Emmaus disciples returned to Jerusalem to tell the Eleven that they had dined with the risen Christ, Jesus appeared to them in a room behind locked doors. They were terrified because they thought they were seeing a ghost. When Jesus showed them the wounds in His hands and feet, they were amazed and overcome with joy. Jesus ate a piece of fish (perhaps to underscore His bodily presence) and commissioned them for their future ministry.

To me, this is one of the most touching scenes in all the Gospels. It must have been a very emotional encounter. Jesus had died, and now He was with them in the flesh, explaining everything that had happened, everything the Scriptures had foretold—He had to suffer and die and on the third day rise from the dead. His mission to them was to preach repentance and forgiveness of sins to all nations, beginning in Jerusalem. He reminded His disciples that they were His witnesses, and told them to stay in the city until His Father sent the Holy Spirit, who would empower them to continue His mission (see Luke 24:36-50). Then, St. Luke records that Jesus led them a short distance (two miles) outside the

Thomas the Doubter/Carl Bloch

city to Bethany, where He lifted up His hands and blessed them. While He was blessing them, He left them and ascended into heaven (Lk 24:50, 51).

In the Bible, even before the creation of man, God blessed all the living creatures and the animals, saying: "Be fruitful and multiply" (Gen 1:22). Blessing was a sign of favor, as when Isaac blessed his son Jacob (Gen 27:27-29). God blessed the patriarchs and the prophets and He commanded His priests to bless the people "in His name" (Deut 21:5). When people blessed one another, they were in fact asking God to continue to extend His generosity and love to that person.

In his book of biblical meditations on the Eucharist, Fr. Luis Alonso-Schoekel gives an unusual and insightful explanation of blessing: "The quantity of water delivered from a reservoir is not just a voluminous mass of matter," he says, "but energy which will become light, which will give power to factories, set machines going and fertilize fields" (*Celebrating the Eucharist, Biblical Meditations*, 149). Looking at it this way, imagine the graces and gifts resulting from one blessing given by the Source of Energy, the creator of life and light Himself, God almighty!

Jesus gave His final blessing to His disciples, and, through them, to us. Lifting up his hands at the end of Mass, the celebrant marks us with the Sign of the Cross, blessing us in the name of the Father, the Son and the Holy Spirit, sending us out to announce to the world that *Christ has died, Christ has Risen, Christ will come again*. Through the Mass, God the Father "has blessed us in Christ with every spiritual blessing" (Eph 1:3).

## Dismissal

The deacon or priest dismisses the congregation "to do good works, praising and blessing God" (*General Instruction of the Roman Missal*, 90). We are invited to go back to our homes, our neighborhoods, our schools, our workplaces and *live* the meaning of the Mass. He chooses one of three phrases:

> *Go in the peace of Christ.*
> *The Mass is ended, go in peace.*
> *Go in peace to love and serve the Lord.*
> The people answer, *Thanks be to God.*

## Veneration of the Altar and Recessional

After the dismissal, the priest venerates the altar with a kiss, just as he did at the beginning of Mass. Before leaving the

Fr. Lawrence Hennessey gives the final blessing.

sanctuary, he makes a profound bow, then joins the ministers of the altar to form a recessional. They process out in the same order in which they entered, the celebrant going last. There is usually a concluding song that sends the congregation home on a high note of joy and thanksgiving.

## HISTORY

In the early Church, the priest announced the end of Mass by saying, *"Ite, missa est,"* or, "Go you are dismissed." (The term was also used to dismiss people from an audience at the Roman imperial palace or from the public courts, as well as from church.) *Missa est* is derived from the Latin verb, *mittere,* meaning to send. The word *"missa"* originally meant "dismissal"; but the sending forth from the holy Sacrifice was so significant, that by the fourth century, the word "Mass" was the name given to the entire Eucharistic celebration. After the priest said, *"Ite, missa est,"* the people responded with an acclamation which signified their agreement: *"Deo gratias"* or "Thanks be to God."

By the eleventh century, the faithful were formally dismissed (*Ite, missa est*) only after Masses of a festive or joyful character, when the *Gloria* was recited. The dismissal was not announced on penitential days, such as during Lent and Advent; in its place the priest said the *Benedicamus Domino,* or, *Let us bless the Lord*, which praised God. On the days of penance, the people remained in church to say the Stations of the Cross.

In the papal Mass of the early Church, the ministers of the altar formed a rather grand procession into the church. There was a thurifer (incense bearer), deacons, banner-bearers, light-carriers, acolytes, cross-bearers and seven torch bearers who walked in front of the pope, who came last. Following Communion, the Pontiff, as he was called then, blessed the congregation by saying a prayer known as a "prayer of blessing." When the prayer was concluded, the archdeacon turned to the Pontiff indicating that he should make the sign of dismissal to the people.

Fr. Josef Jungmann records an event that took place in the year 538 that shows how highly the Roman people valued the blessing at the end of Mass. On the feast of St. Cecilia, in a church named after her, Pope Vigilius had just given out Communion, when an envoy of the emperor came and took the pope into custody and led him to Byzantium. The people followed him to the ship and demanded "that they might receive the prayer from him" (the blessing prayer). The pope recited the oration, all the people answered *Amen*, and the ship got underway (*The Mass of the Roman Rite*, 533).

Pope St. Gregory in the sixth century limited this final blessing prayer to Masses said during Lent, perhaps as a special favor to the penitents who were seeking reconciliation with the Church on Holy Thursday. For years, the privilege of blessing the people at the end of Mass fell to the bishops. This gesture summed up all the favors that God had granted the people during the Eucharist. In the absence of a bishop, priests gave their blessing. According to a document dating from the end of the eleventh century, the priest blessed the congregation before he left the altar because "it would be a disgrace not to do so" (M. Chevrot, *Our Mass Explained*, 233).

Until the nineteenth century, prayers and devotions were often said after the final dismissal. In the early Church, after the final blessing the priest moved to the left side of the altar where he read the Prologue of the Gospel of St. John (Jn 1-14). This practice started in the early Church and continued through the Middle Ages. St. Augustine tells of a man who wanted this text to be written in letters of gold in every church. In the Middle Ages, people wrote it on amulets and wore it as a charm. It became a favorite devotion of the faithful, and of priests, who said it after Mass. They read this Gospel over the newly-baptized and the sick, to fend off damage from storms, and, in general, to protect themselves from all kinds of evil. In 1570, Pope Pius V admitted it as part of the Mass. As a prelude to the Last Gospel (as it was called), the priest said, "The Lord be with you." The people responded, "And with thy spirit." Then the priest said, "The beginning of the holy Gospel according to St. John." The people answered, "Glory be to Thee, O Lord." During the reading, when the priest said, "and the Word was made flesh," everyone genuflected. I have included the Prologue of St. John's Gospel at the end of this book for your prayerful meditation.

In the late Middle Ages and into the latter part of the nineteenth century, intercessory prayers were added at the end of Mass, where they were said at the foot of the altar. Pope St. Pius IX ordered such prayers to be said when the Papal States were endangered. In 1884, Pope Leo XIII extended these prayers to the whole Church. They were mainly for the conversion of sinners, and for the conversion of Russia. Certain prayers were directed to the Mother of God, such as the Hail Mary and *Salve Regina*, begging her protection for the Church.

On October 13, 1884, while consulting with his cardinals after Mass, Pope Leo XIII paused at the foot of the altar and lapsed into what looked like a coma. After a little while, the Pope recovered himself and related the terrifying vision he had of the battle between the Church and Satan. Afterwards, Pope Leo went to his office and composed this now famous prayer to St. Michael the Archangel and asked that it be recited after Low Mass, a position it occupied until Vatican II. Recently, Pope John Paul II recommended it as a prayer for the Church.

> St. Michael the Archangel, defend us in battle; be our defense against the wickedness and snares of the devil. May God rebuke him, we humbly pray. And do thou, O prince of the heavenly host, by the power of God thrust into hell Satan and all the evil spirits who prowl about the world for the ruin of souls. Amen.

## REFLECTION

Collecting books on the Eucharist is my hobby, or, perhaps, addiction. While some people collect stamps, Lladro, or National Geographic magazines (my husband), I am happiest when leafing through a book on the Mass. My fantasy is to line the walls of an entire room with bookshelves and fill them with—you guessed it— books on the Eucharist. I don't remember where I came across *"Eucharist, Celebrating Its Rhythms in Our Lives,"* by Fr. Paul Bernier, SSS, a Blessed Sacrament father; but every time I pick it up I'm rewarded with another insight into the meaning of Eucharist. Father Paul is the superior of his community at the Church of St. Andrew in New York City, and also edits *Emmanuel* magazine, a magazine devoted to the Eucharist published by the Congregation of the Blessed Sacrament. He spent many years in the Philippines, the locale for the following narrative. If there ever was a story that captured the relationship between the Eucharist and our everyday Christian life, this is it.

> One day in Manila I was at our downtown church. There I bumped into two little street children, aged about seven and nine. They were sisters. Home for them was an alley between two office buildings. I knew that they came from a larger family, and that they had no father—which is probably why they enjoyed being held and hugged, or otherwise given attention. On my way to the store for some medicine, I invited them to accompany me.
>
> Fortunately, the medicine cost less than expected, so I had a bit of change left over. I gave the girls a choice: "What would you prefer, ice cream or an apple?" Apples were then selling for about thirty-five cents, about half the price of ice cream. Their eyes lit up and they both chorused, "Apples!" They had probably never had one before.
>
> I bought each of them a nice big apple. They held them out, almost in admiration, all the way back to the church. At length I asked, "Aren't you going to eat them?" Their answer still leaves me ashamed. "No," they said. "We're going to bring them home to share with our brothers and sisters." I myself would probably have succumbed to the temptation to eat the apple and say nothing about it at home. They saw sharing not as a burden, but as an opportunity, a privilege, and a joy. These two uneducated children knew more about sharing and Eucharist than I did. (113, 114)

If we relate this story to the gift we have been given in the Mass, do we first of all really appreciate its enormity and meaning for our lives, and second, do we show our gratitude by sharing what we have received with our family, friends and the new neighbor down the street?

We have a mission: to bring the love of Jesus we have received in the Eucharist home, and share it with our brothers and sisters who are literally starving for lack of spiritual nutrition. When St. Augustine was asked what happens to the people who partake of the bread and wine at Mass, he said that we become what we have eaten. We are called to be bread for others, just as Jesus is Bread for us. Blessed Teresa of Calcutta used to tell her nuns, "Go out there and let them eat you up."

When the celebrant dismisses us with the words, *The Mass is ended. Go in peace to love and serve the Lord,* we walk out of church into a world that doesn't know God and is in desperate need of Him. It was that way in Jesus' time. No one understood this better than the beloved St. John, who grieved because "he was in the world, and the world was made through him, yet the world knew him not" (Jn 1: 10). We are Our Lord's disciples of the twenty-first cen-

St. John the Evangelist/Louis S. Glanzman

tury, whom He has commissioned to bring His Body to life on earth by feeding others with His love. We belong to a society that lives in darkness and seems bent on destroying itself. We are missioned to be the light that shines in the darkness, and trust in the Lord's promise that the darkness will not overcome it (see Jn 1:5).

Pope John Paul II spent his pontificate bringing the light and truth of the Gospel to the world. He has vigorously defended the sanctity of human life and the right to freedom for every person and society, rights that are seriously challenged in the United States as well as in the rest of the world. While religious persecution is on the rise in this country, we still enjoy the privilege and freedom of being able to worship our God on Sundays, and every day of the week for that matter. Celebrating the Eucharist establishes our Christian identity as sons and daughters of a Father, who, as someone has described, is like a parent who patiently waits at the window, straining to catch a glimpse of His child coming home. He has given us the greatest gift on earth, the Mass, "the prayer to the Father that saves the world," as we have already said. It is hard to wrap our minds around the truth that Mass "takes us to the stable, the Last Supper, the Cross, the tomb and into the heavenly Jerusalem." It is a great mystery to be sure, yet a certain reality that we are called to live— and die for.

Pope John Paul II designated October 2004 to October 2005 as a Year of the Eucharist, to reawaken our wonder and amazement at this gift of infinite love. At the same time he reminds us that the Eucharist and mission are two inseparable realities; authentic celebration and adoration of the Eucharist that does not lead to mission does not exist.

How exactly do we live out our mission? Someone eminently qualified to comment on this is Fr. Henri Nouwen who, late in his life, joined L'Arche, a community founded in 1964 by Jean Vanier in response to the need of people with developmental disabilities to find a valid place in society. Father Nouwen's experience changed his life, hallowing it with deep compassion and love for the Body of Christ. He dedicated his life to helping people find a place of belonging where they could reveal their gifts. Isn't this our goal as Christians? His words convey the essential nature of our Eucharistic mission:

> Prayer and action can never be seen as contradictory or mutually exclusive. Prayer without action grows into powerless pietism, and action without prayer degenerates into questionable manipulation. If prayer leads us into a deeper unity with the compassionate Christ, it will always give rise to concrete acts of service. And if concrete acts of service do indeed lead us to a deeper solidarity with the poor, the hungry, the sick, the dying, and the oppressed, they will always give rise to prayer. In prayer we meet Christ, and in him all human suffering. In service we meet people, and in them the suffering Christ. (*Compassion, A Reflection on the Christian Life*)

How we live out our mission is different for each person. Yet, each of us can make our lives a Mass, taken, blessed, broken and given for others. In this way, we glorify the Father. We become a living sacrifice, Christ's presence in the world, as we continue His work of Redemption.

## The Gospel According to John

In the beginning was the Word, and the Word was with God, and the Word was God. He was in the beginning with God; all things were made through him, and without him was not anything made that was made. In him was life, and the life was the light of men. The light shines in the darkness, and the darkness has not overcome it.

There was a man sent from God, whose name was John. He came for testimony, to bear witness to the light, that all might believe through him. He was not the light, but came to bear witness to the light.

The true light that enlightens every man was coming into the world. He was in the world, and the world was made through him, yet the world knew him not. He came to his own home, and his own people received him not. But to all who received him, who believed in his name, he gave power to become children of God; who were born, not of blood nor of the will of the flesh nor of the will of man, but of God.

And the Word became flesh and dwelt among us, full of grace and truth; we have beheld his glory, glory as of the only Son from the Father. (John bore witness to him, and cried, "This was he of whom I said, 'He who comes after me ranks before me, for he was before me.'") And from his fullness have we all received, grace upon grace. For the law was given through Moses; grace and truth came through Jesus Christ. No one has ever seen God; the only Son, who is in the bosom of the Father, he has made him known (John 1:1-18).

# Bibliography

Abeyasingha, N. *The Universal Catechism, A Homily Sourcebook.* Washington, DC: The Pastoral Press, 1993.

Adam, Adolf. *The Eucharistic Celebration.* Collegeville, MN: Liturgical Press, 1994.

Alonso-Schoekel, Luis. *Celebrating the Eucharist: Biblical Meditations.* New York, NY: Crossroad, 1989.

Augustine of Hippo, St. *The Confessions of St. Augustine.* Translated by F.J. Sheed. New York, NY: Sheed & Ward, 1942.

Augustine of Hippo, St. *The Confessions of St. Augustine,* I.1. Translated by R.S. Pine-Coffin, Penguin Classics, 1970.

Bassett, Bernard. *And Would You Believe It? The Story of the Nicene Creed.* London: Sheed and Ward, 1976.

Bernier, Paul. *Eucharist, Celebrating Its Rhythms in Our Lives.* Notre Dame, IN: Ave Maria Press, 1993.

Bird, David. *The Royal Road to Joy, The Beatitudes and the Eucharist.* Mundelein, IL: Hillenbrand Books, 2003.

Bouyer, Louis. *Life and Liturgy.* London & Melbourne: Sheed and Ward, 1956.

_____. *Eucharist.* Notre Dame, IN: University of Notre Dame Press, 1968

Brown, Nadine. *Interceding with Jesus.* Omaha, NE: Intercessors of the Lamb, 2000.

Brown, Raymond. *The Gospel According to John,* I-XII. New York, NY: Doubleday/London: Geoffrey Chapman, 1966.

Burke, John. "The Gift of the Priestly Homilist." *Homiletic and Pastoral Review,* San Francisco, CA. (November 1999.)

Cantalamessa, Raniero. *The Eucharist, Our Sanctification.* Collegeville, MN: The Liturgical Press, 1993.

_____. *The Mystery of God's Word.* Collegeville, MN: The Litrugical Press, 1991.

*Catechism of the Catholic Church.* Washington, DC: United States Catholic Conference, 1997.

Champlin, Joseph M. *The Mystery and Meaning of the Mass.* New York, NY: The Crossroad Publishing Company, 1999.

_____. *The New Yet Old Mass.* Notre Dame, IN: Ave Maria Press, 1977.

Charmot, Francois. *The Mass, Source of Sanctity.* Notre Dame, IN: Fides Publishers, 1964.

Chesterton, G.K. *Saint Thomas Aquinas.* New York, NY: Image Books, Doubleday, 1956.

Chevrot, Monsignor. *Our Mass Explained.* Collegeville, MN: Liturgical Press, 1958.

Cioffi, Paul L., and Sampson, William P. *Gospel Spirituality and Catholic Worship.* Mahweh, NJ: Paulist Press, 2001.

Clare, Francis. *Glory to Glory.* Mineola, NY: Resurrection Press, 1998.

Congar, Yves. *I Believe in the Holy Spirit,* Vol 1 & 2. New York, NY: Seabury Press, 1979.

*Constitution on the Sacred Liturgy. Vatican Council II: The Conciliar and Post Conciliar Documents.* Translated by Austin Flannery. Northport, New York: Costello Publishing Company, 1996.

Coughlin, Peter. *The New Mass: A Pastoral Guide.* Washington, DC: Corpus Books, 1969.

Crichton, J.D. *Christian Celebration: The Mass.* London & Dublin: Geoffrey Chapman, 1971.

Croegart, A. *The Mass, A Liturgical Commentary,* Vol II. Westminster, MD: The Newman Press, 1959.

D'Apolito, Alberto. *Padre Pio of Pietrelcina.* San Giovanni Rotondo, Italy: Our Lady of Grace Friary, 1978.

DeGrandis, Robert. *Healing Through the Mass.* Mineola, NY: Resurrection Press, 1992.

Deiss, Lucien. *The Mass.* Collegeville, MN: The Liturgical Press, 1992.

_____. *Spirit and Song of the New Liturgy.* Cincinnati, OH: World Library Publications Inc., 1976.

De Jaegher. *One With Jesus.* Westminster, MD: Christian Classics, Inc., 1993.

DeLubac, Henri. *Catholicism.* San Francisco, CA: Ignatius Press, 1988.

Dix, Dom Gregory. *The Shape of the Liturgy.* New York, NY: Seabury Press, 1982.

Dunney, Joseph A. *The Mass.* New York, NY:The Macmillan Co., 1947.

Ellard, Gerald. *Christian Life and Worship.* Milwaukee: The Bruce Publishing Company, 1950.

Emmanuel of Medjugorje, Sr. *The Amazing Secret of the Souls in Purgatory.* Santa Barbara, CA: Queenship Publishing, 1997.

Emminghaus, Johannes. *The Eucharist, Essence, Form, Celebration.* Collegeville, MN: The Liturgical Press, 1997.

Eusebius. *The History of the Church.* Translated by G.A. Williamson. New York, NY: Penguin Books USA, Inc., 1965.

Farrell, Edward. *Prayer is a Hunger.* Denville, NJ: Dimension Books, 1972.

Fink, Peter E. *Praying the Sacraments.* Washington, D.C: The Pastoral Press, 1991.

*Vatican Council II.* Translated by Austin Flannery. Northport, NY: Costello Publishing Company, 1996.

Floyd, Gregory. *A Grief Unveiled.* Brewster, MA: Paraclete Press, 1999

Galache, Gabriel. *Praying Body and Soul, Methods and Practices of Anthony De Mello.* New York: The Crossroad Publishing Company, 1997.

Gaudoin-Parker, Michael. "Becoming Eucharist-Hearted." *Emmanuel,* Congregation of the Blessed Sacrament, Cleveland, OH. (Sept/Oct 2003.)
_____. *Heart in Pilgrimage.* New York: Alba House, 1994.
*General Instruction of the Roman Missal.* Washington, DC, United States Conference of Catholic Bishops. 2003.
George, Francis Cardinal. "Easter in the Year of the Eucharist." *The Catholic New World*, Chicago, IL. (March 27-April 9, 2005.)
Gertrude of Helfta. *Gertrude of Helfta, The Herald of Divine Love.* Translated and edited by Margaret Winkworth. New York, Mahwah, NJ: Paulist Press, 1993.
Ghezzi, Bert. *The Sign of the Cross.* Chicago: Loyola Press, 2004.
Graf, Dom Ernest. *The Priest at the Altar.* New York City: Joseph F. Wagner, Inc., 1926.
Grassi, Dominic. *Still Called by Name, Why I Love Being a Priest.* Chicago, IL: Loyola Press, 2003.
Grigus, John. "The Intercessory Power of the Eucharist." *Immaculata,* Libertyville, IL. (February/March 2005.)
Hahn, Scott. *A Father Who Keeps His Promises.* Ann Arbor, MI: Servant Publications, 1998.
_____. *The Lamb's Supper.* New York: Doubleday, 1999.
Howell, Clifford. *Mean What You Say.* Collegeville, MN: The Liturgical Press, 1965.
*Instruction Concerning Worship of the Eucharistic Mystery.* Sacred Congregation for the Sacraments and Divine Worship. St. Paul Books and Media, 1980.
Jeremias, Joachim. *The Lord's Prayer.* Translated by John Reumann. Philadelphia, PA: Fortress Press, 1964
John Paul II, Pope. *Go in Peace.* Chicago, IL: Loyola Press, 2003.
_____. *On the Eucharist in Its Relationship to the Church.* Boston, MA: Pauline Books and Media, 2003.
_____. *The Spirit Giver of Life and Love.* Boston, MA: Pauline Books and Media, 1996.
Jungmann, Josef. *The Mass.* Collegeville, MN: The Liturgical Press, 1976.
_____. *The Mass of the Roman Rite.* Translated by Francis A. Brunner. New York, NY: Benziger Brothers, Inc., 1959.
_____. *The Early Liturgy.* Translated by Francis A. Brunner. Notre Dame, IN: University of Notre Dame Press, 1959.
_____. *The Liturgy of the Word.* Translated by H.E. Winstone. London: Burns & Oates, 1966.
_____. *The Meaning of Sunday.* Translated by Clifford Howell. Notre Dame, IN: Fides Publishers, 1961.
Kavanagh, Aidan. *Elements of Rite.* New York, NY: Pueblo Publishing Company, Inc., 1982.

Kiefer, Ralph A. *To Give Thanks and Praise*. Washington, DC: National Association of Pastoral Musicians, 1980.

Knox, Ronald. *The Mass in Slow Motion*. New York, NY: Sheed & Ward, 1948.

Kowalska, Faustina. *Divine Mercy in My Soul*. Stockbridge, MA: Marian Press, 1987.

Kunzler, Michael. *The Church's Liturgy*. London, New York: Continuum, 2001.

Kwatera, Michael. *Preparing the General Intercessions*. Collegeville, MN: The Liturgical Press, 1996.

*Lumen Gentium*. *Vatican Council II: The Conciliar and Post Conciliar Documents*. Translated by Austin Flannery. Northport, New York: Costello Publishing Company, 1996.

Lussier, Ernest. *Living the Eucharistic Mystery*. New York, NY: Alba House, 1975.

Maloney, Raymond. *Our Splendid Eucharist*. Dublin: Veritas Publications, 2003.

MacNutt, Francis. "A Near Death Experience." *The Healing Line*, Jacksonville, FL. (January/February 2005.)

Manelli, OFM Conv., Stefano. *Jesus Our Eucharistic Love*. Brookings, SD: Our Blessed Lady of Victory Mission, 1973.

Mannion, Francis M. *Masterworks of God: Essays in Liturgical Theory and Practice*. Chicago, IL: Hillenbrand Books, 2004.

Marthaler, Berard L. *The Creed*. Mystic, CT: Twenty-third Publications, 1987.

Martimort, Aime Georges. *The Church at Prayer: The Eucharist*. New York: Herder and Herder, 1973.

Mazza, Enrico. *The Celebration of the Eucharist*. Collegeville, MN: The Liturgical Press, 1999.

McBride, Alfred. *The Second Coming of Jesus*. Huntington, IN: Our Sunday Visitor, 1993.

McCarthy, Thomas. *Forever a Priest*. Oak Lawn, IL: CMJ Marian Publishers, 2004.

McCarthy, William. *The Our Father*. McKees Rock, PA: St. Andrew's Productions, 1999.

McMahon, John T. *Live the Mass*. Perth, Australia: Pellegrini & Co, 1945.

Merton, Thomas. *The Sign of Jonas*. New York, NY: Harcourt Brace, 1953.

Morneau, Robert F. *Paths to Prayer*. Cincinnati, OH: St. Anthony Messenger Press, 1998.

Nouwen, Henri. *With Burning Hearts, A Meditation on the Eucharistic Life*. Maryknoll, NY: Orbis Books, 1994.

_____. *The Return of the Prodigal Son*. New York, NY: Image Books, Doubleday, 1992.

Nichols, Vincent. *The Gift of the Mass*. Mystic, CT: Twenty-third Publications, 1997.

O'Carroll, Fintan, and Walker, Christopher. *Celtic Alleluia*. Portland, OR: OCP Publications, 1985.

Parsch, Pius. *The Liturgy of the Mass*. London: B. Herder and Co., 1957

Pecklers, Keith. *Liturgy in a Postmodern World*. London: Continuum, 2003.

Pennington, M. Basil. *The Eucharist, Yesterday and Today*. New York, NY: Crossroad, 1984.

Petit, Ian. *This is My Body, A Guide to the Mass*. Collegeville, MN: The Liturgical Press, 1991.

Proctor, June. *We Are Eucharist*. United Kingdom: St. Paul's, 1996.

Randolph, Francis. *Know Him in the Breaking of the Bread*. San Francisco, CA: Ignatius Press, 1998.

Ratzinger, Joseph. *The Spirit of the Liturgy*. San Francisco, CA: Ignatius Press, 2000.

*Redemptionis Sacramentum*. Congregation for Divine Worship and Discipline of the Sacraments. United States Conference of Catholic Bishops, 2004.

Revised Standard Version of the Bible, Catholic Edition. San Francisco, CA: Ignatius Press, 1966.

Roguet, A.M. *Holy Mass*. Collegeville, MN: Liturgical Press, 1974.

Rohr, Richard, and Martos, Joseph. *The Great Themes of Scripture: Old Testament*. Cincinnati, OH: St. Anthony Messenger Press, 1988.

Rolheiser, Ronald. "How to Listen and Hear God Say 'I Love you.'" *The Catholic New World*, Chicago, IL. (April 13-26, 2003.)

_____. *The Holy Longing*. New York, NY: Doubleday, 1999.

Schultz, Valeria. "Faith Like a Seed." *America*, New York, NY. (March 7, 2005.)

Sears, Robert. "Christ's Eucharistic Body and Healing." Article prepared for a Regional Meeting of the Association of Christian Therapists, Hinsdale, IL. (February 19, 2005.)

Sheerin, Daniel J. *The Eucharist*. Wilmington, DE: Michael Glazier, 1986.

Silf, Margaret. *Inner Compass*. Chicago, IL: Loyola Press, 1999.

Smolarski, Dennis C. *How Not to Say Mass*. Mahweh, NJ: Paulist Press, 1986.

_____. *Eucharistia, A Study of the Eucharistic Prayer*. New York, NY: Paulist, 1982.

Stravinskas, Peter. *The Bible and the Mass*. Mt. Pocono, PA: Newman House Press, 2000.

Tardiff, Emiliano. *Jesus Lives Today!* Miami, FL: Greenlawn Press, 1989.

Teresa of Avila, St. *The Autobiography of St. Teresa of Avila*. Translated by E. Allison Peers. Garden City, NY: Image Books, 1960.

_____. *The Way of Perfection*. Translated by E. Allison Peers. New York, NY: Doubleday, 1991.

*The Sacramentary*. New York: Catholic Book Publishing Co., 1985.

Weigel, George. *Witness to Hope*. New York, NY: Cliff Street Books, 1999.

Xavier, Leon-Dufour. *Dictionary of Biblical Theology*. Gaithersburg, MD: The Word Among Us, 1967.

# *Picture Credits*

Cover: Reunion des Musees Nationaux/Art Resource, NY; vi-vii Fredericksborg Museum, Denmark; viii Copyright Msgr. Anthony LaFemina; xiii Erich Lessing/Art Resource, NY Kunsthistorisches Museum, Vienna, Austria; xv Copyright Msgr. Anthony LaFemina; 17 Erich Lessing/Art Resource, NY; 18 Frederiksborg Museum, Denmark; 25 Scala/Art Resource, NY; 44 Frederiksborg Museum, Denmark; 51 Erich Lessing/Art Resource, NY; 53 National Trust/Art Resource, NY; 54 Erich Lessing/Art Resource, NY; 58 Bildarchiv Preussischer Kulturbesitz/Art Resource, NY; 62 Scala/Art Resource, NY; 64 Reunion des Musees Nationaux Art Resource, NY; 70 Ricco/Maresca Gallery/Art Resource, NY; 73 Alinari/Art Resource, NY; 78 Copyright Superstock; 88 Brooklyn Museum of Art, NY/Bridgeman Art Library; 94 Frederiksborg Museum, Denmark; 99 Brooklyn Museum of Art, NY/Bridgeman Art Library; 100 Victoria and Albert Museum, London/Art Resource, NY; 103 2005 Courtesy of Trinity Stores, www.trinity stores.com (800.699.4482); 108 Jewish Museum NY/ SuperStock; 110 SEF/Art Resource, NY; 120 Jewish Museum NY/ SuperStock; 121 Copyright Danny Hahlbohm/www.inspired-art.com; 125 Jewish Museum NY/SuperStock; 130 Scala/Art Resource, NY; 139 Erich Lessing,/Art Resource, NY. Louvre, Paris; 141 2005 Courtesy of Trinity Stores, www.trinity stores.com (800.699.4482); 147 Alinari/ Regione Umbria/Art Resource, NY; 2005 Courtesy of Trinity Stores, www.trinity stores.com (800.699.4482); 168 National Gallery of Scotland; 177 Jewish Museum NY/SuperStock; 182 2005 Courtesy of Trinity Stores, www.trinity stores.com (800.699.4482); 188 Bequest of John Ringling, Collection of the John and Mable Ringling Museum of Art, the State Art Museum of Florida; 192 Scala/Art Resource, NY. Coll. Monte dei Paschi, Siena, Italy; 199 Jewish Museum NY/ SuperStock; 205 Jewish Museum NY/SuperStock; 209 Erich Lessing/ Art Resource, NY; 225 San Nicolo dei Mendicanti, Venice, Italy/ Bridgeman Art Library, NY; 229 Jewish Museum NY/SuperStock; 238 Frederiksborg Museum, Denmark; 246 2005 Courtesy of Trinity Stores, www.trinity stores.com (800.699.4482);